Close Readings

CLOSE READINGS

Analyses of Short Fiction

from Multiple Perspectives

by students of

Auburn University Montgomery

EDITED BY

ROBERT C. EVANS

Third Edition

SARAH HARRELL, LISA HARRISON,
AND CATHERINE MERRITT

ASSOCIATE EDITORS

NEWSOUTH BOOKS

Montgomery | Louisville

NewSouth Books
105 S. Court Street
Montgomery, AL 36104

Library of Congress Cataloging-in-Publication Data
available upon request.

Third Edition (Revised), July 2010
ISBN-13: 978-0-9785311-1-9
ISBN-10: 0-9785311-1-6

Originally published in 2001 by Court Street Press with the
ISBN 1-58838-042-4 (trade paper) and the
ISBN 1-58838-046-7 (limited edition hardcover)
and in 2006 by MBF Press.

Design by Ben Beard

Printed in the United States of America

To all the students
whose lively minds
and passion for learning
have made this book possible

Contents

Contributors

Jennifer Adger; Jeff Alexander; Amanda Allen; Debbie Altman; Patricia Angley; Ashley Ashworth; Melissa Baker; Kimberly Barron; Benjamin Beard; Janis Blaesing; Krissy Blankenship; Kathleen Bohen; Shon Boling; Curtis Bowden; Nataliya Bowden; Lara Bridger; Lee Bridges; Spencer Brothers; Jennifer Brown; Sonja Brown; Tanya Brummett; Roger Burdette; Shameka Carroll; Melanie Clark; Ree Ann Clark; Randall Cobb; Andrea Cook; Melissa Crane; Timothy D. Crowley; Mike Cunliffe; Todd Davis; Shannon Dean; Foster Dickson; Paul Duke; Kathleen B. Durrer; Heather Edwards; John Elder; Jeremy Fore; Timothy Francisco; Matt Gilmore; Ashley Gordon; Jacques Grant; Shelly Green; William Greene; Kenneth W. Griffin; Alan Griffith; Kyla Gunter; Drayton Hamilton; Barbara Hartin; Phyllis Hedrick; Charlotte Henderson; Sonjanika Henderson; Amanda Higgins; Deborah Hill; Michael Hitch; Kerrie Hopper; Laketa Huddleston; Connie James; Jamey Johnson; Scott Johnson; Willie Mae Johnson; Steven Jones; Connie James; John Kelley; Angelisa LaVan; Barbara Larson; Barrett Lee; Monica Felicia Lee; Anje Lister; Marty Mace; Katie Magaw; Mia Manning; Kathy Mayfield; John McGaughey; Mary Mechler; Regina Moates; Christy Myers; Kevin Nutt; Kurt R. Niland; Pat Norman; Ann O'Clair; Mike Odom; Margo Paraska; Edward Pate; Karen Worley Pirnie; Eleanor Planer; Lane Powell; Michael Probst; Neil Probst; Will Quincy; Stephanie Reed; Terri Richburg; Denean Rivera; Melissa Roth; Marie Robinson; Dianne Russell; Peggy Russell; Lorelei Jackson Sanders; Jay Sansom; Debbie Seale; Julie D. Sellers; Tawanda Shaw; Brian Shefrin; Claire Skowronski; Durand Smitherman; Charles Solomon; Angela Soulé; Patrick Steele; Frances Stewart; Mark Stewart; Randy C. Stone; Teresa Stone; Tammy Taite; Ondra Thomas-Krouse; Eric Thomason; Barbrietta Turner; Peter Walden; Gwendolyn Warde; Kristi Widner; Geni Williams; Claudia Wilsch; Jonathan Wright; Carolyn Young.

Preface

This book brings together literary analyses submitted by students in a variety of English classes at Auburn University Montgomery during the past few years. By offering detailed examinations of selected short stories by three masters of short fiction (Kate Chopin, Frank O'Connor, and Brian Friel), the book also seeks to illustrate in very practical and specific ways the usefulness of various ancient and modern theories of literary interpretation. The volume is designed to *explain* those theories as clearly as possible and then to show how they can be *applied* to the specific phrasing and features of varied literary works. Although the present volume is limited in its focus to works of short fiction, the same theories and methods can easily be used in reading poetry, drama, and novels.

As the Introduction explains in further detail, this book proceeds from the assumption that any reader of literature *already* uses a theory or theories to make sense of any text, although few of us are consciously aware of this fact. Instead, we assume that we are "just reading." Two main purposes of this book, therefore, are to help make the use of such theories more self-conscious and informed, and also to make readers more aware of the sheer variety of interpretive theories that presently exist. The book seeks to show not only how and why some of those theories conflict, but also how and why they can be used to supplement and complement one another.

By focusing so intently on *students'* interpretations, the volume seeks to show that literary analysis need not be intimidating or remote—that, in fact, rich insights about a text can be offered by anyone with an inquiring mind who is willing to read closely and thoughtfully. It is a pleasure to reproduce in this volume the insights offered by so many thoughtful students at AUM—students who ranged from freshmen majoring in a wide variety of topics to advanced graduate students of literature. Their ideas—whether written down in essay form or jotted down by their instructor as they popped up during class discussion—form the real heart and soul of this volume.

The writings reprinted here were originally published in a number of separate volumes, including the following: *Short Fiction: A Critical Companion*, edited by Robert C. Evans, Anne C. Little, and Barbara Wiedemann (Locust Hill Press, 1997); *Frank O'Connor: New Perspectives*, edited by Evans and by Richard Harp (Locust Hill Press, 1998); *Kate Chopin's Short Fiction: A Critical Companion*, edited by Evans (Locust Hill Press, 2001); and *Brian Friel: New Perspectives*, edited by Harp and Evans (Locust Hill Press, 2001). Enormous thanks are due to Tom Bechtle, publisher of Locust Hill, for permission to reprint the writings included here. Thanks are also due to Brian Friel and his publishers for permission to reprint the full text of his story "Ebb Tide," and to Harriet Sheehy and the estate of Frank O'Connor for permission to reprint the O'Connor stories reproduced in this volume.

Preface to the Revised Edition (2006)

Special thanks are due to Deborah Cosier Solomon and to Irina Traphan for their careful reading and correction of the text.

Acknowledgments

This book would not have been possible without both the passion and the patience of all the students who have contributed to it; to them I owe the greatest thanks.

Thanks are also due to the colleagues who collaborated with me on the several books from which this volume derives, particularly Richard Harp, Anne C. Little, and Barbara Wiedemann.

My colleagues and I in the English Department at AUM, as well as our students, have been enormously lucky to have had Alan Gribben as our department head. Both he and his predecessor, Pat Hill, have shown that good leadership can also be (indeed, must always be) encouraging and humane if it is to be most effective. Colleagues both within and outside the English Department have also constantly reminded me, through the quiet examples set by their everyday behavior, of how lucky I am to be a part of this particular community. Two members of the larger AUM community, Tim Bailey and Carolyn Johnson of the interlibrary loan department, have been enormously helpful (and patient) in their assistance with my work on this book. I owe them many thanks. In addition, for the past several years I have been extremely fortunate to have had as my publisher Tom Bechtle, a man who truly cares about literature, and whose personal generosity and devotion to his craft have been consistently astonishing and astonishingly consistent. Work on this present book, meanwhile, has been a pleasure thanks largely to the efforts of Ben Beard—superb student, outstanding thespian, and master of the Mac.

Much of the work reflected in this volume resulted, directly or indirectly, from a generous grant from the Andrew W. Mellon Foundation, for which I am very grateful.

Finally, my deepest thanks (as always) belong to Ruth, whose love and support mean more to me with each passing year.

R. C. E.

Close Readings

Introduction

Literary Theory and Literary Criticism: What's the Use?

Robert C. Evans

Although literary theory is often considered highly abstract and intellectual and therefore remote from the concerns of "ordinary" readers, any reader of a literary text inevitably uses a literary theory of some sort. Any reader, that is, inevitably makes assumptions about why and how a text should be interpreted, understood, or appreciated. Responding to a text inevitably involves applying these assumptions to the text, whether or not we are consciously aware of doing so. One goal of literary theorists, indeed, is to encourage us to be more conscious of the assumptions we make and use when we read. By being more conscious of these assumptions we can not only use them more insightfully but can also consider their strengths and weaknesses, their relative advantages and disadvantages. We can consider whether and in what ways they seem valid; we can make sure that we better understand their larger implications; we can determine whether we are applying them consistently; and we can help ensure that the theory we use is a theory we have freely chosen rather than one we have merely taken for granted simply because it is practiced by others. Studying literary theory, then, can not only introduce us to different ways of reading texts but can also encourage a fuller development of our minds by prompting us not only to think for ourselves but to make sure that we can explain why we have chosen to think and read as we do.

Studying literary theory, however, has become increasingly difficult as the number of such theories has itself increased, especially during the last century. So many theories now exist, and so many often seem so difficult to grasp, that it is little wonder that so many "ordinary" readers feel intimidated (or even repelled). Trying to make sense of a given theory, and then trying to determine how that theory can be compared and contrasted with others, is a genuinely daunting task. Different theorists seem not only to make fundamentally different assumptions but also, frequently, to speak fundamentally different languages—languages that often seem arcane and highly abstract. It is hardly surprising, then, that many readers, when confronted with the opportunity or need to expose themselves to theory, adopt the response of Melville's Bartleby and would simply "prefer not" to.

The Abrams Scheme

Understanding the assumptions that lie within and beneath various literary theories becomes much easier when we heed the advice of M. H. Abrams, himself a highly influential theorist. Abrams suggested a scheme that is both firm enough and flexible enough to make sense of just about any theory one can imagine.[1] By applying this schematic approach to different theories, we can better understand both how they are similar and how they differ, and because the Abrams scheme encourages a systematic approach to various theories, it also makes it much easier to remember both their common and their distinctive features. Any schematic approach, of course, inevitably involves some simplification; in the final analysis, the best way to understand a particular theorist's ideas will be to examine them with individual care and attention. The Abrams scheme, however, provides a useful way to begin the study of literary theory and

---

[1] Abrams has extended and updated his ideas since they were first published as the "Introduction" to his classic book *The Mirror and the Lamp: Romantic Theory and the Critical Tradition* (Oxford: Oxford University Press, 1953), 3-29. For more recent treatments see, for instance, the essay "Types and Orientations of Critical Theories" in the collection *Doing Things with Texts: Essays in Criticism and Critical Theory*, ed. Michael Fischer (New York: Norton, 1989), 3-30; and also the entry entitled "Poetry, Theories of (Western)" in *The New Princeton Encyclopedia of Poetry and Poetics*, ed. Alex Preminger and T. V. F. Brogan (Princeton: Princeton University Press, 1993), 942-54.

to organize both the tactics and results of our thinking.

Briefly, Abrams argues that any literary theory that attempts to be complete will inevitably make certain fundamental assumptions about several basic aspects of literature. These aspects can be called the writer, the text, the audience, and "reality." To these four categories we can add a fifth: the critic. Any theory of literature, in other words, will tend to make assumptions about the role of the *writer*, the features of the *text*, the traits of the *audience*, the nature of *"reality,"* and the functions of the *critic*. Moreover, assumptions in one category will almost inevitably affect, or be consistent with, assumptions in another. Take an obvious example: if a theorist assumes that "reality" is fundamentally structured by inherent or imposed differences between the sexes, that assumption will in turn affect how the theorist imagines the role of the writer (for example: male? female? sexist? liberationist? free? oppressed? etc.), the features of the text (for example: progressive? conservative? experimental? traditional? flexible? rigid? etc.), the traits of the audience (for example: men? women? repressed? tolerant? conservative? liberal? etc.), and the functions of the critic (for example: a supporter of liberation? an advocate for previously ignored writers? a student of "male" and "female" habits of thinking and writing? etc.).

Or take another example: if a theorist assumes that a literary text is a work of careful craftsmanship, he will automatically assume that the writer will (or should) be a craftsman, that the audience will (or should) appreciate such craft, and that the critic will (or should) help call attention to the highly crafted intricacies of the text. The relationship between these other ideas and the theorist's assumptions about "reality" are not, in this instance, inescapably clear. Thus the theorist may (for instance) assume that "reality" itself is highly complex and highly coherent and that the complex, coherent text therefore reflects reality; or he may assume that "reality" is complex or incoherent and that the text therefore provides either a satisfying or an illusory alternative. The category of "reality," in fact, is likely to be the most difficult category of the Abrams scheme to understand at first. For one thing, "reality" is likely to be defined differently by different theorists: some may emphasize individual psychological "reality"; some may stress social, economic, or political "reality"; some may focus on physical "reality"; some may even question the usefulness of the category (by suggesting, for instance, that an objective "reality" does not exist). Ironically, though, even theorists who doubt the existence of any independent "reality" will still need to use the concept. However, since "reality" can be defined so differently by so many different theorists, it seems best to highlight its debated, provisional status by placing the word in quotation marks. Most theorists can agree that literature involves texts, writers, audiences, and critics, but disputes about the nature of "reality" (or about how to understand it, if it *can* be understood) are often crucial to the differences between various theories. A Freudian critic makes different assumptions about "reality" than, say, a Jungian or Christian critic. Studying literary theory often involves studying different concepts of what is most fundamentally *real*.

Central Emphases in the Abrams Scheme

The Abrams scheme is useful as an analytical tool, however, not only because it breaks literary theories down into some basic component parts and suggests how those parts are interrelated. It is also useful because it suggests that each literary theory will tend to emphasize one component part as the crucial or most important. Some theories, for instance, will tend to emphasize the ways in which literature reflects, imitates, or mimics "reality." Abrams calls such theories *mimetic* (from the Greek word for imitation). In mimetic theories, the writer is judged by her ability to provide an accurate representation of "reality"; the text is judged by its success as such an imitation of "reality"; the audience expects the text to imitate "reality" and responds to it in those terms; and the critic thoroughly examines the work's relationship with "reality." Making one assumption (the need to imitate "reality") thus entails a whole series of related assumptions about writer, text, audience, and critic.

Some theorists, however, focus less on the text as an imitation of "reality" than on its function in affecting an audience. Abrams calls these kinds of theories *affective* theories, because they will tend to look at every other component of the scheme in terms of this emphasis on the audience. The writer will be judged by her skill in affecting an audience, as will the text. "Reality" in this case will be conceived mainly in social terms, and the critic will chiefly be interested in how (and how well) the writer uses the text to affect the audience.

Other theorists tend to focus less on the audience, however, than on the writer herself. Because these theorists tend to be interested in how the text is an expression of the writer, Abrams terms such approaches *expressive* theories. Instead of the text being seen mainly as a reflection of some external "reality" (as in mimetic theories), the text in expressive theories will tend to be seen as a reflection of some important aspect of the writer (such as her mind, soul, values, emotions, or spirit). Expressive theorists will tend to assume that audiences are interested in such self-expression by writers, that the most important "reality" will be "reality" as perceived and expressed by the writer, and that the critic should mainly be concerned with examining the text as a form of the writer's self-expression.

Finally, Abrams notes that some theories tend to emphasize the central importance of the text itself. They think of the text not so much as an expression of the writer, as a reflection of external reality, or as an instrument for affecting an audience; rather, they think of it as having an independent existence of its own, as being an object interesting in its own right. For this reason, Abrams calls such theories *objective* theories, and for objective theorists the text is the most important aspect of literature. The writer is thought of mainly as the craftsman who creates the object; the audience is thought of as the persons who respond to the object; the critic is thought of as the person who studies the object most intently. The object may imitate reality or it may seem to reject such imitation; in either case, however, the focus of objective theorists is on the object (the text) itself.

Applying the Abrams Scheme

The Abrams scheme provides us, then, with a simple but surprisingly adaptable method for making sense of nearly any theory we might confront or wish to use. It offers a means of appreciating both the comparisons and the contrasts between competing theories, and it even gives us a means of studying literature itself. (Abrams assumes, for instance, that every literary work will tend to embody a particular theory of literature. We might therefore analyze a story by asking what the story implies about the role of the writer, the features of the text, the traits of the audience, the nature of "reality," and the functions of the critic.) The scheme makes it easier to help grasp and remember the distinctive features of different theories, and it also functions as a tool for understanding both the most ancient and the most recent theories of literature.

This is not the place to apply the Abrams scheme to the scores of theories that have been used, over the centuries, to make sense of literature. Our focus, instead, will mainly be upon the most influential theories of the last hundred or so years. It seems worth beginning, however, by examining the assumptions that seem to underlie the thinking of four of the most important early theorists of literature: Plato, Aristotle, Horace, and Longinus. Examining these four theorists should be valuable for several reasons. First, doing so will help remind us that the most recent theories are hardly the only ways humans have used to think about literature. To the extent that the newer theories really are *new*, they may only be reflections of a very limited range of human experience and of a very distinct moment in time. Whether they will seem as valuable a hundred or a thousand years from now as they seem today, only time will tell. The ancient theorists, however, have in some sense already passed that test: Aristotle and the rest still have interesting and relevant things to say to us after many centuries, and some of the most basic issues of literary theory were confronted first by the first theorists. That, in fact, is a second reason for including them here. Many of the questions that stimulated Plato and Aristotle stimulate us still today, and many of the answers the ancients formulated have influenced recent theories and theorists. Although some recent theories seem distinctively modern (the Freudian approach, for example), others seem to build on earlier insights. The assumptions of modern "formalists," for instance, have much in common with the assumptions employed by Aristotle.

However, a third reason for examining a few of the ancient theorists is that those theorists themselves so powerfully influenced later critics and theories. Many of the most important critics of the Renaissance, for example, were very obviously influenced by their reading of Plato, Aristotle, and Horace (especially the last two), and the ideas of many Romantic critics have much in common with those of Longinus. Familiarity with the ancient theorists, then, can help us better grasp all the other theorists who followed them, including ones we have neither the space nor the time to study here. The ancient theorists provide certain paradigms and state certain basic positions that recur again and again in the history of literary theory. Once we recognize these basic patterns and ideas in Plato, Aristotle, Horace, and Longinus, we will be in a better position to recognize them in numerous later theorists.

Finally, one more reason for focusing on the four ancients suggests itself. As luck would have it, the thoughts of each one can be associated with a different central emphasis on the Abrams scheme. In other words, Plato tended to emphasize a *mimetic* theory of literature; Aristotle tended to present an *objective* theory; Horace tended to offer an *affective* theory; and Longinus tended to advocate an *expressive* theory. Studying the early theorists, then, can help us better understand some of the most basic arguments it is possible to make about literature and to see how those arguments compare and contrast.

Method and Abbreviations

The following brief descriptions of various theories attempt to present, as clearly and schematically as possible, the different assumptions each theory tends to make about the writer (**W**), the text (**T**), the audience (**A**), "reality" (**R**), and the critic (**C**). As explained above, assumptions in one category will tend to reflect and affect assumptions in the others. Inevitably there will be some repetition of phrasing, but this should have some value in highlighting the connections between different categories. Thus, if a theory regards the text (**T**) as a highly crafted object, it will tend to regard the writer (**W**) as a craftsman and the critic (**C**) as a student of craftsmanship. Laying out the assumptions of the different theories by using these five categories should make it possible to see the connections between categories *within a given theory* but should also make it possible to spot the comparisons and contrasts *between different theories*. Plato and Aristotle, for instance, tend to make fundamentally different assumptions about the nature of the audience; these different assumptions are readily apparent when one reads the summaries of their attitudes in the A categories of each scheme.

Although each category of each theory has generally been discussed in one paragraph each (labeled **W1**, **T1**, etc.), in some cases fuller descriptions have been provided and more paragraphs have been used (labeled, for example, **W2**, **W3**, etc.). Longer descriptions have been provided for theories that seem either unusually difficult, complex, or unfamiliar (such as deconstruction). Some of the most powerful theories, on the other hand, make intuitive sense to most readers (whether or not one accepts their assumptions) and therefore require less explanation. Feminism is a good example: few students have any difficulty understanding the implications and assumptions of feminist criticism.

Brief introductions to each scheme will attempt to provide extremely basic discussions of the sources and influences of each theory and of its historical significance and relations with certain other theories.

Ancient Theories

Plato

Ironically, **Plato** *(ca. 427-347 B.C.) is not only one of the earliest and most influential commentators on literature but also one of its fiercest critics. Partly because he considered the influence of poetry on Greek culture excessive, and partly because he sincerely believed that society should operate according to standards of truth and virtue discovered and confirmed by philosophical reasoning, he was suspicious of the emotionalism and irrationality expressed and encouraged by many literary texts. Many later discussions of literature have been either explicit or implicit attempts to answer his objections, and* *in fact it has been famously said that the whole history of Western philoso-phy is a series of footnotes to Plato. Plato's attacks on literature (memorably expressed in the* Ion *and in Book X of the* Republic*) are the logical result of his theory of REALITY, which is for him the most important component of the Abrams scheme.*

W1. Rather than being creative or possessing any true understanding of their own, writers are likely to be passive copiers or imitators of the external world. Writers are therefore likely to deal with the superficial appearances of things rather than presenting any genuine knowledge of what is truly real. Indeed, writers are often likely to be mere entertainers who appeal to (and thereby incite) the emotions and passions of their audience. Writers are themselves likely to be emotional, irrational, and illogical; they will tend to know how to manipulate words but not how to examine ideas seriously. Some writers will tend to rely on passive "inspiration" and will thus exercise even less rational control over their writings; in this sense such writers might fairly be described as inspired idiots. In general, then, writers will negatively influence society by en-couraging irrationality. Some writers may have some social use, however, if their writings are used to help to make reason and virtue attractive to persons who are not capable of appreciating philosophical arguments on behalf of these ideals.

T1. A text should be judged mainly by how accurately it imitates or represents its subject matter; in this sense, a text's "content" is more im-portant than its "form." However, texts created by poets and other "cre-ative writers" are almost inevitably inaccurate and defective as imitations, partly because they imitate only the most superficial aspects of things. Since truth must mainly be defined in terms of logical propositions and philosophical rigor (rather than in terms, say, of emotional complexity or ambiguity), most "creative writing" is likely to fall short of such standards. To the extent that a text is philosophically untruthful or inaccurate, it is potentially dangerous. Rather than judging an artistic text in terms of the standards of its artistic genre (by asking, for example, whether it is a successful *tragedy*) and rather than judging a work in terms of its individual artistic excellence (by asking, for example, how all its parts fit together into a complex unity), Plato tends to focus on how accurately the text imitates philosophical *truth*. At best, artistic texts can merely present in attractive ways the truths already derived from philosophy. Truly thoughtful persons, however, will not need to rely on artistic texts in order to grasp those truths.

A1. Most members of most audiences are likely to be fascinated, deceived, and misled by the emotionally stimulating texts that creative writers concoct. Rather than using reason to search for genuine truth, most audience members will be content with the superficial appearances and appeals to passion that creative writers offer. Since such writers tend to be more interested in achieving popularity than in stimulating the minds of their audiences, and since most audiences tend to be more interested in being entertained than in truly learning, creative writers and their audiences will tend to encourage each other's own worst impulses. Audience members are unlikely to care that the writers actually know very little about the subjects discussed in their writings; instead, the audience will be satisfied if its emotions are aroused.

R1. True reality cannot be known by relying on the senses, which are almost inevitably deceptive. Instead, reality can only be known through the exercise of reason, intellect, logic, and philosophical inquiry. By using our senses we merely perceive particular physical objects; by using our reason we can discover general *ideas* or *forms* that explain and make sense of those objects. For example, in order to create any individual chair, there must first be a general idea of what constitutes a chair. Only after the *idea* of chair is known can an individual chair (an imitation of that idea) be created. In this sense, such philosophical *ideas* are more real than any individual, physical manifestation of those ideas. In addition, such ideas are eternal and universal: every physical chair that has ever existed (or can ever exist) has been (and will be) an imitation of the single, unchanging *idea* of chair (or "chairness"). Moreover, while individual chairs will inevitably decay and pass away, the *idea* of chair is immutable. Knowing such *ideas*, then, is far more important than knowing any particular imitation or manifestation of them. Unfortunately, however, creative writers tend to focus on just such imitations rather than focusing on the ideas themselves. Such writers therefore tend to distract audiences from the philosophical pursuit of truth. A philosopher, by using his reason, can come to know the "idea" of chairness; a carpenter can, in turn, possess a practical knowledge of that idea in order to create a physical chair; a poet or painter then will tend to imitate the individual chair created by the carpenter (and, to make matters even worse, can see that chair only from particular angles or perspectives). Artistic imitations, then, are inevitably several removes from genuine truth. In contrast, philosophical truth, because it is rooted in universal and immutable ideas or forms, is unambiguous, absolute, and non-relativistic: it does not depend on individual perspective. Plato's ideal model for knowledge tends to be mathematical knowledge. Thus, $2+2=4$ is true now, always has been true, and always will be true; it is just as true in France as in Nigeria or Nepal. It would be true even if no one were bright enough to realize its truth (it was true, for instance, even before human beings had evolved sufficiently to understand its truth, and it would still be true even if all humans vanished). This kind of *absolute truth* is the kind Plato most values, but he believes that it is a kind of truth that creative writing, almost by definition, cannot provide. Indeed, such writing cannot really provide "truth" in the best sense of the word; it can, at best, only make such truth palatable to persons who are either unable or unwilling to think philosophically.

C1. The critic should have a philosophical orientation; he should be a disinterested truth-seeker and should possess rational, disciplined knowledge. To the extent that the critic is a philosopher, he should work to expose the inadequacies of "creative" texts by demonstrating how they fall short of accurate, philosophical truth. To the extent that such texts can never be completely eradicated, the critic should examine their effects on society, particularly on the ways people think (or fail to think). The critic should act as a judge, condemning texts that undermine truth and encouraging texts that endorse truth. Aesthetics (the study of art) is not a separate realm for Plato; it is a branch of philosophy and, like any such branch, has an obligation to promote a true understanding of reality.

Aristotle

*Aristotle (384-322 B.C.) was a student of **Plato**, but in his extremely influential treatise entitled* The Poetics, *he offered one of the most cogent and systematic defenses of literature ever conceived. Although this treatise focuses mainly on tragedy, its implications are far-reaching because Aristotle (unlike Plato) assumes that literature can offer one way of knowing and understanding the world (rather than simply re-packaging knowledge derived from philosophy). Aristotle takes the literary TEXT itself far more seriously than does Plato; for this reason, he has been much admired by modern FORMALIST theorists.*

W1. The creative writer can be a discoverer of meaning; like the philosopher, he can be a truth-seeker, although in seeking truth he will use methods that differ somewhat from those of the philosopher, and he will also present the truths he discovers differently than the philosopher will. Therefore the creative writer should be judged according to the standards appropriate to his own field of endeavor. For instance, if he is a writer of tragedies, he should be judged by how well his work satisfies the requirements of tragedy as a genre or by how well he helps uncover the potentialities of that genre. In any case, the creative writer is, ideally, a conscious, deliberate artist, a skilled craftsman; he is not an inspired idiot or a merely passive imitator of external appearances. Because artistic skill is partly a result of in-born talent and because different writers will be drawn towards different genres (some being more inclined toward writing tragedies, for instance, while others are more inclined toward writing comedies), there will tend to be a definite connection between the character of the writer and the work he produces. At the same time, the successful writer will tend to possess some general insight into the nature of things, and especially into human nature, since human thoughts and actions will tend to be the focus of his art.

T1. The best artistic texts will be both complex and unified: every part of the work will be essential to it and will be linked to every other part. The connections between the different aspects of a successful text will seem natural and inevitable, and the quality of a text will be determined largely by how well it satisfies these combined criteria of *complex unity*. Every aspect of a text must be consistent with every other aspect; anything that is inconsistent is a defect. In the ideal Aristotelian text, everything fits; everything makes sense as part of a larger whole. In this sense, Aristotle places much more emphasis than Plato on the *form* of a text than on its content, although Aristotle also tends to assume that form and content (at least in great texts) are really inseparable: one cannot be discussed in isolation from the other. In judging a text, we must first determine the genre to which it belongs; it would be inappropriate, for instance, to judge a lyric poem according to the standards of a tragedy, or to judge a tragedy according to the standards of a comedy. Genres, however, are not mere artificial conventions; instead, they are logically necessary and natural ways of writing, natural ways of giving order to experience (or, rather, of perceiving the order that already exists in experience). In other words, experience itself is sometimes tragic, sometimes comic; therefore, tragedy can be a useful way of understanding experience, and so can comedy. Indeed, artistic texts help satisfy an innate and inevitable human desire for knowledge: all human beings have an instinctive need for knowledge; they want to perceive how individual facts relate to larger truths. The successful poem helps provide such knowledge and for that reason deserves respect and a valued place in society.

A1. Because the members of the audience have an innate desire to learn and to know, and because they take pleasure in learning and knowing, and because creative writing can be a form of learning and knowledge, art can have real philosophical and social value. The desire to learn is part of a general *human nature*; it is not confined to philosophers. Because human beings tend to learn through imitation, the fact that works of art are rooted in imitation is a potential source of their value; it is not a cause for condemnation. The most valuable works will therefore be those which best satisfy this innate human yearning for knowledge and understanding—works that reveal, for instance, how individual experiences relate to larger, universal truths. Because Aristotle assumes that a general human nature exists and that art can satisfy some of the most basic needs of that general human nature, he focuses on shared responses to texts rather than on individual, idiosyncratic, and relativistic reactions. The ideal member of the audience will be capable of appreciating the work's artistic unity, complexity, and structure (the arrangement of its formal features, the ways every part of the work contributes to the total effectiveness of the whole). In responding to a text, the audience will respond both to its form and to its content (which are, in any case, inseparable for Aristotle).

R1. Reality or nature consists of general forms, patterns, and coherent processes; the philosopher seeks to understand these, but the artist can also understand them and can help the audience know them as well. Whereas Plato tends to think of these forms as static and as somehow existing apart from or above actual things, Aristotle tends to think of these forms as dynamic processes that are inseparable from particular things. Aristotle's philosophy can therefore account for the way a thing can change while still remaining the same thing. As an acorn evolves into an oak tree, for instance, the plant actualizes the potential inherent in it from the beginning; in other words, it *achieves its form*. Every part of this process is related to every other part; the total process forms a complex and dynamic unity. One purpose (and need) of human life is to dis-cover the forms (the universal truths) that inhere within reality: those meaningful patterns already exist (they are not human concoctions), and philosophers and artists can help us come to know them more fully. Since Aristotle thinks of reality as dynamic, and since works of art (especially literary texts) tend to focus on human *actions* (i.e., meaningful patterns of behavior), literary texts can help illuminate human nature. For Aristotle, to know a particular aspect of reality is to perceive how it relates to some larger pattern or universal truth. Reality is a complex unity; to understand reality is to understand how all its parts fit together. Similarly, the work of art is a complex unity, and to understand it is to understand how all its parts contribute to the whole.

C1. Ideally the critic should have an integrated, systematic understanding of the work of art, including the history of the art form, the particular genre in which the artist is working, and the ways in which each part of the work relates to every other part and how the work as a whole satisfies both the requirements of its genre and the inevitable human need for meaningful knowledge. When examining a tragedy, for instance, she should ask such questions as these: how does this work meet the generic requirements of a tragedy? how does it perhaps reveal new potentials inherent in the tragic genre? how does the plot of the tragedy relate to its characters or diction? Because the critic ideally possesses a systematic understanding of the art she examines, her responses are rational and objective rather than idiosyncratic or impressionistic. She should be able, that is, reasonably to explain why and how a work is successful. The critic is in some sense simply a more self-conscious member of the audience as a whole: her response to a work of art will be similar to the response of the whole audience, but she will simply be able to explain that response more articulately. Just as the creative writer uses her art to help us see the meaningful patterns that exist within reality, so the critic uses her skills to help us see the meaningful patterns that exist within the individual text *and* how those patterns help illuminate reality as a whole. Because critics make it their business to think about art in general and specific genres in particular, critics can even help suggest the as-yet unrealized potential of various genres. In this sense, critical knowledge can even help generate new works of art.

Horace

Horace (65-8 B.C.) was less a literary theorist than a practicing, professional poet. Because he wrote during a period in Roman history when the value of literature was taken for granted, he felt no great need to defend literature from philosophical attacks or to ponder its underlying nature or purposes. His great statement about poetry, often called the Ars Poetica, *was in fact a poetic epistle addressed to members of an influential family interested in writing. In the epistle, Horace focuses mainly on giving very practical advice about how a writer should effectively appeal to an* **AUDIENCE** *(or at least avoid arousing their ridicule). Horace's ideas, which were influenced by Aristotle's and which were sometimes later even more explicitly combined with them by subsequent theorists, were extremely influential during the middle ages and Renaissance and into the eighteenth century. Some similarities exist between Horace's ideas and those of recent READER RESPONSE theorists.*

W1. The writer needs to keep the tastes and preferences of the audience in mind if he wishes to create an appealing work of art. In general he should follow customary practice, since custom is a generally reliable indicator of what the audience will accept. He can depart from custom if he does so moderately; extreme departures are likely to offend the audience. Moderate innovation, however, can please an audience by giving a touch of novelty to familiar themes or styles. The writer thus enjoys license within limits, and, in general, moderation is a worthy ideal: the writer should avoid taking on tasks to which his powers are unequal, since failure will result in public ridicule. The writer should be familiar with the customary practices and features of various genres, since these will affect his audience's expectations. He should know what is appropriate to each genre, and in general he should be careful not to violate decorum. If he depicts a young boy, for instance, the boy should act and speak as boys do. The writer should be a careful craftsman, and he should aim either to please his audience, to instruct them, or to do both. [Later interpreters of Horace tended to blend these goals, arguing that the writer should please *and* instruct or instruct *by* pleasing.] Although writers will need to depend on innate talents, they are also obligated to develop and refine those talents: here, as in much else, balance and moderation are important.

T1. The text should observe the basic rules of its particular genre—rules passed down by custom or tradition. It should be unified and not too complex, and it should be self-consistent. Violations of consistency (for instance, having a god suddenly appear on stage to solve problems in a plot) will seem ridiculous to the audience. The text should be carefully crafted; nothing should seem out of place. It should be a generally faithful imitation of real life and should use generally familiar language. It should convey wisdom, but it must also please. The most successful works tend both to please and to instruct (partly because they thereby appeal to the widest range of audience interests).

A1. Satisfying the audience is crucial; failure to do so will result in ridicule. The audience will be familiar with customary practices, social decorum, and the standards of real life. By violating any of these, the artist risks making a fool of herself. The audience will consist of different segments (the young and old, for instance, or those interested in entertainment and those interested in instruction). The writer who hopes to be successful should therefore try to appeal to as many audience interests as possible (without, of course, being inconsistent or violating custom). Because the audience will not tolerate mediocrity in a writer, the writer must seek to eliminate as many flaws as possible from his work. In general the writer should keep his potential audience constantly in mind and should do nothing that might provoke their ridicule.

R1. Horace tends to emphasize custom and tradition as reliable guides to "reality," and he also tends to stress the poet's need to imitate "real life"—i.e., the common standards of contemporary behavior. The writer should not depart too far either from what is customary or from what seems "realistic." For instance, she can create fictions and fictional characters, but these should seem real and credible. They should not wildly violate the audience's expectations. Similarly, the language the writer uses should be close to the language spoken in real life; it should not seem in any way excessive.

C1. The critic should act as an advisor, almost a father-figure, for the writer. He should give the writer honest advice about what will and won't work. He should try to help prevent the writer from making a fool of himself. In this sense the critic also acts as a spokesman for the audience in general: he articulates the standards by which the work will publicly be judged. The critic should be familiar with the requirements of various genres and with customary practice. He should be tolerant of minor failings and should not expect perfection, but he should judge how well the poet meets the requirements of his craft and the expectations of his audience.

"Longinus"

"Longinus" (first century A.D.) is the name traditionally given to the author of the important treatise entitled On the Sublime, *although the actual identity of the author is unknown. The treatise, written in Greek, was not printed until 1554, after which its influence became increasingly powerful. It became especially important in the late 1600's and had a great impact on eighteenth-and early nineteenth-century ideas about literature. Its strong emphasis on the crucial role of the character, spirit, and genius of the* **WRITER** *makes it a central document in the history of "expressive" theories, particularly those associated with Romanticism.*

W1. The writer who hopes to achieve sublimity (an effect of heightened, almost irresistible power and force) must herself have a sublime mind and sublime character. She must be a good person whose thoughts and feelings are lofty, elevated, and exalted; she must transcend trivialities and strive to achieve ethical and artistic perfection. She must set ambitious goals for herself and for her art, and if her art occasionally falls short of absolute technical perfection, she will still win the respect of her audience by aiming high and achieving much. She should strive to embody, cultivate, and express a genius that will make her seem almost more than human. This same genius, however, will also make her an inspiring example of the best that human beings can achieve. Like an Olympic athlete, she should strive to excel the accomplishments of her predecessors and contemporaries, not so much to achieve personal glory as to show the potential that humanity possesses and thereby give her fellow human beings goals for which to strive. Her achievements will thereby not only constitute personal triumphs but will also inspire artistic and ethical achievement in others. Again like an athlete, she must have natural gifts but must work diligently to develop those gifts to their highest pitch. She should not only imitate the works of sublime writers of the past but should thereby try to model her own character on theirs. Thus she should not only write as Homer would write but try to be the kind of person Homer was. The sublime writer has an important role in her culture: through her work and through her own example, she encourages her contemporaries to strive for spiritual and ethical perfection and to reject shallow, materialistic desires.

T1. The text will inevitably reflect the character of the writer; a debased writer cannot produce a lofty, powerful, or inspiring text. The sublime text will express the genius of the sublime writer, but it will also be the result of his trained and disciplined skills. The great work will express great and noble ideas in powerful, compelling, elevated language that is neither too ornate nor too colloquial, plain, or trendy. Unity and harmony contribute to the sublime effect of a work; the writer must know how to exploit and combine all the standard devices of rhetoric. A sublime thought, expressed in sublime language, will have an over-powering effect on an audience; they will feel themselves transported, uplifted, almost ravished by it. A sublime style will usually result only from long experience and practice, and especially from long exposure to the sublime writings of lofty predecessors. The truly sublime work will achieve a kind of immortality by appealing to intelligent readers always and everywhere. (Shakespeare, for example, might be taken as an example of a writer whose power transcends the limits of his own language, nation, and era.)

A1. Although human beings can become caught up in and enslaved by the trivialities of materialism and selfish pursuits, the sublime writer has the ability to inspire us, to remind us of our true spiritual and ethical potential, to encourage us to strive for elevation in our own souls. The truly sublime work appeals to yearnings that lie deep in our nature; it brings out the best in us; it transports and overwhelms us, allowing us to experience a kind of ecstasy that is closely associated with a feeling of immortality. We instinctively feel that the truly sublime work will cheat death, that it will appeal to the best in human beings everywhere and always, and we therefore feel a kind of awe in its presence. The fact that a human being has been capable of producing such a powerful work makes each member of the audience proud and joyful, and the work will have this powerful effect no matter how many times we experience it. The sublime work hits us with the force of a lightning bolt. The sublime simultaneously enthralls us and enhances our sense of freedom and power by showing us the excellence of which human beings are capable. An audience is usually willing to forgive small technical faults in a work that is otherwise powerful and grand.

R1. Human nature is fundamentally the same in all times and places. Although humans can allow themselves to become distracted by base desires (such as the pursuit of money or self-gratification), they are always capable of being roused and inspired by a truly great work. Such a work reminds them of what it truly means to be human in the best sense; it reminds them of the lofty potential human beings possess. Because such a work appeals to what is best in the human spirit, it achieves a kind of immortality, and it appeals to a fundamental human desire to transcend death—to create (and experience) something that is immortal. The appeal of the sublime transcends race, creed, sex, nationality, or other divisions; it unites in a common sense of humanity's capacity for greatness.

C1. The critic will possess a sophisticated knowledge of the devices (metaphor, simile, etc.) on which a writer can draw, and she will evaluate how successfully the writer combines such devices to produce a unified, concentrated effect. Achieving that effect, however—specifically, the effect of sublimity—is the writer's most important goal, and it is her success in achieving this effect that determines the value of her work. Because the sublime is both an ethical and an artistic quality, the critic is inevitably a judge both of the writer's skill and of her character, just as she is also an advocate of what is ethically best for her society. The critic should try to help foster the kind of noble, elevated society in which noble, elevated writers can flourish; by the same token, she should try to encourage the production of noble, elevated works in order to help encourage society at large to achieve its fullest ethical and spiritual potential. In judging the worth of a work, the critic will attempt to function as a representative of humanity at its best; she will try to stand outside of her own class, sex, race, nation, and time and imagine how the work will be received by the best readers everywhere and always.

Recent Theories

Traditional Historical Criticism

*As the study of modern (as opposed to classical) literature became increasingly professionalized in the late nineteenth and early twentieth century, university departments of literature tended to emphasize the importance of understanding the historical contexts of writers, texts, audiences, and critics. Historical study of literature, which still is (and is likely to remain) one of the most central theoretical approaches, tends to emphasize social **REALITY** as the most important component of the Abrams scheme. A more recent brand of historical theory, usually called the NEW HISTORICISM (see below) makes some fundamentally different assumptions than the ones underlying traditional historical criticism.*

W1. Because the writer's personality and values help shape the text, and because her personality and values are likely to reflect ideas, tendencies, or influences common during her time, historical study can help us understand not only those influences but also the writer and the text.

T1. Because the meaning of the text is likely to reflect meanings that

existed (or were at least capable of existing) at the time the text was created, studying the era in which a text was produced can help us better
understand the meaning(s) of the text. We will be in a better position to
grasp the significance of the text if we know something about its historical contexts, because those contexts inevitably tend to exert a very strong
influence on both the writer and the text.

A1. Audiences of the past differed in significant ways from audiences of
today, and since the writer created the text partly with that past audience in mind, to understand the meaning of the text we must be able
to look at it as its original audience(s) did. Past audiences often made
different intellectual assumptions than we do; they often held different
ideas and felt differently about important topics than do we. Studying
and appreciating these differences can help us appreciate the text's original meanings and can help prevent us from imposing our own modern
prejudices on old texts.

R1. People in the past tended to perceive reality differently than we tend
to perceive it today; they often made significantly different assumptions
than we do about what was real. Their view of reality was shaped (as every
view of reality is shaped) by their particular historical circumstances, by
what seemed true or important or meaningful at the time. To understand
a text properly, we must try to recapture that earlier sense of reality;
we must, in a sense, try to "get inside the heads" of the writer and her
contemporaries.

C1. The critic is capable of learning about the past and of sharing that
knowledge with us. She is a scholar who tries to discover the truth about
the past by examining objective evidence. Her knowledge is disciplined
and her reactions are informed; she is not a dilettante and does not express
merely personal beliefs or idiosyncratic impressions.

W2. By studying surviving evidence from the author's life and lifetime,
it is possible to gain knowledge about the author's beliefs, circumstances,

connections, and general involvement with the ideas of his time and with his contemporaries. Such knowledge is important, because the more we know about the author and his times, the more likely we are to know what he intended his text to mean.

T2. The text cannot be understood apart from the context of ideas and other influences that helped shape it and that helped determine its meaning.

A2. In some respects, audiences that lived at the time a text was created were in the best position to understand a text, because they shared so many of the author's basic assumptions and so much of her basic under-standing of the world. On the other hand, historical investigation can sometimes reveal aspects of the past that were not known at the time to all of the author's contemporaries but that nonetheless influenced the intended meaning of the text.

R2. Subsequent historical investigation can sometimes help us to achieve a valuable sense of perspective on, and therefore a rich understanding of, the past. For example, we may know, thanks to our hindsight, how one historical event led to another; we may be able to see connections between events that seemed to have no necessary connection to persons living at the time the events took place. Therefore, paradoxically, our understanding of their historical "reality" may be even more complicated (at least in some respects) than was their own understanding at the time. The possibility of gaining such knowledge is one justification for historical study in general and for the historical interpretation of texts in particular.

C2. The historical critic should ideally have some understanding of all the multifaceted contexts that may have affected not only the writer but also the creation and reception of the text. In other words, the historical critic ideally seeks to understand the text in as broad a context as possible, knowing as much as possible about all the influences that may have af-fected the original creation and meaning of the text. Only through such broad knowledge of different influences can a historical critic determine which particular influences were *most* important.

W3. No writer is likely to be able to stand completely apart from her own era. Even if she attacks or rejects that era's most basic values or assumptions, she is thereby influenced by them. What she is capable of thinking and feeling is likely to be influenced by the thoughts and feelings common during her time. In any case, her material circumstances—how much money she makes, how much freedom she enjoys, how much recognition she receives, how and where and why she is educated—will all influence her creativity, and these factors are all in turn matters for historical investigation.

T3. No text is likely to be completely unique; each text will tend to have been influenced by the texts that came before it and by texts composed at approximately the same time. In particular, the paraphrasable meaning of the text is likely to reflect what it was possible to think and say at the time the text was composed. Since the meanings of words change, and since new words come into the language over the course of time, historical investigation can help reveal much valuable information simply about the vocabulary a text uses and thus about what the text could have meant at the time it was written.

A3. By attempting to understand a text as it was (or could have been) understood by its contemporaries, we help to overcome (or get outside of or beyond) our own limited personal and present-day perspectives. In a sense we show our respect for the dead by trying to recreate, at least mentally, the world in which they lived. By doing so we can discover what we have in common with them but also how we differ, and both kinds of knowledge are valuable.

R3. Trying to discover the truth about past realities can help to explain the truth about the present; doing so can help us appreciate the factors that have helped influence the modern world. Past views of "reality" can be known by studying the various documents or texts or other pieces of evidence left behind.

C3. The historical critic will profit from the investigations of other kinds of historians—political, economic, social, cultural, etc. Historical investigation is ideally a cooperative enterprise in which each investigator tries to add some new piece of evidence to the total puzzle that comprises the past. By assembling the pieces and by being open to new evidence and to new interpretations of them, the historian can move closer and closer toward an "accurate" or "true" version of the past and of the texts that past helped influence.

Thematic Criticism

Thematic criticism is less a specific approach than a general tendency; there have been (and can be) many different types of thematic approaches. This is because thematic criticism tends to emphasize a view of literature as a means of expressing abstract ideas. Such criticism tends to look for the central theme, the controlling idea, of a work; for this reason, there tends to be a thematic component in almost every other theoretical approach, especially those (such as Marxism, Freudianism, myth criticism, etc.) which explicitly focus on abstract ideas. To the extent that thematic critics emphasize such ideas as highly important aspects of REALITY, they bear some similarity to Plato and to other theorists who measure a text by the value of the concepts it expresses.

W1. Whether he consciously intends to or not, the writer inevitably produces texts that can be understood in terms of abstract ideas. Most thematic critics tend to assume that the best writers are themselves interested in such ideas and that they use their texts to express or explore such concepts. Some thematic critics will explore a writer's consistent exploration of a particular idea over the course of his career, while others will tend to show how the writer's attitudes toward the idea change over time. In either case, thematic critics will tend to assume that the writer has some measure of control over the ideas he expresses and that writers will tend to explore the ideas that are personally most important to them.

T1. The text expresses, explores, examines (etc.) abstract ideas such as appearance vs. reality, the imagination, justice, prejudice, the nature of morality, etc. Such ideas help give the text its meaning, interest, and unity; the text is organized around such ideas. Texts that express such ideas are literally more significant or meaningful than texts that do not. Many thematic critics assume that one idea will tend to be the most important or defining focus of the text; this idea is often called the "central theme" or "central motif." In a sense, a text then becomes a way of making or exploring arguments about such ideas. Most thematic critics will assume that the text is intended to provoke thought about abstract ideas and that the most significant meaning(s) of a text will involve such ideas. Thematic critics tend to treat texts as (to some degree) philosophical or argumentative—i.e., as statements or explorations of different intellectual propositions or positions.

A1. Most thematic critics will tend to assume that the ideal audience will (or should) be interested in the abstract ideas a work explores. The audience will be less interested in the specific structure(s) or details of the text itself than in how the work relates to "larger" ideas that exist apart from the text itself. Indeed, they will be interested in how these larger ideas help to explain or make sense of specific details whose function is not immediately obvious.

R1. Thematic critics tend to assume that human beings have a tendency (and perhaps even a need) to understand their experiences in terms of large, meaningful patterns or abstract ideas. The richest experiences will be those that tend to disclose some larger meaning that can be applied to other experiences, whether in the past, present, or future. Abstract ideas help us to make sense of our lives, to understand our places in society or in the universe, and literary texts often deal implicitly with the most important of these ideas (for example, good vs. evil; right vs. wrong; the purpose of living; the nature of happiness; fate vs. free will; war and peace;

crime and punishment; the nature of love, or of justice, or of duty, or of truth, etc.). Such ideas give us insight into the nature of human existence, and it is partly to gain such insight that we read literature.

C1. Thematic critics tend to emphasize the importance of abstract ideas; these ideas help to make sense of human life and therefore can also be used to help make sense of literary texts. Determining which idea(s) a text most emphasizes is one of the key tasks of the thematic critic. Ideally, such an idea should help explain the most important details of a work and the relations among and between those details. Because the idea will not be immediately apparent or strikingly obvious, the critic, by making the idea explicit and showing how it helps explain various details of the text, serves the useful task of making the text more comprehensible and therefore even more satisfying. Thematic critics will often assume that the best texts can help teach valuable lessons about (or at least provide valuable insights into) the ideas they explore. For this reason they often assume that literature has some social, intellectual, or even moral value above and beyond any value it may have simply as art.

Formalism (Anglo-American "New Criticism")

*Formalism has been one of the most widespread and most influential kinds of criticism practiced in the twentieth century. As its name suggests, it tends to focus on the **TEXT** itself (and, in this respect, has much in common with Aristotelian theory). It was often called "new criticism" when it first began to exercise real influence (especially in the 1930s and 40s). It was often considered opposed to TRADITIONAL HISTORICAL CRITICISM and to other kinds of theory which failed (in the formalists' view) to give sufficient emphasis to the literary text. By the 1950s and 1960s it had become perhaps the dominant approach in the professional study of literature, but almost from the moment it was born it was attacked by proponents of other approaches, including advocates for just about every other approach mentioned below. Although the "new criticism" is now considered by many to be distinctly old-fashioned, its central emphasis on texts and on the need for "close reading" is always likely to exert a strong appeal. Formalism is most* *vulnerable to criticism to the degree that it sees texts as being unified and harmonious wholes—complex unities. Many later approaches attack this central formalist assumption.*

W1. The writer who creates complex, unified texts probably possesses a complex, unified mind or sensibility. However, although the text may reflect a complex unity already present in the writer's mind, what is in the writer's mind can ultimately never be known. All we can know is what the writer got down on paper—i.e., the text itself. Formalists therefore tend to be relatively uninterested in the psychology of authors.

T1. Formalists value texts that are both complex and unified—texts in which every part seems to "fit" or contribute to the larger whole. Therefore the text itself (specifically, how all its parts fit together) is the primary focus of formalist concern.

A1. The ideal audience takes pleasure in the text's complex unity, admiring the artistry with which the parts are arranged into a harmonious whole. Just as formalists tend to be uninterested in the psychology of writers, so they tend to be uninterested in the psychology of audiences. Their chief interest is in the arrangements and patterns of the words on the page.

R1. Reality itself is complex, but it is not chaotic; the writer, by composing complexly unified texts, helps us discern the meaningful patterns that can be found within reality. Appreciating the complexities of texts can thus help us better appreciate the complexities of the reality those texts reflect.

C1. The critic, like the ideal member of the audience, takes pleasure in appreciating the work's complex unity. The critic's job is to explain how all the parts fit into a harmonious whole. She helps illuminate the complex relations among the different parts of a text.

W2. The writer is highly skilled, and each text she creates is absolutely unique. A writer fails if her text fails to achieve complex unity.

T2. Each text is as individual as (for instance) each human being; no two texts are ever exactly alike.

A2. The audience should be willing to look for and appreciate the individuality of each text and should begin by assuming that everything in a text somehow fits. A text that *seems* to fail should be given some benefit of the doubt before it is dismissed. In trying to appreciate the text, audience members can benefit from the insights of other audience members. Ideally, they will participate in a genuine dialogue in order to appreciate the rich harmony of the text as fully as possible.

R2. Appreciating the uniqueness of each text should help encourage us to appreciate the uniqueness of other components of reality. Just as we contemplate the beauty of a text, so we can learn to contemplate the beauty of reality.

C2. Just as a priest helps us appreciate the intricacies of the divine, so the critic helps us appreciate the intricacies of a text. The critic serves the text by helping us appreciate its complex unity and harmonies.

Psychoanalytic Criticism

Psychoanalytic criticism is closely associated with the theories and influence of Sigmund Freud (1856-1939). Freud's approach to human psychology was strikingly original, especially in its emphasis on the personal unconscious and on sexual motivations. It was not long before Freud's ideas began to affect the interpretation of literature, and indeed Freud himself was quite interested in art and artists. In one sense the component of the Abrams scheme most emphasized by Freudian critics is the WRITER, for such critics are often fascinated by the psychological roots of creativity. More recent Freudian critics, however, have emphasized the ways each member of the AUDIENCE recreates the text in his or her own psychological image. Perhaps it is best to argue, then, that for Freudians the key Abrams component is "REALITY,"

because they focus on the central role of the psyche in perceiving and inter-
preting experience.

W1. The mind of the writer consists not only of her conscious awareness but of her unconscious drives and motives. The latter influence the
former in numerous ways. The unconscious mind is therefore a powerful
influence on a writer's creativity and on the texts she creates. Many of
our strongest unconscious drives are sexual and are formed during our
early development. Although many of these highly personal drives are
often later repressed in the interests of social conformity, they are never
extinguished; instead, they often find expression in indirect ways. Within
the mind of each person, including each writer, three basic elements
jockey for dominance: the *id* (strong instinctive desires dominated by
the pleasure principle); the *ego* (conscious rationality, which helps organize and control and channel the impulsive *id* to useful purposes and
which tries to accommodate the individual to external realities); and the
superego (the expression of social values and expectations, which encourages moral behavior—behavior that works to the advantage of society at
large). The *id* can be associated with the unconscious mind; the *ego* can
be associated with the conscious mind; and the *superego* can be associated with the conscience, especially with the conscience as shaped and
defined by social values.

T1. For some psychoanalytic critics, the text is inevitably an expression
of the mind of its creator; attempting to study the text without knowing something about the writer is therefore misguided. The language
and symbolism of the text will therefore often be full of psychological
(especially sexual) significance. Just as a person's deepest unconscious
motives will often be indirectly implied in the images and symbolism
of his dreams, so the literary text functions in some ways like a dream:
meanings are not obvious but are implied and must be interpreted by
examining the clues provided by images and symbols.

A1. For some psychoanalytic critics, the unconscious motives, drives, and desires of the audience are at least as important as those of the writer. Such critics may focus on the unconscious desires of a large group of readers in a particular historical era; such a focus is often called "psychohistory." For example, Victorians may as a group have shared certain psychological motives that were not shared by "hippies" from the 1960's, and vice-versa. Similarly, seventeenth-century Puritans may have shared a set of psychological motives that differed from those of seventeenth-century "libertines." Different groups of people, then, may be motivated by particular sets of unconscious drives. However, some psychoanalytic critics would argue that each individual person is motivated by his or her own set of psychological drives or needs. For instance, Norman Holland argues that each person tends to have a particular "identity theme"—a particular way of interpreting experience based on his or her own psychic desires and repressions. Each reader will therefore tend to read a text in a manner that makes sense according to his or her own "identity theme" and will tend to overlook or reject interpretations that do not accord with that theme.

R1. Psychic reality is the most important kind of reality; our knowledge or experience of everything else (including the "external," "material" world) is filtered through our minds. Focusing on how the mind (or how individual minds) work, therefore, will be a main focus of psychoanalytic criticism.

C1. The psychoanalytic critic will focus on the psyches (especially the unconscious elements thereof) of such entities as writers, readers, and characters. Moreover, to the extent that a text itself may have hidden or submerged layers of meaning, the text itself may be said to have an "unconscious," and the psychoanalytic critic may therefore focus on analyzing the unconscious patterns latent within the text.

W2. According to some theorists (such as Harold Bloom), each author tends to be motivated by (partly) unconscious rivalry with other authors, especially with writers of the past. Each present-day writer is in creative conflict with his predecessors, and writers tend to follow certain patterns in attempting to deal with this "anxiety of influence." In attempting to establish their own independent identities as writers, they adopt various strategies, including denial, repression, and resistance and also an effort to surpass previous writers. The relationship between writer and audience can be similarly complicated.

T2. Some theorists, especially those influenced by the French psycho-analyst Jacques Lacan, argue that each text possesses an "unconscious"; therefore, interpreting the text will involve studying the complicated relations between the text's surface meaning and its underlying implica-tions. According to Lacanian theorists, the various aspects of texts will tend to reflect the different stages through which humans ordinarily pass, including an initially strong identification with the mother (in which the mother is seen almost as an extension of the child, her only function being to satisfy the child's desires) and then a later loss of this sense of completeness as the child enters the social world, identified with language, law, and the father. Whereas some psychoanalysts seek to "heal" this split, others argue that such "healing" is by definition impossible and that healthy adults must accept and embrace their fragmentation and alienation, their conflictedness. For this reason, such psychoanalytic critics value texts which explore and expose fragmentation rather than pretending that it doesn't exist.

A2. Psychoanalytic critics tend to be especially concerned with issues of *gender*—i.e., with how not only writers but also readers come to adopt certain sexual roles or identities. Whereas some early psychoanalysts assumed that certain gender roles were "normal" or "healthy" and oth-ers not (or at least less so), more recent writers are likely to assume that particular gender roles are potentially fluid positions on a vast spectrum or continuum. For such writers, the simple opposition of "male" and "female" is too simple. Each writer, and each member of the audience, is likely to possess a far more complicated psyche than such a simple opposition can describe. In any case, the ways an audience responds to a text is likely to be strongly affected not only by the text's presentation of gender roles but also by each audience member's gender identity.

R2. Some psychoanalytic theorists believe that all human beings have the potential to confront the same basic stages of psychological development and encounter many of the same kinds of psychological influences, especially at the earliest ages. Some theorists believe that certain phases of development are healthy or "normal" and that others are self-destructive or unhealthy. Other (more recent) theorists are less likely to regard a particular psychological response as "normal" or "healthy." In either case, psychoanalytical theorists tend to stress that each individual's particular development is likely to be highly specific and distinct, depending on the influences or environment he encountered. Therefore, to assume that there is such a thing as a general "human nature" is to engage in a gross over-simplification. The psychological "reality" of each individual— whether he is a writer, a character, or an audience member—is likely to be highly personal and idiosyncratic.

C1. Psychoanalytic critics tend to focus on the psychological *complexities* of writers, characters, readers, and texts. They will assume that very little in any of these entities is simple or uncomplicated, and they will rely on larger theories, usually developed by theorists whose main interest is not literature *per se*, to help explain the ways these entities function. The psychoanalytic critic tries to penetrate beneath the surface of the entity he studies. Whether psychoanalytic criticism can ever provide "objective" or "scientific" analyses, or whether such criticism necessarily reflects the psychological complexities of the individual critic, is open to debate; different theorists have taken different positions on this issue.

Archetypal or "Myth" Criticism

Archetypal or "myth" criticism takes much of its inspiration from the work of the psychologist Carl Gustav Jung (1875-1961). Just as Aristotle was a student of Plato but later disagreed with his teacher in fundamental ways, so Jung was at first a follower of Freud but eventually rejected the latter's heavy emphasis on the personal and sexual unconscious. Instead, Jung tended to emphasize the common psychological habits and tendencies human beings share. He argued for the existence of a "collective unconscious"—a common reservoir of responses to common stimuli. "Archetype" is the term commonly used to describe a stimulus that provokes this kind of common, almost automatic response. Archetypal criticism is sometimes also called "myth" criticism, because certain basic stories or mythic figures are believed to structure the ways humans commonly try to make sense of their experience. In this sense, the aspect of the Abrams scheme most emphasized by myth critics is "REALITY." Like Freudian theorists, they tend to stress the interaction between the mind and experience, but because they emphasize the collective more than the personal unconscious, archetypal critics are more likely to be interested in the broader AUDIENCE than in the individual WRITER.

W1. The writer is able through her words to evoke universally shared thoughts and feelings that we cannot control or resist; she therefore exercises a kind of influence over her audience, but her power to exploit such feelings also suggests *some* measure of control or mastery over them. At the same time, the writer must be in tune with—or swayed by—these feelings in order to evoke them in others.

T1. The great text is highly complicated and possesses many levels of psychological significance and resonance. To describe only the surface level of the text (its "obvious" or paraphrasable meaning) is to give only a superficial account of it. The archetypal or myth critic is concerned with deeper levels of meaning; she explores patterns of imagery or of theme. These patterns, although not necessarily obvious on first reading, will probably deeply stir the reader's feelings.

A1. There *is* a general human nature; there are general habits of thought and feeling, typical human responses to certain basic stimuli. The successful text appeals to or stimulates these general and basic human responses. These responses are not necessarily ones of which we are consciously aware; indeed, they may be all the more powerful the more they are unconscious or preconscious. Fear of absolute darkness, for instance, is one common human response that a writer may exploit.

R1. Myth critics tend to be mainly concerned with general *psychological* reality, with "human nature." Our psychological responses, however, are largely the products of our interactions (as individuals and as a species through the eons) with physical nature. If artists can exploit references to darkness to suggest danger or evil, they can do so partly because human beings have always tended to respond fearfully to the dark. If springtime can be used to symbolize rebirth or to suggest comedy, that is partly because throughout the ages spring has tended to call up those kinds of associations in the human mind. Myth critics are very interested in the interactions between humans and nature, since those interactions are often at the root of our responses to literary works, no matter how "sophisticated" or "intellectual" those works (or our responses) may seem at first.

C1. Because the myth critic will tend to look for the deeper patterns in a work, he must be at home in, or at least have a profound interest in, numerous other disciplines, including psychology, anthropology, comparative religion, etc. He will be interested in any discipline which can help explain the underlying psychological traits or patterns of behavior common to all human beings.

W2. Although the writer exploits archetypal patterns or responses in her text, she need not consciously do so. Indeed, she probably cannot entirely or deliberately control the number or nature of the archetypal patterns the text reveals.

T2. Appreciating the archetypal patterns in a text can help us comprehend its deeper unity or coherence. Doing so may be especially useful when more obvious kinds of unity seem lacking or when the poem seems, on the surface, to be full of contradictions and incoherence. The significance of a particular image will largely depend on the specific description of it and on the larger context of the entire work. For instance, fire might be used in one work to symbolize destruction (as in a raging inferno) or it might be used in another work to symbolize security and comfort (as in a crackling fireplace). Similarly, a blizzard would suggest different meanings than a gentle snow-fall. Thus, there is no simple, one-to-one correspondence between a particular archetype and a particular meaning; the context of the symbol and its specific features must be explored before the symbol's significance can be explained.

A2. Archetypal habits of mind are part of the deep structure of the human psyche; they are not thoughts or feelings we can easily or consciously choose either to have or to reject. Myths or archetypes appeal to or exploit our deepest collective fears and desires, our most tenaciously rooted instincts. Great texts tend to grapple with the worries and problems that trouble us most (e.g., death, alienation, powerlessness, etc.) or to celebrate those feelings that give us the greatest joy (love, security, community, etc.). The successful text appeals to us on an emotional, psychological level before it appeals to us intellectually. A text that lacks this kind of basic psychological power will be relatively unsuccessful, no matter how "cultivated" or "sophisticated" its superficial structure or phrasing or intention may seem.

R2. In a sense, our response to archetypes is pre-linguistic. A baby does not need to know a specific language in order to fear the darkness or to enjoy the sensation of suckling at its mother's breast or to take satisfaction in the feeling of warm water on its skin or to feel terror at being plunged into water that is either ice-cold or steaming hot. Presumably it also does not matter whether such a baby later ends up speaking Russian, Swahili, or English. Language is less important in determining our response to literature than these basic human reactions to common stimuli.

C2. The myth critic's familiarity with a wide range of texts (and not necessarily just "literary" texts, but also religious texts, folklore, etc.) will make it easier to appreciate both the uniqueness of any particular text *and* the general traits it shares with other texts.

W3. The writer should obviously be a conscious artist, but unless he is in touch and in tune with mythic patterns or with archetypal habits of mind, the text he produces will seem simple, sterile, and superficial. Such a text may strike us as clever but not as moving, powerful, or profound. In a sense the successful text is as much the product of the collective mind of the whole human race as it is the result of any individual's conscious effort.

T3. A work achieves its individuality partly from the unique ways in which it exploits or combines mythic images or patterns of significance. The more one knows about the common patterns that underlie most works, the better equipped one is to appreciate the genuine uniqueness of any given text. The great text may exploit (indeed, probably must exploit) many of the very same patterns, symbols, etc. found in "common" or "popular" literature. By giving especially powerful expression to these archetypes, the great text achieves its greatness. Sometimes the best way to study archetypal images or patterns is in fact to study popular literature, because in such literature those features are likely to be most easily and obviously visible.

A3. The successful work appeals to psychological traits all humans share, not simply to traits confined to particular social classes, genders, or interest groups. The appeal of the successful text transcends particular eras and even, ideally, particular cultures, because the archetypal aspects of the text also transcend these limits. The great work touches chords that resonate powerfully in the hearts and minds of people everywhere and in every era.

R3. Myth critics tend to assume that some of the most important feelings or responses are the ones we can't ever quite put into words or that transcend the words we use in trying to describe them. The same basic myths and archetypes may (in fact, almost inevitably *will* be) used by writers of different times, places, nationalities, races, genders, etc., because the basic patterns of human interactions with each other (social reality) and with nature (physical reality) almost always are, have been, and are likely to remain the same.

C3. Since any individual text involves a re-working or exploitation of images of patterns common to other works, myth critics greatly emphasize these commonly shared traits. They are less concerned with the absolute uniqueness of any individual work than with the features a work shares with many other texts. Thus they are much concerned with genres (different *kinds* of writing, such as comedy or tragedy). Paradoxically, the more one knows about the common patterns that underlie most works, the better equipped one is to appreciate the genuine uniqueness of any given work, especially if the work departs from or alters an underlying, expected pattern. Creating such changes may be one of the most effective ways for a writer to achieve maximum impact. Thus if we have been led from most of our past experiences with texts to expect that the sheriff will win the final gunfight (or that the daring knight will finally slay the ferocious dragon), but instead the sheriff bites the dust and the dragon eats the knight for dinner, we will know that the writer is deliberately toying with our expectations to achieve a particular effect.

Marxist Criticism

Marxist criticism is obviously indebted to the political philosopher Karl Marx (1818-1883), who emphasized the ways in which material or economic conditions affect every other aspect of human life. Marx not only sought to explain the historical rise of capitalism but also sought to explain why capitalism would necessarily give way to socialism and then to communism. His ideas became increasingly influential in the late nineteenth and early twentieth centuries; Marxist political parties, professing dedication to the interests of the working class, sprang up everywhere, and Marxist philosophy developed many subtle variations. The triumph of Lenin in Russia and the consequent formation of the Soviet Union made Marxism the official philosophy of a huge portion of the world's population—a proportion that became even larger when China and many countries in Eastern Europe also became officially communist following World War II. By the 1990s communist philosophy was no longer the official doctrine of the Soviet Union (which had now dissolved back into Russia and a number of other separate nations) or of the previously Marxist nations in Eastern Europe. Marxism in China, meanwhile, had become in some ways quite different from its former self. Marxist ideas, however, are still attractive to many persons and are always likely to have some appeal as long as conflicts exist between different economic classes. This emphasis on class conflict, indeed, is central to the Marxist understanding of "REALITY," which is probably the defining component of the Abrams scheme for Marxist theorists. In its heavy emphasis on changing social reality, Marxism has much in common not only with traditional historical criticism but also with the more recent "New Historicism." Important differences, of course, also exist.

W1. The writer himself, like the text he "creates," is the product of a particular set of social circumstances; he is implicated in a (class) power-structure whether he is consciously aware of this or not. He is himself shaped by social pressures and social conditions, and there is a sense in which his role is just as much "written" and "pre-scribed" as the works he supposedly creates. This is one reason that the Marxist critic will tend to be less interested in either the text itself or in the writer himself than in the social circumstances that helped produce both. The Marxist critic is likely to ask, "what are the *practical, social* causes, functions, and consequences of any particular 'work of art'?"

T1. Marxist critics assume that no text can be understood apart from the historical and social conditions that helped shape its production. They are less concerned with studying the formal relations among the parts of the "work itself" than with studying the ways in which the text reflects or implies or distorts or falsifies or criticizes or endorses (either tacitly or explicitly) the social (class) power-structure of its day or of the era in which it is being read.

A1. There is no monolithic "audience." The people who make up the audience for any text are necessarily members of particular (often different and conflicting) social classes. A given text will either help strengthen or help weaken the interests of a particular class. A given member of the audience is likely to value works which reflect or strengthen the interests of her class. By the same token, she will tend to dislike texts which seem foreign to her class interests or which threaten them in some way. Often, audience members may not be fully aware of the political reasons for their likes and dislikes. They may honestly believe that their tastes are "objective" or "disinterested."

R1. Marxist critics tend to be very suspicious of claims that any particular beliefs or social arrangements or values are "natural" or "eternal." It is usually in the interests of the dominant class to treat certain conditions or beliefs as if they were "natural" or "God-given" or "permanent," since doing so obscures the extent to which such conditions or beliefs serve their particular interests. A Marxist, however, will tend to believe that the conditions or beliefs of a certain society are shaped by its *history* and that they are therefore capable of being changed.

C1. Marxist critics will often attempt to "de-mystify" or undermine traditional beliefs and values, to rob them of their allure and mystique, to show that they are not neutral or "spiritual" or non-political or "objective" but to show that they are in fact rooted in power-politics and class-conflict. Marx, for instance, called religion "the opiate of the masses" because he believed that it tended to pacify the masses, to turn their attention away from the real (usually economic) problems of the real (material) world and from possible solutions to those problems. Any values or systems of belief that work (whether deliberately or not) to stifle or prevent or dilute radical progress can be seen as regressive or reactionary and should be opposed.

W2. Some Marxists believe that socially conscious (and conscientious) writers have an obligation to write works that will help to promote social progress. Others believe that a work can be made to promote such progress if it is properly interpreted, even if promoting progress was not the writer's explicit goal. Even a deliberately reactionary writer can provide evidence for diagnosing (and thus imply ways of remedying) a culture's social problems.

T2. A work can be seen either as reflecting a dominant ideology (system of beliefs), as undermining that ideology, or even as inadvertently doing the latter by doing the former. In other words, by *writing down* ideological assumptions and thus formulating them in a more explicit and noticeable way than is usually the case, the writer may (perhaps even without intending it) expose their vulnerabilities, contradictions, incoherences, etc. A text that is intentionally conservative or "reactionary" (or one written by a "reactionary" writer) may ultimately be more valuable than one that offers simplistic revolutionary propaganda, *if* the reactionary work exposes or inadvertently reveals the problems, contradictions, and illogic inherent in the system it endorses.

A2. Audiences, like writers, are the products of particular social circumstances. Social institutions (such as the school system) help to produce certain kinds of audiences; education, to a great degree, is simply indoctrination. All interpretation and reading is inherently political; to pretend otherwise is to be either deceptive or naive.

R2. Marxists will tend to reject the concept of an unchanging "human nature" as an invention of the dominant class to keep those beneath them more firmly under control. If people are led to believe that "human nature" is fixed and unchangeable, they will not be tempted to make a radical break with past or present social conditions.

C2. Some Marxists see the critic's role as exposing the ways in which literary texts are implicated in oppressive power arrangements. They may point out, for instance, how a given work expresses the class interests of its author or of the audience to whom it most strongly appeals. Every text necessarily has political implications, because every text necessarily either ratifies or challenges the existing social structure, or perhaps it ratifies the structure in some ways and challenges it in others, or perhaps it *seems* to ratify the structure but can actually be used to undermine it.

Structuralist Criticism

Structuralist criticism typifies the very strong interest in the twentieth century in the issue of language—in the ways in which our experiences of (and attempts to understand) "REALITY" necessarily involve coming to terms with language. As their name implies, structuralists assume that "reality" is structured like (or even by) language; therefore, the techniques used in studying how languages function can also help us understand how other systems of meaning operate. Just as a linguist studies the structures by which language achieves "meaning," so a structuralist anthropologist might study the structures by which a culture operates, and a structuralist literary critic might study the structures by which a text operates or becomes meaningful. In this sense, structuralism (like many other literary theories) is not chiefly or primarily a theory of literature, although it can be applied to literature. Structuralism began to influence English-language criticism in the 1960s and 1970s especially, but even as it began to gain influence it began to come under attack from so-called post-structuralist thinkers (especially deconstructors). These thinkers tended to express strong skepticism about the structuralist ambition to provide "true," "scientific," "objective" explanations of the subjects they studied.

W1. Just as an individual word only makes sense when it is seen in relation to the larger language of which it is a part, so an individual text only has meaning in terms of the larger structure(s) in which it participates. For this reason, knowing the structure of the larger system is crucial to understanding the individual text. The word "amo" will make no sense unless one knows Latin; similarly, *Paradise Lost* cannot be understood apart from knowledge of certain structures or codes, which include (for instance) the English language; the genre of epic poetry; the Christian religion; classical literature, etc. To interpret any specific text is to relate that text to the larger codes or structured languages of which it is a part. Whereas formalism focuses on individual texts, structuralism focuses on the larger structures in which individual texts are embedded.

T1. Knowing about the individual writer is less important than knowing about the larger cultural codes the writer used. Only in relation to those codes can the writer's work have meaning. In this sense, it is impossible to communicate an entirely personal or private meaning. Just as structuralists are less interested in individual texts than in the larger codes that allow those texts to have meaning, so they are less interested in individual producers of meaning (writers) than in the larger codes by which meaning is produced. The codes, in fact, are what give meaning to the work: meaning is not the product of a single mind but of larger cultural structures or patterns of meaning.

A1. In the process of interpretation, audiences relate individual texts to larger codes, just as they understand individual words because they know the larger language of which those words are components. Without an understanding of the larger language or code, it would be impossible to understand the single word. Because these codes are largely social and shared, structuralists tend to emphasize the larger codes or language-systems rather than the personal responses or "private psychology" of individual audience members.

R1. Reality is interpreted in terms of structures which are imposed by the human mind; meanings do not exist inherently in things or independently of the interpreting mind. However, individual minds will be structured by shared languages or shared cultural codes. The same "things" will have different significances according to these different codes or languages. There is no "natural" reason, for example, that a red light should signify "stop"; it could just as easily signify many other meanings (even "go"). In our culture a red light (often) signifies "stop" only because that meaning is part of a larger social code. Knowing that code is crucial to making correct interpretations; failing to know it can produce very serious mistakes. Our lives are structured in terms of numerous overlapping codes; the process of living is largely a process of learning these codes and then using them to interpret our experiences. In this sense, knowing the larger code is more important than having (or responding to) any single experience. Most codes will tend to function in terms of *differences* or in terms of *binary oppositions*. For instance, a red light is significant (that is, literally signifies something) partly because it is *not* a green light or *not* a yellow light. We respond differently to a novel because we can see that it is *not* a lyric poem; expecting a novel to function like a poem would simply make no sense because we would be using an inappropriate code.

C1. The structuralist critic focuses less on individual works than on the larger codes or languages in terms of which a work achieves meaning. The critic's job is to understand the intricacies of those codes—to understand how they work, how their component parts fit together, what rules govern them, how and when they are applied, etc. Since any individual work may be meaningful in terms of any number of possible codes, the critic should explore many different possible codes in seeking to interpret a work. In writing about the work, the critic will focus as much on explaining the larger codes as on interpreting the individual text, especially since knowing how the larger codes work can help one interpret numerous other individual texts. The critic's goal is to achieve objective knowledge of how the codes function. (Deconstructionists and postmodernists doubt that such objective knowledge can ever be achieved. Deconstructionists believe, for instance, that the structuralist can never get completely outside of the codes or languages by which he himself interprets meaning; therefore his interpretations can never be objective or neutral.)

Feminist Criticism

Feminist criticism has been one of the most influential of all recent theories, and its influence is unlikely to recede. Since half the population of the world is female, feminist criticism of one variety or another is always likely to have some relevance to the ways people write and interpret. Of course, many *varieties of feminism are imaginable: Marxist feminism, Freudian feminism, Jungian feminism, poststructuralist feminism, multicultural feminism, etc., etc. Feminist critics often disagree among themselves about specific issues and techniques, but almost all share the assumption that "**REALITY**" (whether social, psychological, political, economic, etc.) is structured in terms of sexual or gender differences. Whether these differences are innate or culturally imposed, they are real, and whether a feminist seeks to erase them or emphasize them, they are always likely to be at the center of the feminist enterprise. In European and Anglo-American criticism, feminism became an increasingly important movement in the 1970s, '80s, and '90s.*

W1. The writer will inevitably be influenced, in one way or another, by the assumptions his or her culture makes about sexuality and gender. The writer will tend either to accept or resist (or some combination of the two) the sexual and gender stereotypes that the culture prescribes for writers, readers, plots, characters, genres, etc. The opportunities a writer possesses may in fact be affected by the sexual stereotypes of his or her culture.

T1. The text will inevitably be influenced, for good or ill, by the sexual and gender roles common in the culture in which the text is created. A text will inevitably either affirm or subvert (or some combination of the two) the stereotypes taken for granted in that culture. The best texts will subject such stereotypes to scrutiny and perhaps even criticism, whether explicitly or implicitly. Even texts that are deliberately sexist or reactionary may be useful in exposing stereotypes to view and therefore to potential criticism.

A1. The audience will inevitably be influenced, in various ways, by its culture's gender and sexual assumptions. The audience is also inevitably divided into different interest groups, depending on the sexual or gender identities of the audience's members. A woman reader, for instance, will almost certainly approach a text differently than a male, because women and men tend to have different cultural experiences and to have been exposed to different kinds of conditioning. By the same token, a lesbian reader may respond differently to a text than a heterosexual woman, and an underprivileged African-American woman may respond differently than a prosperous white lesbian. The audience will inevitably consist of different audiences made up of different kinds of men and women with different kinds of experiences and orientations.

R1. Our experience of reality is inevitably affected by our culture, and our experience of our culture is inevitably determined in part by our sexual identities and gender orientations. "Reality" is not a neutral descriptive term; our experience of reality can never be completely "objective" or disinterested. Our views and experiences of reality are inevitably affected by our sexual roles or gender identities (among other factors). Literary texts inevitably influence these roles and identities and are influenced by them.

C1. One role of the critic will be to explore the various ways in which texts influence, and are influenced by, sexual roles and gender identities. If such influence is repressive, the critic will ideally use his or her criticism to help subvert such stereotypes and thereby help promote social progress and individual freedom. The critic is not merely an "objective" student of literature but is ideally a force for positive social change.

Deconstruction

Deconstruction is one variety of poststructuralism and therefore has a complicated relationship with structuralist thought. Often identified with the philosophy of Jacques Derrida (1930—), deconstruction accepts the structuralist emphasis on the importance of language but rejects the structuralist effort to achieve an objective, scientific understanding of language or of much else. To achieve such an understanding would necessarily require the ability to stand somehow outside of or apart from language, but such an objective position, by definition, can never be obtained. Paradoxically, then, deconstructors would tend to emphasize "REALITY" as the most important component of the Abrams scheme, but for them "reality" can never be grasped apart from the language(s) by which we attempt to grasp it. Language is a maze from which we can never really escape in order to achieve a "clear perspective" on something outside the maze. Deconstruction, then, is less a philosophy than a tactic or technique of interpretation—one that provides no final answers but, instead, one that keeps returning us to the insoluble problems posed by language. Deconstructive theory thus has implications for any aspect of human life involving language—which is to say, for nearly all aspects of human life. Deconstruction was especially influential in the late 1970s and 1980s and was considered by many to pose a devastating threat to formalism. Marxist and new historicist critics, however, saw deconstruction itself as a kind of formalism because of its alleged lack of interest in historical and social issues. Some Marxists and feminists, however, attempted to use deconstruction itself as a political tool, useful in undermining more traditional points of view.

W1. The writer who produces a text is himself the product of a larger language system. In this sense, it is that system rather than any particular individual that really produces the text. (Structuralists also tend to share this assumption.)

T1. Because the text is part of a larger language system that is full of contradictions, instabilities, irresolvable paradoxes, and gaps, the text itself can never be completely harmonious, stable, unified, or non-contradictory. (Structuralists are much less likely to emphasize contradictions and gaps; this is one important way in which deconstruction parts company from structuralism.)

A1. Since no real unity exists *within* the text, any unity or pattern of consistent meaning will necessarily be imposed by the audience. Ideally, the audience should realize that these patterns *are* externally imposed; they should not assume that the patterns are objectively present in the text. In other words, they should not assume that the patterns they impose reveal any real "truth" about the text. (This assumption directly contradicts a major tenet of formalism.)

R1. "Reality" itself can never be objectively known. All of our experience of "reality" is filtered through a language system (or "discourse"). Because many different language systems exist, many different versions of "reality" exist. We can never possess "true," "objective" knowledge of "reality"; deconstruction radically questions all of these standard categories. (Although deconstructors share with structuralists a belief that we interpret reality in terms of different "codes," deconstructors are much less likely than structuralists to assume that we can ever know or understand those codes objectively—that we can ever get fully outside them to see them from a neutral point of view.)

C1. Because the text possesses no inherent meaning or unity, the critic in a sense creates any meanings she finds in the text. In this sense, the critic herself is a kind of author, a kind of creator. By producing a critical, deconstructive reading of a text, she produces another creative text, which can itself be further criticized or deconstructed. (Whereas structuralism sees the critic as a kind of scientist who pursues objective knowledge of the codes she studies, deconstruction denies the possibility of such knowledge; the critic is less a scientist than a creative writer herself.)

W2. Whereas traditional theories almost all assume that the author is a unified, single subject with a unified, single sensibility, deconstruction assumes that the author is herself largely a product of the language system she happens to use. What an author is capable of thinking and writing is largely determined by the language system available to her, with which (and through which) she necessarily thinks and writes. Rather than individual consciousness determining language, individual consciousness is determined *by* a pre-existing (and unstable) language system. Deconstruction thus poses a radical challenge not only to conventional theories of interpretation but also to conventional humanistic notions such as individuality, the unified self, and personal creativity.

T2. Deconstruction emphasizes the paradoxes, contradictions, or gaps in texts (and not only in "literary" texts but in *all* texts). However, it does not attempt to resolve or harmonize or unify these contradictions. Rather, it tries to show how such contradictions exist at the heart of any work (indeed, at the heart of language in general and of any piece of language). A text can have no single, stable, unified pattern of meaning. Any patterns found in the text are not inherent *in* the text but are imposed by readers. Whereas traditional critical theories tend to eliminate or reduce multiple, conflicting, and contradictory readings of a single text, deconstruction acknowledges the inevitability of such a proliferation of meanings and indeed seeks to release it and make it possible.

A2. Each reader is himself the product of a language system (or of competing language systems). Therefore, the reader himself is less important than the language system(s) that influence(s) his responses to a text. Just as deconstruction undermines the common notion of an individual creative "author" who has "authority" over a text, so it also undermines the common notion of an individual reader who has personal control of his responses to a text.

R2. Almost all traditional literary theories assume that literature imitates (or "re- presents") a reality outside itself. Deconstructors assume that a text can never really get beyond or above the web of language to imitate an external "reality." The text's connections to "reality" are less interesting to deconstructors than are its connections to and with other texts, which are themselves largely responsible for shaping our notions of what "reality" is. Thus, deconstructors are very much concerned with the question of *inter-textuality*—with the ways in which a particular text is a re-writing and revision of previous texts. The connection between the text and context ("history") is complicated for deconstructors because "history" is itself already textual: the only way we "know" history is through texts. "Historical events" are not simple givens (data) to be known; rather, "history" is itself constructed by, in, and through language ("discourse"). We cannot know "history" directly; we know only our *construction* of history. The problem of the relation between "text" and "history" suggests again that in interpreting one text, we must fall back

on other texts, and to interpret them we must fall back on others, and
to interpret them we must fall back on others, and so on and on in an
infinite regress of textuality. Here as elsewhere, deconstructors focus on
a hierarchical pairing (such as "history/fiction") in which one term ("history") is privileged over, or seems superior to, another ("fiction"). They
then *subvert* or de-stabilize the hierarchy, showing how "history" is itself
already a kind of fiction. Normally we try to suppress or escape this kind
of paradox, but this is precisely the kind of puzzle which deconstructors
look for and emphasize.

C2. The complexities a critic finds in a text will inevitably be irresolvable
contradictions, not complex unities. The critic should look for (and tug
on) these "loose threads," and he should also look for the ways in which
one text re-writes (i.e., both replicates and alters) previous texts. Unlike
the formalist critic, the deconstructor is less concerned with elucidating
the author's *skill* in constructing a harmoniously unified work than with
scrutinizing the text for those points at which its self-contradictions become most apparent. The critic is less concerned with *how* the text means
than with showing how it implies something that seems to contradict or
subvert its "obvious" or "intended" meaning.

W3. Whereas traditional theories almost all assume the author's control
over his text and its meaning(s), deconstruction presumes that the text's
operations and significances are largely determined by the functions of
language itself. The author cannot control or suppress the contradictions
embedded in the text because they are embedded in language itself. The
best authors will be those who are aware of the inherently contradictory
and unstable nature of language and who will highlight and emphasize
those very features of language in their texts: they will emphasize the *lit-
erariness* of the text rather than offering the text as the accurate transcript
of some supposedly external reality.

T3. The distinction between "literary" language (on the one hand) and
"normal" or "philosophic" or "scientific" language (on the other) is a

fiction. All language is, at root, "literary" (metaphorical, figurative). All language imposes structures on reality rather than discerning "true" or "objective" structures beneath or within "reality." We cannot stand outside of our system(s) of language ("discourses") and view "reality" with an "innocent eye." Deconstruction radically questions all of these concepts, all of these "hierarchies," in which (for instance) "philosophy" is presumed to be different from (and superior to) "literature," or in which "reality" is presumed to be distinguishable from (and more trustworthy than) "language." One typical deconstructive move or tactic is to take a standard hierarchy of concepts, such as

philosophy

———————

literature

and reverse it, showing how the "inferior" concept infects or taints the "superior" one. Thus, "philosophy" normally pretends not to be "literature," but it cannot itself escape all of the ambiguous qualities or features it attributes to literature. Similarly, since literature is a way of using language in which the metaphorical, figurative, fictional aspects of language are most openly acknowledged and embraced, "literature" may, paradoxically, be the most "philosophic" (or "truthful") kind of language-use. The point of this deconstructive tactic is *not* to construct a *new* hierarchy, not to "privilege" the old "inferior" term and topple the old "superior" one. Rather, the point is to show how the hierarchy is *unstable*, and to insist on and preserve a sense of that radical instability. Once we realize that the hierarchy is wobbly, we do not try to pretend that it is stable; instead, we always look for the wobbling.

A3. On the one hand, deconstruction gives the audience a much more active and important role in determining the meaning(s) of a text. Since the text's meanings are not determined by the text itself or by the author, the reader has a much more prominent role to play in determining the meaning. On the other hand, since the individual reader is herself the product of discursive (linguistic) systems, since her very role as reader is something that is partly determined by the nature of the discursive system which she has imbibed and literally *embodied* since her earliest days, and since her individual consciousness is shaped and conditioned by the language by which that consciousness is constituted, the reader's autonomy and independence are radically problematized. Deconstruction is usually thought to undermine the hierarchy "text/reader," in which the text is presumed to present a determinate or definite meaning to the reader. But the deconstructive process can also work the other way. Thus, the hierarchy "reader/text," in which "reader" is the privileged term and which assumes that readers determine the meanings of texts, can be deconstructed by raising the issue of the extent to which readers are *themselves* "texts" constructed and constituted by language-systems. By deconstructing in both directions, we achieve not a hierarchy but an unstable pairing in which neither term is privileged.

R3. Just as the meaning of a text cannot be pinned down or delimited or controlled by appealing to the "intention" of the "author" (for reasons mentioned above), so that meaning cannot be pinned down by appealing to the "context" of the "text." For instance, it is not possible to ascertain the clear, unequivocal meaning of a Shakespeare sonnet by appealing to its "historical context" (such as "Elizabethan ways of thinking" or "Renaissance assumptions") because that context is not a neutral, objective, unquestionable description of an historical *reality* but is *itself* a constructed text which can itself be deconstructed. Such a "context" is a partial, incomplete, subjective selection of all the available data from the period in question. Notice again the typical deconstructive procedure: paired concepts (in this case, "text"/"context"), which seem simply neutral and descriptive, are actually shown to exist in a kind of hierarchy in which one part of the pair is implicitly assumed to be superior to and in control of the other part ("context" is assumed to control the meaning of a text). Once this hierarchy has been shown to exist, the deconstructor undermines it (shows how it wobbles), in this case by showing that "context" is actually "text," that what seems *real and objective* is actually *constructed, invented, imposed.* It therefore becomes impossible to stabilize the "meaning" of a "text" by appealing to its "context," since that "context" is itself a "text."

C3. If all language is inherently "literary" or "fictional" or "figurative," then criticism cannot distinguish itself entirely or absolutely from the literature which is ostensibly the object of its attention. Criticism is a kind of literature; literature can be a kind of criticism. The critic is no longer a sort of scientific, objective truth-seeker; instead, she should be aware of her own role as a kind of creative writer, someone who uses language in a creative, figurative, "literary" way. On the one hand this new view of criticism gives the critic a kind of new dignity and enhanced status, since she is no longer simply a kind of parasite on the literary text but is herself the creator of richly interesting texts of her own. On the other hand, this new view robs her of her pretensions to scientific objectivity. Her own texts are themselves susceptible to further deconstruction, by herself or by others. The patterns she once claimed she "discerned" in texts are patterns she herself *imposes*; the meanings she used to claim to "find" or "discover" in texts are meanings partly of her own invention. Rather than being embarrassed by this fact, however, she should freely acknowledge it and embrace it. The best critics are those who are aware of the contradictions inherent in what they are attempting to do.

Reader-Response Criticism

Reader-response criticism is one of the most obvious results (and causes) of the decreasing influence of FORMALIST theory. Whereas formalism emphasizes the text as a self-contained object in its own right, reader-response criticism, as the name implies, highlights the reactions of individual members of the AUDIENCE. To the extent that it assumes that each reader will tend to respond uniquely, it has much in common with PSYCHOANALYTIC criticism; to the extent that it assumes that responses will be broadly similar, it bears some resemblance to TRADITIONAL HISTORICAL criticism (this is especially true of so-called "reception theory," which studies how and why texts have traditionally been received or understood in different times

and places). Reader-response criticism tends to share with DECONSTRUC-
TION a skepticism about the possibility of offering "neutral" or "objective"
interpretations. Reader-response theory became especially influential in the
late 1970s and 1980s and is likely to remain attractive to anyone who sees
the audience's experience as central to literature.

W1. Writers have, at best, only a limited amount of control over how
their texts are interpreted. Indeed, for some reader-response critics, there
is a sense in which the author is himself the creation of the reader, because
the reader inevitably makes certain assumptions about the author's values,
intentions, and performance. The reader perceives the author through
the text, but the reader also perceives the text through his own mind or
consciousness. In a sense, the author is himself only another reader of the
text he produces; the fact that he is the author does not guarantee that
his interpretation of the text is "correct," and in fact it probably makes
little sense to speak of "correct" interpretations at all. However, some
reader-response critics (phenomenologists) argue that the reader can in
a sense enter into the mind or consciousness of the author and perceive
the text through the author's eyes; in this sense the text provides an
opportunity to perceive from another's point-of-view. Still other reader-
response critics see the author and reader as cooperative co-creators of the
text, each contributing something to the reading experience, while other
reader-response critics see the relationship between writer and reader as
inherently antagonistic.

T1. Texts exist not as autonomous objects of study but rather as events
in the minds of those who read them. In important respects, a text does
not exist until it is read or perceived. Therefore the minds, perceptions,
and responses of individual readers are the sources of textual "meaning."
Reader-response critics disagree about the extent to which a text (or its
author) can control the responses a text elicits, but they tend to concur
that such responses are the most important subjects of critical attention.
Some reader-response critics see the text as a fluid and dynamic *process*
rather than as a static object; in this sense, the text is more like a piece of

music (which unfolds in time) than like a painting (which in a sense can be perceived all at once). By breaking the text down into small unfolding moments of time, such critics enhance the possibility that different readers will perceive each moment (and therefore the total experience or event) in different ways. Some reader-response critics argue that the text itself shapes, moment-by-moment, our unfolding understanding of its meaning: by providing new information, by clearing up or creating ambiguities, the text shapes our response. Other reader-response critics would argue, however, that the text can never really control our responses to it; for these critics, the responses shape the text rather than vice-versa.

A1. Some reader-response critics focus on the specific reactions of individual readers; for critics who adopt this approach, no two readings of a given text (even if those readings are done by the same reader at different points in time) are ever exactly the same, so that no text can ever mean quite the same thing to different readers (or even to the same reader at different times in his life). Each reader brings to the text her own unique personality and consciousness, and because the text is filtered through her mind, each reading of a text produces, in a sense, a unique text. In this sense, the audience member is as much the "creator" of the text as the author. However, some other reader-response critics focus on the general or *shared* responses of large groups (or communities) of readers. These critics argue that no reader reads in complete isolation; rather, each reader is part of an interpretive community, whose informal and often unstated rules of interpretation she has learned. The existence of interpretive communities with shared rules of interpretation helps explain why different readers can largely agree about the "meaning" of a text.

R1. Reader-response critics tend to agree that there can be no neutral, objective perception of reality, especially of reality as embodied in literary texts. The perspective of the observer will always help determine what, exactly, the observer sees, and since different observers will look at reality from different (even, in some respects, unique) points of view, in a fundamental sense "reality" will be different for each observer. Any similarities in persons' perceptions of reality will result from prior similarities in the points-of-view from which they observe. The kind of "reality" emphasized by reader-response critics will tend to be a "reality" defined by individual or social *psychology*. Since both individual and social psychology are partly shaped by historical and cultural forces, some reader-response critics are interested in how different perceptions of "reality" are created by cultural conditions and institutions.

C1. Since interpretation is necessarily subjective to one degree or another, the critic should not pretend that his reading of the text is the only possible or the only valid reading. The best critics, in fact, will try to be as self-conscious as possible in their employment of interpretive strategies. In other words, they will never assume that their interpretations are perfectly "natural" or are dictated by the "text itself." Agreement with other critics should be seen as indicating that one shares (for whatever reasons) the same interpretive assumptions as those critics; agreement indicates not that objective truth has been discovered but rather that those in agreement are part of the same basic interpretive community and share the same basic interpretive paradigms. Some reader-response critics (particularly those with an interest in history) will try to study changes in interpretive communities over time. In studying a Shakespeare play, for instance, they might study the range of possible interpretations that were available to Shakespeare's contemporaries; they might study the actual recorded *reception* of the text—not in order to arrive at a "true" interpretation of the text but precisely to show, in part, how differing interpretations evolve and even co-exist.

Dialogical Criticism

*Just as DECONSTRUCTION is inextricably linked with the work of Jacques Derrida, so dialogical criticism is inevitably tied to the work of its founder, Mikhail Bakhtin (1895-1975). Like many twentieth-century thinkers, Bakhtin was interested in the nature of language, but his emphasis on how language functions (as different voices within the **TEXT**) gives* *his theory some important connections with FORMALISM. However, his tendency to think of the text as a dialogue, cacophony, or polyphony of voices differs from the formalist emphasis on artistic unity, while his interest in the ways the text interacts with history makes his theory comparable, in some ways, to the NEW HISTORICISM. Dialogical criticism became especially influential in the late 1970s and 1980s.*

W1. The writer is always engaged in actual or potential dialogue with actual or potential readers and also with the different "voices" that find expression in his work. These different "voices" may reflect different aspects of his own being, since the writer, like the text, is the result of and reflection of dialogue between different voices or discourses. Every work is inherently rhetorical; that is, it attempts to affect (and is therefore affected by) its audience.

T1. The text is less the expression of a single, authorial point of view than a site of dialogue, conversation, debate, and negotiation between different points of view. The voices of characters in a work, for instance, may be just as important as the voice of the narrator or author in determining how a work is interpreted. The best texts are rarely monological—i.e., rarely the expression of simply one point of view. In this sense, texts never possess absolute unity and coherence; rather than being static objects they are dynamic processes of dialogue.

A1. The audience is not simply external to the text; rather, the writer inevitably takes the potential reactions of potential audiences into account while shaping the text, so that the very process of writing the text involves a kind of dialogue with anticipated audiences. In this sense, the audience has a hand in the composition of the text, so that even before the text is read it has already been affected by points of view other than those of the author alone.

R1. Social reality is crucially important in influencing the traits of writers, readers, texts, and critics. All these entities are embedded in society and are necessarily engaged in dialogue, interaction, and negotiation with actual or potential audiences. Words are always *addressed*. Observing the interaction of points of view within a work can help us appreciate the complex interchange of points of view in society itself.

C1. The critic will not try to reduce the text to the expression of a single point of view but will show how the text articulates different, sometimes competing voices. The critic must pay attention not only to what a text explicitly says but also to what is left unsaid and/or to what is only implied. The critic will not try to force one monologic interpretation on a text but will keep her ears open for the different voices a text articulates.

New Historicism

Just as other recent theories have attacked the FORMALIST emphasis on unity and artistic harmony, so does the new historicism, but new historicism is also suspicious of unifying explanations generally, especially in literary history. Rather than finding sameness in the past (by claiming, for instance, that most people at a particular time tended to act or think alike), new historicism tends to focus on conflict, contention, domination, and resistance. In this sense it has much in common with Marxism; both tend to focus on changes in social "REALITY." However, new historicism tends to differ from Marxism in having a less obvious or consistent political agenda. New historicism was explicitly formulated mainly in the 1980s and became very influential by the end of that decade.

W1. Whereas traditional historical criticism tends to emphasize the writer as the most important influence on the text, new historicism tends to emphasize multiple and often contradictory influences. Traditional historicism assumes that by studying the historical context that influenced the writer, we can better understand the text the writer produced. New historicism tends to assume that there is no such thing as a single or coherent historical "context" that can help to explain either the writer or the text in any simple, single way. Rather, the historical forces that influence a writer and text are likely to be so numerous, so diverse, and so potentially conflicting that studying a writer or text historically will complicate, rather than simplify, our understanding of them.

T1. The text is not only influenced by contemporary forces but is itself also a social force that inevitably exercises some influences in return. In other words, the text is not so much a thing as an *act*, a social deed. Whereas traditional historical criticism tends to emphasize the writer and text as the essentially passive objects of historical influences, new historicism is interested in exploring the dynamic relationship—the give *and* take—between the text, its own era, and even later eras. Once a text is created, it exerts multiple and largely unpredictable influences of its own. Because any text consists of elements of the larger codes a particular society uses to structure itself and to communicate, any text can potentially be useful in the attempt to understand any other text produced by that culture. Therefore, even texts that seem to have nothing to do with literature can be useful as jumping-off points for the study of literary texts. Similarly, literary texts can offer points of departure for reflections on an entire culture.

A1. The text will inevitably reflect many of the influences that also affected contemporary audiences; for this reason, literary texts can be highly useful in studying past societies, since the codes or assumptions by which those societies operated are inevitably embedded in such texts. Contemporary audiences responded to literary texts in ways shaped by larger codes of meaning, larger ideologies or fundamental assumptions. However, these codes themselves are likely to have been diverse, multifaceted, incoherent, and even conflicting. For this reason, no single code or ideology is likely to explain the contemporary audience. Indeed, such a single entity—*an* audience—is unlikely to have existed; instead, it makes more sense to think of varied, conflicting, and unstable audiences. No single interpretation of a text is therefore likely to do justice to the complex responses of actual contemporary audiences.

R1. New historicist critics tend to assume that our experience of reality is inevitably social: that is, no individual exists in isolation or in a vacuum, and therefore one's experience of "reality" is never truly private. That experience instead is shaped by the larger codes and discourses by which one's society is structured. However, those codes and discourses are themselves numerous, unstable, and often conflicting. A culture is not a single or coherent entity but is instead a dynamic process of constant conflict and negotiation among different interests. For this reason, cultural questions are always in some sense questions of power. To a great degree, new historicists are interested in how texts affect and are affected by shifting relations of power. Every text (indeed, every aspect of culture) is in this sense enmeshed in politics (in the broadest sense of that term).

C1. The critic herself can never be a disinterested observer or a neutral investigator. Inevitably she herself is enmeshed in her own contemporary culture—in her own contemporary set of power-relations. Inevitably her own writing is influenced by political motives and has political effects, although neither these motives nor these effects are likely to be completely simple, entirely conscious, or entirely under the critic's deliberate control. Because the relations between a text and its surrounding culture are likely to be so complex and multifaceted, no field of study is irrelevant to a critic's work. Profitable insights can be gleaned from anthropology, sociology, philosophy—indeed, from any discipline that can offer insights into the ways a culture operates. Like any writer, the critic herself is caught up in a larger dynamic process of negotiation over which she can exert only *some* degree of influence. The best critics will be those who are as self-conscious as possible about the political dimensions of their work and who do not try to pretend that such dimensions do not exist.

Multiculturalism

Multiculturalism is less a particular critical theory (with a routine series of practices and methods) than a general orientation. Like a number of other recent approaches it emphasizes social "REALITY" as the key component of the Abrams scheme, and like them, too, it acknowledges the differences that exist within society, especially differences involving group identities. In Anglo-

*American criticism, multiculturalism has become increasingly important
since the 1960s as different groups have asserted and explored their separate
ethnic, sexual, and linguistic identities.*

W1. The writer is not merely a person but is inevitably a member of a
particular group; membership in this group inevitably affects how and
what he writes and how his writing is received by others (who are also
members of various groups). Is the writer black or white? Gay or straight?
English-speaking or Spanish-speaking? A mulatto? A mestizo? Lesbian or
bisexual? A black lesbian, a white lesbian, a chicana lesbian? The answers
to such questions will inevitably affect the writer's experiences and thus
also his work. Even a writer who seeks to write simply as a "human being" will thereby inevitably be adopting a position toward one or another
group; no writer, then, can ever completely adopt a "neutral" or "objective"
stance or transcend social differences or group identities.

T1. The text will inevitably reflect the experiences of the writer—
experiences shaped by the writer's relations with the various groups that
constitute her society. The text may express the values and perspectives
of the minority group to which the writer belongs, or it may attempt to
express the values and perspectives of the dominant or majority group,
or it may challenge majority values, or it may try to accommodate or
reconcile minority and majority values, or it may express any of a number
of other possible relationships between the majority and minority culture. Inevitably, though, it will be affected in some way by the existence
of these alternative cultures. In a society composed of different groups
who adhere to different values, any text will inevitably have a political
dimension; it will inevitably either affirm or undermine the values (and
therefore the relative social power) of the group.

A1. Just as writers are inevitably members of various groups within a
larger society, so the same thing is true of the audience. Membership
in such groups inevitably affects how a particular reader experiences
or responds to a particular text. The reader, for instance, may value a

text that affirms the values of her group, or she may disdain a text that seems to undermine the values of her group, or she may respond in less obvious ways. In responding to a given text, an audience member will inevitably be expressing her sense of her identity, particularly her degree of identification with one or another of the groups that compose society. A reader who assumes that her values are natural or inevitable or objective or neutral is either deceiving herself or is trying to impose her values on others.

R1. The most important kind of reality for multicultural critics is social reality—the existence of persons in society and particularly in social groups. These groups may *seem* natural and inevitable (for example, male/female; black/white; young/old) but inevitably they are to some degree *socially constructed.* For example, to be born as a woman in a sex-ist society is one thing; to be born as a woman in a "liberated" society is another. To be gay in a small, rural Southern town will probably involve a different set of experiences than being gay in San Francisco. Similarly, to be a young, attractive woman in a sexist society will probably involve a different set of experiences than being an elderly, unattractive woman in the same society. Multicultural critics assume that one's experience of "reality" is always shaped, to one degree or another, by the cultures to which one belongs or with which one is associated by others. Identity will often involve complex, overlapping membership in various groups: one might, for instance, be an elderly, attractive, Spanish-speaking black lesbian in a small Southern town.

C1. The multicultural critic is suspicious of the claim that there is a general "human nature." He will tend to examine how a writer's membership in a particular group (or groups) affects how he writes and how his writing affects (and is affected by) members of his own and other groups. He will tend to examine how texts explore (or attempt to ignore) human differ-ences. He will tend to value works that take such differences seriously. He will be very interested in the *political* dimensions of texts—i.e., in how texts affect (and are affected by) the status and power of the groups to which their writers and readers belong. His approach will tend to be interdisciplinary—drawing, for instance, on history, psychology, anthropology, sociology, linguistics, or any other field that can help illuminate the differences between human groups.

Postmodernism

Postmodernism is less a well-formulated theory than a recent intellectual trend that has affected thinking about society, interpretation, and the arts. It is similar in important ways to POST-STRUCTURALISM OR DE-CONSTRUCTION, especially in its skepticism about large-scale "truths" or "objective" interpretations of "REALITY." By its very nature postmodernism is fluid and difficult to define, and as one of the most recent of critical orientations, it is still in the process of evolution. It became a subject of widespread discussion in the late 1980s and 1990s.

W1. Ideally the writer adheres strictly to no stable system of thinking but actively explores (or is passively open to) a variety of positions, roles, attitudes, stances, often in the same work. While formalism would tend to seek an underlying order in such diversity, postmodernism is comfortable with and even celebrates complexities, contradictions, ambiguities, and the potential freedom they exemplify. Rather than nostalgically mourning for a lost sense of coherence and/or for a stable system of larger values, then, the postmodern writer ideally embraces what might strike a formalist as incoherent and chaotic. Rather than being disengaged from or hostile to popular culture, the postmodern writer interacts with it, recognizing no rigid distinctions between "high" and "low" art.

T1. Whereas previous approaches to texts have often sought to find underlying patterns of unity or coherence (whether formal, psychological, thematic, social, etc.), postmodernism shares with deconstruction a belief that texts will be (and even should be) full of contradictions, gaps, incoherences, and randomness and will reveal unexpected, startling, and even unsettling juxtapositions of styles, genres, and modes of thought. Postmodernism also shares with deconstruction a belief that every aspect of reality is in some sense simply a "text" or "sign," so that a text's most important relations will not be with reality *per se* (which we can never truly or fully know) but only with other texts. The text can never accurately "mirror" the external world except insofar as the world itself is full of contradictions or incoherence. Since a text can never really imitate a coherent external reality (partly since no such coherent reality exists), the text will always in some sense be referring back to itself and will never really get "beyond" or "outside" itself.

A1. Rather than appealing to the audience's sense of logic or reason or to its beliefs in particular ideologies or world-views, postmodernism will implicitly undermine or subvert all these stable systems. Ideally the audience will cooperate in and welcome this sense of disruption; ideally audience members will find the confrontation with postmodern art liberating (even if disillusioning). Ideally the audience will not search for the "deeper, underlying" meanings of a text but will delight in its surfaces, in its ironic juxtapositions of apparently contradictory meanings. Rather than feeling threatened by the chaotic qualities of the postmodern text, the audience ideally will adopt the same playful, tentative, ironic attitude that helped produce the work in the first place. Just as the text is full of contradictions, so is the "identity" of each audience member; indeed, the notion of a coherent, stable "identity" is implicitly disrupted by postmodern art.

R1. Previous kinds of writing and thinking had placed great confidence in the possession of (or at least the search for) large "meta-narratives" that would make sense of diverse phenomena. Postmodernism is suspicious of all such totalizing (and ultimately reductive) explanations. Marxism, for instance, cannot explain all the phenomena it attempts to encompass; nor can Christianity or structuralism or Freudianism or Islam or science or any other coherent system of thought. Attempts to see the world in terms of such larger ideologies almost inevitably result in oppression of ideas, persons, cultures, works, etc., that "don't fit." Postmodernism is therefore suspicious of any large-scale ideology that tries to make sense of the world by *imposing* sense on it. Rather than trying to penetrate beneath the surface of things to disclose some more important underlying reality, the postmodern writer doubts the existence of such a reality and thus sees all things as in some sense ornamental, decorative, illusory. Giving up the search for "meta-narratives" means feeling comfortable with diversity, uncertainty, and toleration and also means accepting and even enjoying the contradictions one finds within oneself and others. Reality (or in any event our experience of reality) is inherently fragmented and incoherent.

C1. The postmodern critic will call attention to and revel in the (inherent) contradictions, (unintended) ironies, and (irresolvable) paradoxes in the texts she examines. Rather than faulting a text that is full of contradictions (as would a formalist), she will acknowledge the inevitability of such contradictions or tensions and will indeed value texts that highlight them or that do not attempt to disguise, ignore, or disparage such "incoherence." The critic will be at least as interested in how texts can be *used* by different persons as in what those texts "inherently" *mean*, since inherently they "mean" no single thing (i.e., have no stable significance). The critic will be suspicious of, and skeptical toward, any text that claims to set forth an all-embracing explanation; like the deconstructor, she will interrogate such a text to expose its heterogeneity—its lack of a simple, single, coherent meaning.

Pluralism

The most influential spokesman for critical pluralism has been Wayne Booth, who has been defending this approach since at least the 1960s. Like any critical theory, pluralism makes important assumptions about the nature of reality, but perhaps the most important component on the Abrams scheme for a pluralist involves the role of the **CRITIC** *herself. This is true because pluralism is not itself an interpretive approach but rather a way of coming to terms with the vast variety of approaches that have been (and will undoubtedly continue to be) proposed. Pluralism assumes that each approach, by asking different questions about literature, will provide different kinds of* *answers and that each kind of answer is at least potentially valuable in its own right. Pluralism does not attempt to harmonize competing ways of thinking, nor does it radically doubt the validity of all ways of thought. Rather, it emphasizes that each separate theory can provide insights consistent with the questions the theory asks and the assumptions it makes. Pluralists encourage practicioners of a given theory to be as logical and consistent as possible in developing and applying their theories, and it also encourages practicioners of rival theories to give their rivals a fair hearing. Pluralism thus shares with POSTMODERNISM a suspicion of dogmatic, all-embracing explanations, but it encourages an intellectually responsible use of any particular interpretive approach.*

W1. A writer can be viewed from multiple perspectives—as a craftsman, as an individual psyche, as a representative human being, as a member of a particular culture, as an advocate of a particular politics, as a member of a particular gender, etc., etc. The kinds of questions we ask about a writer and the kinds of answers we find to those questions will therefore vary, depending on how we happen to be approaching the writer at any particular moment. Different kinds of approaches or questions will inevitably elicit different kinds of results or answers. We need to be careful, then, to understand exactly which approach we are adopting and need to realize that that approach is not the only one that might be used.

T1. Everything just said about the writer is also true of the text. A text can be treated, for instance, as a formal object; as a historical, social, or political document; as a revelation of the author's psyche or of some underlying psychology of humans in general; etc. No single approach is either totally right or completely comprehensive; each is appropriate in its own way; each ideally reveals a different aspect or dimension of the text. A text can be seen to make or possess some coherent sense *within* the specific terms of a particular approach, but no single approach can tell us everything about the text's significance(s). Whereas formalists might seek to harmonize these approaches or find their common ground (thus producing an integrated or coherent, even if complex, reading of the text), pluralists feel no strong urge to harmonize or homogenize divergent readings. Indeed, there is real value in being able to ask fundamentally different kinds of questions of the same text.

A1. Ideally each audience member will be as conscious as possible of the kinds of questions she is asking of a text and of the larger assumptions those questions take for granted. Ideally each audience member will realize that the answers she elicits when interrogating a text will be only partial answers (answers that are relevant to and from one perspective), not absolutely complete or final explanations. Ideally, each reader will try to understand thoroughly the rules, procedures, and interpretive methods of whatever approach(es) she adopts and will be able to recognize when and how a particular interpretation either satisfies or falls short of the standards appropriate to that particular approach. The reader will try to provide as rigorous, logical, and intellectually responsible a reading as possible *according to the standards of the approach she adopts*. If she chooses a Marxist perspective, for instance, she should not simply assume that that perspective is, in and of itself, superior to any other. Rather, she should recognize that different Marxist readings of the same work will do fuller or lesser justice to the ideal potential of a Marxist reading of that work. Whatever approach a reader adopts, she should try to use it intelligently and thoughtfully and should be vigilant to avoid errors or mistakes. She should be aware of the premises from which she is arguing, should scrutinize those premises as much as possible, and, assuming that she still finds them valuable after scrutinizing them, should apply them with consistency and rigor to her reading of the work. Finally, she should avoid assuming that her way of reading is the *only* legitimate way.

R1. Reality can be approached only from particular perspectives or angles or assumptions or premises. A complete and impartial and thoroughly objective understanding of reality seems impossible. Our questions about reality, and our answers to those questions, make sense only in terms of the assumptions that underly both the questions and the answers. Whereas a "monist" assumes that there is only one way of understanding reality, and whereas a skeptic assumes that there is no valid way of understanding it, and whereas eclecticism tries to pick and choose among different approaches in order to construct a comprehensive approach, a pluralist assumes that different approaches will spotlight different aspects of reality and that there is some value in using many different approaches.

C1. The pluralist critic does not believe that "anything goes." He does not assume that any particular interpretation is valid simply because it is unique. Rather, he tries to test each particular interpretation against the standards implied by the interpreter's own assumptions. He tries to determine whether a particular reading does justice to the potential inherent in that kind of reading. Some formalist interpretations, for instance, may be more thorough and exacting than other formalist interpretations. The same would be true of Marxist, deconstructive, structuralist, psychoanalytical approaches, etc. Within the terms of a given system of thought, it is possible to determine how close a particular reading comes to an *ideal* reading *within that system*. Thus, a pluralist critic is neither a complete skeptic nor a complete relativist: he does not assume that all interpretations are just as valuable as any others. Rather, he tries (1) to determine the premises from which a critic is working; (2) to decide whether those premises are coherent or contradictory (i.e., whether they are self-consistent); (3) to assess whether an interpreter using those premises has applied them rigorously and consistently and has seen as much with them as they will allow him to see. The pluralist critic assumes that no single perspective has any monopoly on the truth, and he is suspicious of systems that claim to be able to explain everything.

Applications

Diverse Responses to Kate Chopin's "The Story of an Hour"

Contributions by: Kathleen B. Durrer, Scott Johnson, Barbara Larson, Jonathan Wright and by Lara Bridger, Randall Cobb, Mike Cunliffe, Foster Dickson, Amanda Higgins, Mary Mechler, Dianne Russell, and Geni Williams

One good way to grasp a literary theory is to see it in action—to witness how it might be applied to a particular work. Kate Chopin's brief tale "The Story of an Hour" provides excellent material for such a litmus test. Chopin's work, composed in 1894, typifies the style and concerns of an author famous mainly for her great novel *The Awakening*. Yet the present story is not only brief and clear but also compelling and complex, and it easily lends itself to a variety of critical approaches. In the text printed below, the passages numbered and highlighted in boldface are ones that actual students were asked to analyze as part of a final examination in a course in literary criticism. Some passages from the story are approached from single perspectives; others are approached from several varying points of view.

Excerpts from some of the student responses (keyed to the numbered passages) follow the story itself. These responses, of course, are meant to be suggestive rather than definitive; they are meant to show, for instance, not how *a* feminist critic *would* react to a particular passage but rather to suggest how *one* feminist reader *might* respond to a specific selection. For this reason, more than one response to each passage has been provided whenever possible. Critics adopting the same basic theoretical approach often reach divergent interpretations of identical data, and the diverse student responses reprinted here are intended to illustrate that fact.

"The Story of an Hour"

by KATE CHOPIN

Knowing that Mrs. Mallard was afflicted with a heart trouble, great care was taken to break to her as gently as possible the news of her husband's death.

It was her sister Josephine who told her, in broken sentences; veiled hints that revealed in half concealing.[1] Her husband's friend Richards was there, too, near her. It was he who had been in the newspaper office when intelligence of the railroad disaster was received, with Brently Mallard's name leading the list of "killed." He had only taken the time to assure himself of its truth by a second telegram, and had hastened to forestall any less careful, less tender friend in bearing the sad message.

She did not hear the story as many women have heard the same, with a paralyzed inability to accept its significance. She wept at once, with sudden, wild abandonment, in her sister's arms. **When the storm of grief had spent itself**[2] she went away to her room alone. She would have no one follow her.

There stood, facing the open window, a comfortable, roomy armchair. **Into this she sank, pressed down by a physical exhaustion that haunted her body and seemed to reach into her soul.**[3]

She could see in the open square before her house the tops of trees that were all aquiver with the new spring life. The delicious breath of rain was in the air. **In the street below a peddler was crying his wares.**[4] The notes of a distant song which some one was singing reached her faintly, and countless sparrows were twittering in the eaves.

There were patches of blue sky showing here and there through the clouds that had met and piled one above the other in the west facing her window.

She sat with her head thrown back upon the cushion of the chair, quite motionless, except when a sob came up into her throat and shook her, as a child who has cried itself to sleep continues to sob in its dreams.

She was young, with a fair, calm face, whose lines bespoke repression and even a certain strength. But now there was a dull stare in her eyes, whose gaze was fixed away off yonder on one of those patches of blue sky. It was not a glance of reflection, but rather indicated a suspension of intelligent thought.

There was something coming to her and she was waiting for it, fearfully. What was it? She did not know; it was too subtle and elusive to name. But she felt it, creeping out of the sky, reaching toward her through the sounds, the scents, the color that filled the air.

Now her bosom rose and fell tumultuously. **She was beginning to recognize this thing that was approaching to possess her, and she was striving to beat it back with her will—as powerless as her two white slender hands would have been.**[5]

When she abandoned herself a little whispered word escaped her slightly parted lips. **She said it over and over under her breath: "free, free, free!"**[6] The vacant stare and the look of terror that had followed it went from her eyes. They stayed keen and bright. Her pulses beat fast, and the coursing blood warmed and relaxed every inch of her body.

She did not stop to ask if it were or were not a monstrous joy that held her. A clear and exalted perception enabled her to dismiss the suggestion as trivial. **She knew that she would weep again when she saw the kind, tender hands folded in death; the face that had never looked save with love upon her, fixed and gray and dead. But she saw beyond that bitter moment a long procession of years to come that would belong to her absolutely.**[7] And she opened and spread her arms out to them in welcome.

There would be no one to live for her during those coming years; she would live for herself. **There would be no powerful will bending hers in that blind persistence with which men and women believe they**

have a right to impose a private will upon a fellow-creature.[8] A kind intention or a cruel intention made the act seem no less a crime as she looked upon it in that brief moment of illumination.

And yet she had loved him—sometimes. Often she had not. What did it matter! What could love, the unsolved mystery, count for in face of this possession of self-assertion which she suddenly recognized as the strongest impulse of her being!

"Free! Body and soul free!" she kept whispering.[9]

Josephine was kneeling before the closed door with her lips to the keyhole, imploring for admission. "Louise, open the door! I beg; open the door—you will make yourself ill. What are you doing, Louise? For heaven's sake open the door."

"Go away. I am not making myself ill." No, she was drinking in a very elixir of life through that open window.

Her fancy was running riot along those days ahead of her. Spring days, and summer days, and all sorts of days that would be her own. She breathed a quick prayer that life might be long. It was only yesterday she had thought with a shudder that life might be long.[10]

She arose at length and opened the door to her sister's importunities. There was a feverish triumph in her eyes, and she carried herself unwittingly like a goddess of Victory. She clasped her sister's waist, and together they descended the stairs. Richards stood waiting for them at the bottom.

Some one was opening the front door with a latchkey. It was Brently Mallard who entered, a little travel-stained, composedly carrying his gripsack and umbrella. He had been far from the scene of accident, and did not even know there had been one. He stood amazed at Josephine's piercing cry; at Richards' quick motion to screen him from the view of his wife.

But Richards was too late.

When the doctors came they said she had died of heart disease—of joy that kills.[11]

1. *"It was her sister Josephine who told her, in broken sentences, veiled hints that revealed in half concealing."*

Barbara Larson: A **FEMINIST** critic might respond negatively to this sentence, not only because it implies the stereotype of the "weaker sex" but also because that stereotype is reinforced by another female character. This last problem might be particularly troubling to the feminist critic, since the reference to "sister" could have suggested a deeper, even more positive sense of sisterhood if the words that followed had not presented the character as weak and tentative. Her "broken sentences" reflect the unease with which she accepts the role of messenger. The word "veiled" implies a stereotyped feminine delivery, while the word "hints" suggests that the recipient of the message will be unable to accept the straight truth. Indeed, the phrase "revealed in half concealing" reiterates that inability. **Kathleen B. Durrer**: A **FEMINIST** critic might decry this presentation, . . . since, despite the story's feminist theme and female author, Josephine represents the stereotype of women as weak, ineffectual, and emotional. Whether she is motivated by a desire to avoid the unpleasant or by a fear of Louise's reaction, Josephine is portrayed as weak. Had the story been written by a man, a feminist critic might argue that Josephine illustrates male writers' tendencies to portray women as characters who are unable to confront reality directly and who must therefore resort to "broken sentences" and "veiled hints" in ineffectual efforts to convey news that is best delivered quickly and concisely. **Amanda Higgins**: Even the diction seems to stutter, mirroring a common perception of women as being unable to communicate effectively and without hysteria. A **FEMINIST** critic might be especially disturbed by the fact that this stereotypical vision of women was penned by a woman, since Chopin would thus be providing further evidence that patriarchy has programmed even feminist writers to remain within certain acceptable limits in depicting female behavior. **Dianne Russell**: A **FEMINIST** critic might cringe when reading this sentence because it implies that Josephine is chosen over Richards to bear the tragic news simply because she is a woman. Because our patriarchal society teaches us that women are more emotionally supportive and nurturing than men, it comes as no surprise that Chopin depicts Josephine as knowing how to relate the news *gently* to Mrs. Mallard, using "broken sentences" and "veiled hints" to soften the shock.

2. *"When the storm of grief had spent itself . . ."*

Kathleen B. Durrer: An **ARCHETYPAL** critic might respond to this phrase by highlighting the reference to "the storm." Storms have often been used to symbolize tremendous outpourings of emotion, the cleansings of the spirit that must occur after powerful disturbance before life can continue. Coupling this image with "grief" calls to mind the various rituals of grief that have existed throughout history. All societies have developed formal ways to acknowledge grief, thereby suggesting to an archetypal critic that this need is innate and universal. **Barbara Larson**: An **ARCHETYPAL** critic might respond to this phrase by arguing that it evokes a universal response from the audience. Since almost all humans have had repeated personal experiences with storms, almost any audience would react to the word "storm" by imagining a violent commotion or outburst of passion, and the word "grief" would similarly convey to anyone the common emotion resulting from a deep sorrow caused by a painful loss. In this phrase, Chopin thus draws on experiences and reactions to which almost all human beings can relate. **Dianne Russell**: An **ARCHETYPAL** critic might appreciate this passage not only because grief is an emotion that can seem uncontrollable and that afflicts people of all races, cultures, and genders, but also because a storm similarly stimulates feelings that all people can share. **Amanda Higgins**: By using an **ARCHETYPAL** image associated with powerful natural forces, Chopin implies that Mrs. Mallard grieves adequately and sincerely, not easily shrugging off her husband's death. **Lara Bridger**: An **ARCHETYPAL** critic would appreciate Chopin's use of an archetypal image both to portray and to elicit an emotional response. The "storm" image evokes both the fear of destruction and the promise of renewal. A reverence for nature (a force beyond human power) is instinctual, and it informs Louise's intense emotion as she confronts the overwhelming power of her own nature. As Louise's shelter, or marriage, is destroyed by her husband's death, the "storm" of her inner turbulence indicates the destruction of old ideas. Ultimately, as the archetype also implies, a cleansing effect results. Louise's "storm of grief" washes away the emotional deadwood of her marriage and allows her to begin anew. **Mike Cunliffe**: An **ARCHETYPAL** critic might note that in Mrs. Mallard's case, the storm descends, unleashes its downpour, and then vanishes. Louise's storm is brief and singular; it spends itself totally, not to return. Moreover, Chopin's use of the storm image is archetypally appropriate in another way. The end of a storm generally brings sunshine and tranquillity, just as Louise experiences calm after her thoughts turn from her husband to herself.

3. *"Into this she sank, pressed down by a physical exhaustion that haunted her body and seemed to reach into her soul."*

Kathleen B. Durrer: A Freudian **PSYCHOANALYTIC** critic might respond to this report by arguing that Mrs. Mallard's physical exhaustion is evidence of the tremendous battle occurring in her unconscious mind. Louise is experiencing a powerful conflict of the three zones of her mind—the id, the ego, and the superego. Presumably she has led a sexually repressed life, as was not uncommon among women in traditional households of her time. Her reaction to her husband's death may imply that their marriage did not abound in sexual passion. A Freudian critic might focus on Louise's presumed sexual repression and argue that the news of Brently's death touched off an internal battle in her unconscious mind. Upon learning the news, the id might immediately begin scheming to take control, to seize the freedom offered by Brently's death and begin a quest for pleasure. The superego, however, might be appalled by the thought of any pleasure being derived from the death of a husband and might fight to impose the proper social behavior expected of a grieving widow. The ego, of course, would attempt to mediate between these two extremes in order to prevent a complete mental breakdown from resulting. Although Louise is not aware of the battle raging within her unconscious, it physically exhausts her. **Barbara Larson**: A Freudian **PSYCHOANALYTIC** critic might note that almost every word in this sentence can suggest feminine sexuality, especially "sank," "pressed down," "her body," "reached into her soul," and "physical exhaustion." Here, however, the sexuality is passive and implies domination.

Lara Bridger: A Freudian **PSYCHOANALYTIC** critic might contend that Louise's marriage has imposed such strict limitations on the expression of her deepest desires that a violent release of primal energy is now inevitable. **Geni Williams**: A Freudian **PSYCHOANALYTIC** critic might respond to this sentence by arguing that it almost seems as if Mrs. Mallard has been controlled by her super-ego for most of her life. She has had to strive for social perfection: to be the perfect wife, to be the perfect upper-class wife, and to be the perfect woman in general. Now that these pressures have subsided, it is almost as if the adrenaline has stopped pumping through her body and exhaustion has set in.

4. *"In the street below a peddler was crying his wares."*

Barbara Larson: A **MARXIST** critic might note how this sentence tacitly reflects the class power structure of Chopin's day. By placing the vendor in "the street below," Chopin reminds us of the social distance between the vendor who is below and the potential buyer who is above. By calling the vendor a "peddler," Chopin encourages us to view the seller as a wanderer, thus underscoring the "lower class" connotations of his profession. The mere presence of a figure "crying his wares" reminds the audience that the lower class does not have the means to visit distant stores and select expensive items of their choice; instead, they must accept whatever is available from the "peddler" on the street. A Marxist critic might see such phrasing as reflecting the author's own position of relative power in the socio-economic structure of her day. **Kathleen B. Durrer**: A **MARXIST** critic might respond to this sentence by noting that it provides evidence of the class structure of Chopin's America. The fact that Louise looks down on the street might imply her social superiority and condescension toward the working class that provides for her day-to-day needs. Although the Mallards' social class is not explicitly stated, the story suggests that they are members of the upper class. Their financial status is implied in the description of their home, since Louise looks out on an open square from a comfortable, roomy chair in her second-floor bedroom. Her status is also implied by her complete lack of financial concerns as she contemplates her future. A Marxist might contrast the social condition of a street peddler in the late 1800s with the social condition of the Mallards and might assert that such inequity typifies the evils of capitalism. **Amanda Higgins**: A **MARXIST** critic might view such a sentence as an impediment to social progress because it uses the image of the peddler merely as an ornament, to create a mood, thereby underemphasizing the real hardship inherent in being a member of a lower socioeconomic class. **Lara Bridger**: A **MARXIST** critic might suggest that Louise, as a member of the upper class, is aware of, but unconcerned with, the peddler. She gazes out the window from her over-stuffed chair, rediscovering her identity, as the peddler diligently struggles to fuel an economy which affords Louise's self-indulgent contemplation. Conversely, the peddler is never afforded personal identity but is defined only as a member of the working class. **Dianne Russell**: A **MARXIST** critic might note how casually this sentence assumes that the existence of different social classes is the norm and will always be the norm. The existence of such a class system is made to seem as inevitable as the weather.

Kathleen B. Durrer: A **DECONSTRUCTOR** might respond to this sentence by emphasizing the contradictions inherent in its phrasing. Perhaps a deconstructor would focus, for instance, on the relationship between the words "peddler" and "crying." At first glance the relationship seems clear, because a peddler must sell items on the street; he must "cry" or orally advertise his goods. Therefore "crying" might be seen as a tool the peddler uses to accomplish his role in life. However, "crying" may also subtly suggest a public voice raised in protest or an inarticulate utterance of distress, rage, or pain. Therefore, instead of signifying a relationship of tool to job, "crying" and "peddler," taken together, may imply the pain or injustice of the peddler's lowly position in life. Or perhaps a deconstructor would focus on Mrs. Mallard's elevated position and the peddler's lower position and argue that although the story appears to concern Mrs. Mallard's freedom from repression, she is still repressed by her social status. Therefore, her subordination to Mr. Mallard has only been replaced by her subordination to the dictates of upper-class society. The peddler, on the other hand, despite his lowly status, has more real freedom than Mrs. Mallard because society does not mandate his behavior to the degree that it mandates hers. **Barbara Larson:** A DECONSTRUCTOR might use this sentence to illustrate the inevitability of a multitude of interpretations being offered of any text, whatever meaning the author may have intended. Although this sentence does not seem particularly important to the story as a whole, by exploring various possible interpretations of it, a deconstructor could argue that it typifies the instability of all language. Perhaps the author included the sentence to remind the audience that while the main character is faced with a monumental event in her life, for others life goes on as usual. A reader, on the other hand, might view the introduction of the peddler as a distraction from grief or as an annoyance to one who is suffering. Another reader might see the peddler as more free than Louise, while another might see Louise as more free than the peddler. Still another reader might see Louise as a person who has just escaped one kind of oppression but who is herself implicated in the oppression of the peddler. A deconstructor would not fear such conflicting interpretations but would instead see them as evidence of the unstable meanings of any text. **Lara Bridger:** A DECONSTRUCTOR might emphasize the inconsistencies embedded in this sentence. Apparently the sentence implies that the peddler is "below" Louise, both literally and figuratively. He hawks his wares in the street while Louise relaxes in the safety of her home. However, while seemingly at a disadvantage, the peddler is a male and a participant in the economy, while Louise must depend on the financial support of her husband. The peddler's presence might suggest a similarity between these two oppressed persons, but their genders and different economic positions also create an unresolved friction. The peddler, as a male, participates in the oppression of Louise;

Louise, as a member of the upper class, participates in the oppression of the peddler. A deconstructor would probably see this contradictory relationship as inevitable in a text which is, by its very nature, intrinsically unstable.

5. *"She was beginning to recognize this thing that was approaching her, and she was striving to beat it back with her will—as powerless as her two white slender hands would have been."*

Kathleen B. Durrer: LONGINUS might respond to this sentence by recognizing Kate Chopin's talent for using beautiful, powerful language to express Louise's feelings. Chopin's phrasing is concise yet manages to create a vivid image in the minds of her readers. Longinus advocated the use of "elevated language" to transport an audience, and he felt that to achieve the "sublime," a writer must use noble diction and dignified, elevated composition. A word such as "striving" and a phrase such as "white slender hands" add touches of sublimity here. **Barbara Larson**: Although the style of this sentence is not particularly elevated, LONGINUS would probably approve nonetheless because the phrasing does have the potential to capture the audience and sweep it dramatically along. By presenting the unseen invader so mysteriously, Chopin enthralls the audience and gives the passage a somewhat frenzied quality. By using such words as "approaching," "possess," "beat," "will," and "powerless," Chopin demonstrates her ability to use language to captivate her readers. Even the length of the sentence is worth noting, and the simile, full of adjectives, heightens the audience's response to the author's words. **Lara Bridger**: LONGINUS might consider this sentence a sublime illustration of Louise's sublime moment of inspiration. Louise's "possession" by a powerful force epitomizes Longinus's belief in the overwhelming power of beautiful truths. Louise, confronted with the truth of her nature, cannot resist possession by it.

Kathleen B. Durrer: A FEMINIST critic might object to this passage if it were analyzed as a single sentence, separated from the story as a whole, because this sentence portrays Louise as both mentally and physically weak (a typical stereotype of women at the turn of the century). Louise is presented as mentally weak because she lacks the needed will power to combat "this thing" that is approaching her. Louise is also presented as physically weak because her "two white slender hands" would probably be "powerless" to defend her from a physical assault. Both images reinforce the stereotype that women are unable to deal effectively with threats in their world. Women allegedly needed to be shielded from the harsh reality of the world and protected by males, who supposedly were both physically and mentally stronger. However, within the context of the story as a whole this passage might be applauded by a feminist critic because it serves to "set up" the reader for the shocking revelation that follows. The passage helps to convince the reader that Louise is the typical weak and submissive woman of her time. This image, however, is then shattered in the paragraphs that follow. The overall effect is a startling, perhaps shocking, yet insightful look into the feminine psyche and might thus be praised by feminist critics. **Barbara Larson**: A **FEMINIST** critic might object to this sentence not only because the character is portrayed as timid and as hesitant to welcome or even accept her new-found freedom, but also because the author's words seem to support the stereotype of the "weaker sex" to the detriment of women in general. Because the author in this case is herself a woman, a feminist might find such phrasing especially painful. By using the phrase "beginning to recognize," Chopin implies that a woman such as Mrs. Mallard could hardly conceive of a freedom such as she now faces. It is a "thing" unknown to her. The phrase "this thing that was approaching her" almost suggests that this future freedom seems a threatening monster of some sort, an impression reinforced by her "striving to beat it back." Emphasizing that both ("two") hands would not be enough to defend Mrs. Mallard, Chopin goes even further by describing the hands as "slender" and "white," implying that they have known little work or hardship and can provide no effective resistance. On the one hand, a feminist critic might be bothered by Chopin's perpetuation of the stereotype of a weak female; on the other hand, such a critic might argue that Chopin shows how such weakness inevitably results from the kind of sheltered life forced upon Mrs. Mallard and other women like her.

6. *"She said it over and over under her breath: free! free! free!"*

Kathleen B. Durrer: A READER-RESPONSE critic might react to this sentence by acknowledging that different audiences might react to it differently. For example, the majority of Chopin's contemporaries in 1894 would probably have considered her story rebellious and revolutionary in its questioning of traditional women's roles. However, another audience, consisting of women in the 1890s who were struggling for greater rights and freedom, might have viewed Louise's outburst as an inspirational rejection of a woman's traditional role. Even today, Chopin's words can elicit different reactions from different kinds of readers. Many women readers, for instance, can probably sympathize with Louise's desire for freedom. Many men, however, would probably be repelled by the idea of a woman rejoicing that her marriage has ended, especially by a tragic accident. However, the wide range of potential reader responses need not be limited by differences in sex. A woman of the religious right, for example, might also react negatively to Louise's words, viewing them as degrading to the institution of marriage. Similarly, many other reactions can be imagined from many different kinds of readers. **Barbara Larson**: One kind of READER-RESPONSE critic might react to this sentence by noting how Chopin uses her powers of persuasion to encourage readers to respond as the author wishes. By using the phrase "She said it over and over," Chopin hints that the words have become a consoling mantra for the bereaved widow, thus implying a positive interpretation of them. The words "under her breath" might also encourage the reader to feel an intimacy with Louise and thus regard her sympathetically, since the reader is allowed to share a very personal moment. Likewise, by placing exclamation marks after each use of "free," Chopin may be encouraging the reader to share Louise's excitement about this new-found liberty. Of course, different kinds of readers may have differing reactions. One sort of reader, for instance, might be repulsed by the secret joy (expressed "under her breath") this woman feels at the death of her spouse. Reader-response critics, then, might try to show how Chopin *attempts* to shape her readers' responses, although these critics concede that no author can ever exercise absolute control over the text she creates. **Dianne Russell**: A READER-RESPONSE critic might suggest that different readers might respond in differing ways to this sentence. For instance, a man who has never been oppressed would be unlikely to respond to the sentence in the same way as a woman who had spent her life under the rule of a strict, domineering father and then under the control of a strict, domineering husband. Such a woman would fully understand Louise's feeling of emancipation.

7. *"She knew that she would weep again when she saw the kind, tender hands folded in death; the face that had never looked save with love upon her, fixed and gray and dead. But she saw beyond that bitter moment a long procession of years to come that would belong to her absolutely."*

Barbara Larson: A DIALOGICAL critic might note that although this passage relates Mrs. Mallard's thought processes to the reader, it also exemplifies a dialogue between the voice of her old life as a subservient wife and the voice of her new life as an independent woman. One voice (the widowed Mrs. Mallard) remembers her role as a recently married woman, while the other voice (the single Louise Mallard) recognizes that the time for sustained grieving is over. The words "tender hands" and "never looked save with love" are obviously provided by the woman who at least thought she was content with her married life. The phrase "fixed and gray and dead" is somewhat neutral and serves as a transition to the voice of the newly liberated Louise, who looks forward enthusiastically to a life without marital bonds. The words "that bitter moment" is a final concession to the voice of the old life before the new voice finally echoes far into the future by referring to "the long procession of years to come that would belong to her absolutely." By presenting this diversity, Chopin also perhaps implies a conflict (or dialogue) between at least one side of the character and the authority of the author herself, or perhaps

Chopin inadvertently reveals a conflict or dialogue between competing perspectives within her own mind. Finally, a dialogical critic might also interpret this passage as epitomizing a dialogue between character and reader, in which the character is implicitly arguing her case for the right to feel liberated, conceding to the reader all of her husband's kindnesses before she gives way to complete ecstasy at the new life that fate had presented her. **Kathleen B. Durrer**: A **DIALOGICAL** critic might respond to this passage by first noting that it presents an intimate look into Louise's consciousness. Louise's thoughts are presented as they unfold. Dialogical critics often prefer works that allow their characters a kind of "freedom of speech" that permits a reader to respond to the character without direction from the author. Mikhail Bahktin, discussing Dostoevsky, argued that a writer could dramatize the internal conflicts and developmental stages of a single character by involving the character in dialogues with doubles, alter egos, or other beings. A dialogical critic might therefore note how the quoted passage (and indeed the majority of "The Story of an Hour") implies an internal dialogue within Louise as she reacts to the news of her husband's death. **Lara Bridger**: A **DIALOGICAL** critic might suggest that the dialogue of voices in this passage indicates social conflict. Louise is torn between her duty to her husband and her desire to live for herself. Furthermore, responsibility to an institution which has repressed her is also compounded with her genuine feeling for her husband.

8. *"There would be no powerful will bending hers in that blind persistence with which men and women believe they have a right to impose a private will upon a fellow creature."*

Kathleen B. Durrer: A **NEW HISTORICIST** critic might respond to this sentence by noting that it not only provides evidence of the social structure which existed at the time Chopin's story was written but that it also contributes to a movement to change that structure. Up until the late 1800s, the dominant role of men in society went widely unchallenged. Men were "in power," and nowhere, perhaps, was their dominance more evident than in marriage. Women were usually expected to submit to their husbands' wishes even when they disagreed with them. This passage is especially intriguing because it not only illustrates the social structure that existed but because it also provides insight into the psychological stirrings that were emerging in the minds of many women who were subjected to such oppression. Even today, the new historicist might emphasize the applicability of this passage to the struggle of women to free themselves from subordinate relationships in a male-dominated work force. **Barbara Larson:** Because **NEW HISTORICIST** critics generally define reality in terms of power relations (including dominance and submission), this passage would offer an abundance of opportunities for close examination. In addition, the passage can be seen as an attempt to undermine the accepted male/female power positions of Chopin's time. The words "powerful will" are especially important because they suggest, through contrast, the subservient position Mrs. Mallard has heretofore occupied. Obviously her will has been previously bent. The words "blind persistence" remind the reader that often there is no examination of the appropriateness of one person's dominance of another; rather, the dominance is successfully perpetrated (and perpetuated) because it is traditional. Words such as "right" and "impose" again suggest the struggle for power that pervades so much writing (according to many new historicists). **Foster Dickson:** A **NEW HISTORICIST** might emphasize the stress on power in this passage, concentrating especially on the words "powerful" and "impose." Interestingly, although Mrs. Mallard obviously feels oppressed, her husband probably lacks any consciousness of oppressing her or any deliberate desire to do so. **Lara Bridger:** A **NEW HISTORICIST** might note how Louise's continued submission is ultimately maintained by the inevitable return of the establishment, embodied by her husband. Although the story seems at first to affirm Louise's escape, it finally reveals the victory of the status quo. **Dianne Russell:** A **NEW HISTORICIST** critic might suggest that this sentence depicts human beings as they typically behave—that is, trying to impose their wills on one another.

9. *"And yet she had loved him—sometimes. Often she had not. What*

did it matter! What could love, the unsolved mystery, count for in face of this possession of self-assertion which she suddenly recognized as the strongest impulse of her being!

"'Free! Body and soul free!' she kept whispering."

Scott Johnson: A **STRUCTURALIST** critic might point out the paired opposites (or "dyads") implicit in this passage, such as dependence and freedom, indifference and love, and material and spiritual ("body and soul"). In fact, the story as a whole has a dualistic structure, based on a contrast in the location of the action—between upstairs and downstairs. When Mrs. Mallard is downstairs the first time, she hears of her husband's death and is struck with grief. The second time she is downstairs, she discovers that her husband is alive, and subsequently dies of a heart attack. When she is upstairs, on the other hand, she experiences almost an epiphany or revelation. Furthermore, the language in this part of the story abounds with connotations of life and vitality. The upstairs-downstairs dyad therefore symbolizes more basic contrasts: between exultation and grief, and between life and death. This contrast could also be seen—in terms of the Western culture of which the story is a part—as a reflection of the binary opposition of Heaven and Hell.

Jonathan Wright: A **THEMATIC** critic might suggest that this passage contributes to the story's central theme of "freedom," for within these lines, Mrs. Mallard, although having been initially reluctant to think of freedom following the news of her husband's death, now boldly embraces it. Indeed, when Mrs. Mallard thinks about how "she had loved him— sometimes" and confesses that "often she had not," she seems actually to exercise a freedom previously unknown to her. As the lines of "repression" on her face suggest, she may previously have quieted her thoughts of dissatisfaction with guilt, but now she seems guilt-free.

Scott Johnson: A **POSTMODERNIST** critic might highlight Mrs. Mallard's shifting attitudes and her willingness to accept new roles. Despite our culture's frequent treatment of love as undying (or at least as fairly resilient), this text shows Mrs. Mallard's love to be fluid and indeterminate. The contradictions implicit throughout this passage provide further evidence of the inevitable instability of Mrs. Mallard's convictions. For instance, the last two sentences of the first paragraph are phrased as questions, but they end with exclamation points rather than question marks. The exclamation points suggest a forceful declaration, but their interrogative phrasing exposes their actual tentativeness. Also, if Mrs. Mallard's "self-assertion" is truly "the strongest impulse of her being," why has she just "suddenly recognized" it as such? In fact, the description of her "self-assertion" as an "impulse" is enough to show that it is no more real, or lasting, than her love for her husband. It is also unclear, in the phrase "possession of self-assertion," whether Mrs. Mallard possesses the self-assertion or if she is possessed by it. If the former is true, then self-assertion is shown to be something which she has acquired, and can therefore lose, rather than an inherent part of "her being." If the latter is true, then how can she be said to be asserting herself at all, if she is allowing herself to be possessed by a mere "impulse"? **Jonathan Wright:** A **POSTMODERNIST** might note that this passage accurately reflects reality because it shows how individuals not only perceive and react to situations differently, but also because it demonstrates how they often vainly attempt to resolve the contradictions that invariably surface in life. A postmodernist might also suggest that because Louise Mallard's reaction to her husband's death is uniquely her own, she should be allowed to react according to her own feelings, without incurring harsh condemnation by an audience that can know her mind only in part. Although she initially tries to rationalize the fact that "often she had not" loved her husband, she eventually abandons such attempts when she decides that love is an "unsolved mystery." A postmodernist might argue that Louise is wise to recognize the futility of trying to resolve internal contradictions and self-doubt because life's problems are too complex to be resolved by simplistic rules or unambiguous explanations.

Scott Johnson: A **TRADITIONAL HISTORICAL CRITIC** might look at the influence the transcendentalist movement may have exerted on this passage. The diction of the passage, for instance, is extremely reminiscent of the language of Emerson. It also resembles the phrasing of Walt Whitman, who was himself strongly influenced by Emerson. The passage especially brings to mind Whitman's "Song of Myself" and Emerson's "Self-Reliance." Like Whitman, Mrs. Mallard is celebrating herself and her freedom. Also like Whitman, she expresses sentiments that seem deeply American. Furthermore, her focus on "self-assertion" is much like that of Emerson, who eschewed bland social conformity and strove for independence with a mystical fervor. Also, the many exclamation marks in this passage suggest an excitement and vitality that would have been appreciated by both Emerson and Whitman.

Jonathan Wright: A **MULTICULTURALIST** might wonder how Louise's views of "freedom" would be different if she were not a young, financially secure white woman. For instance, if Louise were an African-American woman whose parents and grandparents knew the harshness of slavery, she might not perceive her husband's death as "freedom." Furthermore, although an African-American woman at the end of the nineteenth century would probably have experienced financial difficulties even while enjoying the support of her husband, it would have been especially difficult for most black women to survive completely on their own at the turn of the century. Thus, if Louise were a poor black woman who viewed her husband's death as a bittersweet moment, a reader might well suspect the worst of Brently Mallard's character. **Scott Johnson**: A **MULTICULTURALIST** critic might wonder how Mrs. Mallard's situation would be affected if, say, she were a lesbian or had latent lesbian tendencies. Such feelings might, to some extent, explain the power of her feeling of liberation at the death of a husband she may have felt compelled to marry. After all, Mrs. Mallard lived during a time when she would have been considered quite abnormal if she had attempted to live openly as a lesbian. She might feel more free after Brently Mallard's death, then, because her new role as a widow with lesbian feelings would be less constricting than her previous role as a married lesbian. As a widow, for example, she would not be chided for turning away the advances of men.

Alternatively, a multiculturalist might also point out that a black woman reading this story probably would not be affected in the same ways as a white woman. An African-American woman from Chopin's period could not completely share in Mrs. Mallard's new feeling of freedom, because if Mrs. Mallard were African-American, she would be no more free after her husband's death than before.

Scott Johnson: A **NEW HISTORICIST** critic might use this passage to illustrate that every individual exists within a social context defined in part by relationships of power. Mrs. Mallard believes that she has discovered a kind of absolute freedom. It is significant, however, that she has to leave the presence of other people to express this feeling. Her sister and Richards both expect her to be utterly devastated by her husband's death. If she reveals the exhilaration she feels to the outside world, she knows that she will be criticized. In fact, the very cause of her exhilaration is social. Before, she had lived through her husband because she was expected to do so. After her husband's death, however, that particular social restriction would be lifted. What she doesn't seem to realize, however, is that other restrictions would come to take its place. A widow would be expected to act in certain ways, just as a married woman would. Her joy at her husband's death also reveals her to be upper-class, for it would be impossible for a woman without strong economic support to rejoice over the death of a husband. There were not, after all, many good jobs for women in the late nineteenth century. If Mrs. Mallard were from the working class and were left to fend for herself economically, she might well be chained to a sewing machine for sixteen hours at a stretch, making barely enough to survive. If Louise is free at all, then, it is in large part because she is free from being a worker during an extremely oppressive period in American history—a period in which relations of power were quite important.

10. *"Her fancy was running riot along those days ahead of her. Spring days, and summer days, and all sorts of days that would be her own. She breathed a quick prayer that life might be long. It was only yesterday that*

she had thought with a shudder that life might be long."

Kathleen B. Durrer: A **FORMALIST** might respond to this passage by first noting how effectively it contributes to the form of the story. A powerful meaning is conveyed in a relatively short, simple paragraph. Then the critic might note the irony in the passage, especially since it suggests that Brently's death has given Louise the will to live. Finally, a formalist might look at the words themselves in an effort to discover the story's complex meaning. For example, a formalist might examine the use of the word "fancy" and note that as a noun "fancy" comes from the middle English word for "fantasy." This use might imply that Louise's perception of freedom is (as the reader finds out in the end) only a fantasy, a creation of her imagination. Then a formalist might look at the words that follow, especially "running riot," and point out that the word "riot" may imply indulging in revelry, wantonness, or profligate behavior. This sentence might then be viewed as implying Louise's intent to flaunt the standards of society and focus only on her own pleasure. Such close analysis would continue until all the significant words in the passage had been analyzed. Then the formalist would attempt to bring the results of such analysis together to formulate a harmonious but complex interpretation of the work. **Barbara Larson**: A **FORMALIST** critic might respond to this passage by concentrating on its language, paying relatively little attention to the story's social or cultural contexts. Chopin's words can be taken to imply rebirth and an exciting new life for Mrs. Mallard; the reference to "her fancy," for instance, suggests that she is limited only by the limits to her imagination. Chopin encourages the reader to accompany Mrs. Mallard on her fanciful rebirth by continually repeating the word "days," modifying it first with "spring" (suggesting new birth), then with "summer" (implying mature vitality and satisfaction), and finally with "all sorts" (again implying limitless possibilities). The words "would be her own" confirm Mrs. Mallard's transformation from dependence on her husband to independence, while in the next two sentences words such as "quick," "prayer," and "shudder," along with the repetition of "long," remind the reader of the life/death pattern that permeates and helps organize the story. **Dianne Russell**: A **FORMALIST** critic would appreciate this passage because of its use of implication, subtlety, and irony. All three qualities are especially present in the final sentence.

Kathleen B. Durrer: A **TRADITIONAL HISTORICAL CRITIC** might respond to this passage by relating it to social developments occurring at the time the story was written. It was a period of unprecedented change in the opportunities available to women. For the first time in history women were being admitted into universities and being allowed to participate in professions such as medicine. For the first time in history many women had significant choices beyond marriage and spinsterhood. For a woman such as Louise (an intelligent woman who felt repressed) the sudden release from the role of wife might seem to offer the opportunity to sample many of these new opportunities. For the first time in the history of women, these opportunities were now available to her.

Barbara Larson: A **FEMINIST** critic might feel some conflict in responding to this passage. On the one hand, such a critic might note and appreciate the description of a woman relishing the idea of independence. On the other hand, such a critic might feel uneasy at the somewhat flippant language ("fancy," "running riot") used to describe this reaction. Such language, after all, might contribute to the stereotype of the frivolous female. The contrasting diction might be interpreted as reinforcing this stereotype by implying the fickle nature often attributed to women.

Kathleen B. Durrer: **LONGINUS** might react to this passage by admiring how quickly and effectively Chopin conveys Louise's ecstatic reaction to her new freedom. Longinus distinguished between rhetorical amplification (which he associated with an abundance of words) and sublimity (which is often comprised in a single thought). Chopin excels in presenting an extremely complex experience in concise yet beautiful language. Here, for instance, she describes Louise's sudden transformation from despair to hope. Longinus compares sublimity to a lightning bolt that scatters everything before it, and something of that effect is certainly achieved here. **Barbara Larson**: Although **LONGINUS** might value the slightly elevated diction of this passage, he most certainly would applaud Chopin for using language to make the audience share the powerful emotions of the character. Like the formalist, for instance, Longinus would appreciate the hypnotic repetition of the word "days" to emphasize the emotion of the character and enthrall the audience. **Amanda Higgins**: LONGINUS might contend that the heightened, passionate nature of the language here allows the reader to associate Mrs. Mallard's new-found freedom with a victory over death (although that victory is ironically short-lived in her case).

Kathleen B. Durrer: A **MARXIST** critic might respond to this passage by noting how it implies the class interests of Kate Chopin. Here as elsewhere in the story, Chopin seems to challenge the subordinate role of women while nevertheless accepting the larger social structure. In this particular passage, for example, Louise voices no financial worries. Clearly she is of the upper class. This position allows her to revel in the possibilities of her situation, while a widow of a lower social class (such as the wife of the peddler mentioned earlier) would face the prospect of a life of poverty and struggle. However, a feminist Marxist might note that Louise has finally found freedom from the repressive relationship of husband and wife which subordinates and demeans women. **Barbara Larson**: A **MARXIST** critic might note the phrasing that suggests the character's class privileges. A "fancy" capable of "running riot" can develop most easily within comfortable environs. The description of Louise's future as "days that would be her own" places her firmly in a privileged society. Her changing attitude toward the "long" life ahead of her may reflect a self-centeredness rooted in whim rather than a worry anchored in poverty.

Kathleen B. Durrer: An **ARCHETYPAL** critic might respond to this passage in several ways. First, she might focus on the use of "spring days, and summer days" as images suggesting birth and harvest. Spring is typically seen as a season of new beginnings, and Louise is contemplating a rebirth from a life of repression to one of freedom. Summer is often viewed as a time of abundance, a time when labor comes to full fruition. Louise is looking ahead to enjoying the results of her rebirth. From another archetypal perspective, however, Louise herself might be seen as a symbol of the Jungian "anima"—a female invested with unusual power. Louise might here be seen as archetypally symbolizing life and vitality of soul, without which any person would feel dead.

Kathleen B. Durrer: PLATO would probably be distressed by "The Story of an Hour" and particularly by this passage. Plato believed that human emotions must be controlled because they interfere with the search for the truth about reality, a search that can only be successful if guided by facts and reason. "The Story of an Hour" is a story of emotions. This passage, for instance, not only expresses Louise's exhilaration in her freedom but also encourages an emotional response from readers.

11. *"When the doctors came they said she had died of heart disease—of joy that kills."*

Kathleen B. Durrer: ARISTOTLE might respond to this final sentence of "The Story of an Hour" with great appreciation. Aristotle viewed tragedy as "an imitation not only of a complete action, but of events terrible and pitiful." He felt that such events are best presented so that they "come on us by surprise." In these last words, the story of Louise's short freedom is complete. The ending is unarguably surprising. Yet when the reader stops to analyze what has occurred, she discovers that the events are not improbable. Mrs. Mallard's weak heart is mentioned in the first line of the story and thus provides a logical cause for the tragic surprise at the end. Aristotle felt that the element of surprise was strengthened when it, like everything else in a work, had a necessary connection to the rest of the work. In the closing words of her story, Chopin achieves a surprise that does not violate the work's unity but instead strengthens it. **Barbara Larson: ARISTOTLE** might note that the story has depicted a change in fortune and that this final ironic twist, although surprising, is completely consistent with the story's very first words. **Amanda Higgins**: ARISTOTLE might appreciate the fact that this short sentence wastes no words but is completely efficient in bringing the work to an intricate, complex conclusion. **Dianne Russell**: ARISTOTLE would value this sentence because it epitomizes the complex unity of the story. He would also applaud the sentence because it exemplifies his assertion that recognition and reversal are most effective when they coincide. Here we learn of Mrs. Mallard's death (reversal) at precisely the moment that we recognize the inadequacy and irony of the doctors' explanations.

Kathleen Durrer: HORACE might have responded to the final sentence in "The Story of an Hour" by advising Chopin to moderate the shocking impact of the sudden closure. In discussing every element of the literary text, Horace advised the writer to consider its potential impact on the audience. For this reason, Horace tended to counsel moderation in presenting a story. He advised writers to avoid taking risks that might shock or repel the audience. Chopin's story challenged the conventions of her society. This final sentence conveys an especially shocking meaning (that death may be preferable to life as a married woman), and that message would have been seen by many as almost revolutionary in the 1890s. Horace would have frowned upon the use of literature as a tool of social reform. Such reforms are often unpopular, and since Horace emphasized the writer's need to please an audience, he would have been reluctant to advise the writer to offend them. However, the final judge in Horace's theory of literature is always the audience. Perhaps this fact would help redeem Chopin in Horace's opinion, since "The Story of an Hour" is now viewed as a classic model of the short story. In other words, it has won audience approval. **Barbara Larson**: HORACE might commend Chopin for the simplicity with which she depicts Mrs. Mallard's tragic end. The irony of the phrase "the joy that kills" is moderate enough to please an audience rather than confuse them, and the ironic twist shows a desire to please and amuse them. **Amanda Higgins**: HORACE might appreciate the final sentence because it affects the audience; it packs a powerful punch. He would praise Chopin's efficient use of language, and although she violates stereotypes of female behavior by showing Mrs. Mallard's happiness at her husband's death, Chopin does so in moderation (for instance, by stressing Louise's appreciation of Brently). Horace would admire this restraint.

Kathleen B. Durrer: A FEMINIST critic might applaud the tremendous irony in the final words of "The Story of an Hour." The irony results because the reader knows that Louise's death occurs not from joy but from the horrible realization that she has lost the freedom she thought she had achieved. Louise's death emphasizes the oppression she has suffered, for she dies not "of joy that kills" but because, having once captured a brief glimpse of freedom, she refuses to return to a life of repression. **Lara Bridger:** A FEMINIST critic might be disturbed by the implications of this conclusion, preferring instead an ending that affirmed the possibility of female empowerment. **Amanda Higgins:** A FEMINIST critic might consider it tragic not only that Mrs. Mallard never lived the freedom she desired, but also that no one ever knew her brief happiness. **Foster Dickson:** A FEMINIST critic might find it ironically fitting that her husband's mere presence kills her at her moment of greatest triumph. It is almost as if a free woman must die. **Barbara Larson:** Because the "doctors" are not identified explicitly as feminine and are therefore presumably males, a FEMINIST critic might note their patriarchal assumption that Mrs. Mallard would die from joy at seeing her husband again. Feminists might see the doctors' response as typically condescending and ignorant.

Kathleen B. Durrer: A READER-RESPONSE critic might respond to this sentence by arguing that different audiences would interpret it differently. Both feminists and formalists, for instance, might admire the irony of this conclusion, but for varying reasons. Also, a reader-response critic might note that reactions to Chopin's ending would probably have been different in 1894 than in 1994. **Barbara Larson:** A READER-RESPONSE theorist might note the multitude of possible responses that even one word of this passage—"doctors"—might evoke in different readers. Different readers might imagine the doctors, variously, as caring or pompous or solicitous or skilled or inept or any number of other possibilities. **Lara Bridger**: A **READER- RESPONSE** critic might observe, for instance, that while a conservative male reader might take some satisfaction in Louise's end, a sympathetic feminist might lament her tragic demise.

Kathleen B. Durrer: A Freudian **PSYCHOANALYTIC** critic might respond to this sentence by arguing that Louise's death was caused by her tremendous guilt at the pleasure she had experienced at the news of her husband's death. All of Louise's repressed desires had emerged and had been recognized and embraced. When Louise is confronted with her living husband, all of society's conventions return to her mind, and she feels extreme guilt for her earlier thoughts. Louise cannot balance her inner feelings with the conventions of society and marriage. Instead of continuing to live a life wracked by guilt, she therefore chooses death. **Amanda Higgins**: A Freudian **PSYCHOANALYTIC** critic might argue that Louise dies from the realization that she would never be able to live a life that would fulfill the desires of her id and the needs of her ego. A Freudian might argue that she died not from literal heart disease but from psychic conflict. **Mary Mechler**: A Freudian **PSYCHOANALYTIC** critic might contend that Mrs. Mallard's death demonstrates the destructiveness of the repression forced upon her all her life by social conventions.

Kathleen B. Durrer: A **DIALOGICAL** critic might respond to this sentence by noting that in the final line of the story the narrator intrudes upon the form of the work by relating Louise's death in an emotionless voice. Readers are thus closed off from Louise's direct final thoughts and must form their own interpretations of what has occurred. **Amanda Higgins**: A **DIALOGICAL** critic might note how the doctors ultimately speak for Mrs. Mallard, telling her story and in effect having the last word. Such a critic might find the absence of Mrs. Mallard's voice the most intriguing part of this passage, since it links her death and her life. Mrs. Mallard is as voiceless in death as she had been while alive—an ironic illustration of one way that dialogue does define life and literature for the dialogical critic. **Mary Mechler**: A **DIALOGICAL** critic might appreciate this passage since it concludes a secret dialogue with the reader. Although the surviving characters in the story believe that Mrs. Mallard died from the joy of realizing that her husband was still alive, the reader knows a secret to which the other characters have not been privy. **Lara Bridger**: A **DIALOGICAL** critic might note how even the phrase "heart disease" can express two divergent voices or points of view; in more ways than one, perhaps, Mrs. Mallard dies of a disease of the heart. The words of the doctors are truthful in ways the doctors do not realize.

Kate Chopin's "Caline":
General Comments
from Diverse Critical Perspectives

by KIMBERLY BARRON and DEBORAH HILL

The following comments attempt to suggest, in general terms, how particular kinds of critics *might* respond to "Caline," given the basic assumptions that different kinds of critics tend to take for granted about literature. No claim is made that these comments represent the *only* ways a given critic might react; rather, the comments merely indicate how such critics *could* plausibly respond. For fuller explanations of the critical approaches mentioned here, see the introduction.[1] Numbers in brackets refer to the numbered paragraphs in the text of the story included in this volume. (RCE)

PLATONIC CRITICISM: Because a PLATONIC critic is absorbed in searching for philosophical truth and an accurate understanding of reality, he might condemn this story for its *relative* triviality, since it deceives the reader by offering frivolous descriptions and transient emotions as a worthy imitation of reality. For example, Caline's body is presented in considerable detail as she is described as having "yawned and stretched her long brown legs and arms, lazily," and again as she "arose, never minding the bits of straw that clung to her black hair, to her red bodice, and the

---

[1] See also the "Introduction" to Robert C. Evans, Anne C. Little, and Barbara Wiedemann, *Short Fiction: A Critical Companion* (West Cornwall, CT: Locust Hill Press, 1997), xv-lxxvi.

blue cotonade skirt that did not reach her naked ankles" [1]. Plato might consider this description merely an artist's impressionistic conception of reality—a conception that distracts the reader from the pursuit of genuine truth. Also, a PLATONIC critic might have misgivings about this narrative since Caline's emotions, which are relatively trifling in relation to the universal truths of life, are presented as the central focus of the story. For instance, once the train leaves, taking with it her first glimpse of culture and wealth, Caline "could not feel the same after that" [8], and a PLATONIST might note that she cries in sentimental hopelessness when she finally realizes that her desire in going to the city was to meet again "the pleasant-faced boy, who had made her picture that day under the mulberry tree" [14]. Thus, because this story is merely an artistic portrayal of one young girl's emotional experience and fails to teach any universally valuable lesson regarding truth or reality, a PLATONIC critic would probably find little to commend in this tale (DH).

ARISTOTELIAN CRITICISM: Because an ARISTOTELIAN critic is interested in the artistic unity of a literary text and in how it illuminates human nature, he would commend Kate Chopin for her skill in arranging the clutter of Caline's experiences and emotions to create a vivid, unified work of art. For example, the story begins by reporting that something awakened Caline from slumber "as suddenly as if it had been a blow" [1], and it ends by noting the sudden awakening of her heart as she encounters the pleasure and pain of love. An ARISTOTELIAN critic would appreciate the artistic craft demonstrated by this kind of implied connection. However, not only is Caline awakened physically and emotionally, she is also awakened mentally as she observes the finely-dressed, sophisticated men and women from the train and then later experiences life in the city. An ARISTOTELIAN critic would appreciate and seek to reveal to other readers the significance of Caline's awakening and the unity this theme helps give to this story (DH).

HORATIAN CRITICISM: Because a HORATIAN critic is interested in how effectively a writer satisfies the myriad tastes of a wide audience, he might possibly reproach Chopin for limiting her talent to a very slight range of interests. For instance, most young boys who are attracted to adventure and excitement might find the subject of a girl's emotions very dull. Religious men or women who value literature for its didactic qualities might disapprove because this story contains no effective moral, nor does it provide any obvious instruction. Many young women fascinated by romantic affairs might find the story disappointing in that Caline never meets the pleasant-faced boy again, and her love remains unfulfilled. A child unaware of love's misery might miss the pathos of Caline's experience, while an older man or woman whose heart has suffered countless such losses might find the tale relatively insignificant. Although a more selective audience could appreciate the story for its artistry, the wider majority might choose other stories for entertainment or instruction. Therefore, a HORATIAN critic might advise Chopin to concentrate her talent in gratifying her audience's diverse expectations (DH).

LONGINIAN CRITICISM: Because a LONGINIAN critic is interested in truly sublime (i.e., uplifting) works of art that are capable of elevating readers to heights of spiritual ecstasy and inspiring them to pursue nobler lives, such a critic might consider this story picayune, even vain. Although Chopin chooses each word with marvelous detail, her simple, straightforward style might seem to lack the lofty sublimity a LONGINIAN critic admires. Her descriptions of Caline, for example, present us with no lofty ideals or nobleness of character, only a young country girl slowly losing her naiveté. Readers may admire her unaffected beauty or sympathize with her hopelessness, but her experiences do not inspire spiritual or mental exultation. Thus, a LONGINIAN critic might consider this story ineffective in achieving what should be the goal of all literature, namely to inspire the reader's desire for spiritual and ethical perfection (DH).

TRADITIONAL HISTORICAL CRITICISM: Because a TRADITIONAL HISTORICAL critic is interested in studying such matters as the writer, the writer's era, and the original audience's reaction to the text, s/he would thoroughly investigate any historical clues offered in "Caline."

For instance, Chopin's mention of the Texas and Pacific railroad invites
extensive research. A TRADITIONAL HISTORICAL critic might note, for
instance, that the expansive Texas and Pacific Railroad, acquired in 1880
by the infamous "robber baron," Jay Gould, rendered service from El
Paso in the west to New Orleans in the east. Under Gould's control it
eventually operated feeder lines supplying cotton and other Southern
crops for the Missouri Pacific. A TRADITIONAL HISTORICAL critic might
also report that the latter 19th century produced not only the extremely
wealthy railroad magnates but also class conflicts and poverty—issues
obviously relevant to this story. Additionally, such a critic might show
how Chopin's sympathetic depiction of Creole and Cajun life in Louisiana earned her immediate renown as a local colorist. Herself of Creole/
Irish descent, Chopin painted daringly intimate portrayals of Creole
culture and the feminine heart that often shocked her contemporary
audience. "Caline," although seemingly simple and uncontroversial in
itself, would doubtless have impressed the late 19th Century reader as a
rare glimpse into the life of a poor Acadian girl. By thus delving into the
past, a TRADITIONAL HISTORICAL critic would attempt to provide a better
understanding of the author's intentions and of the text's significance to
its original audience (DH).

THEMATIC CRITICISM: Because a THEMATIC critic is interested in
the abstract ideas that a literary work emphasizes, he might focus on the
central theme of Caline's innocence. For example, the story describes
how, when the train stopped in its tracks, Caline looked "stupid at first
with astonishment," for "such a thing had not happened before within
her recollection" [3]. She stares in wonder at the travelers, and when a
young man begins sketching her, she fastens "wide eyes . . . earnestly
upon him" [6]. Once the train leaves, taking with it her first glimpse of
elegance and culture, Caline views the railroad with "new and strange
interest" [8]. She wonders with almost childish curiosity "whence these
people came, and whither they were going" [8]. In the city, she is bewildered and must "readjust all her preconceptions to fit the reality of it"
[13]. Not only is Caline innocent of worldly behavior and mannerisms,

but she is also innocent of her own subconscious desire for emotional attachment. It is her simplicity and inexperience in matters of love that prevent her from recognizing that what she had so eagerly sought was not the city or its crowds of people but, in fact, "the pleasant-faced boy, who had made her picture that day under the mulberry tree" [14]. By pointing out the recurring theme of Caline's innocence, the THEMATIC critic would seek to offer the reader a more comprehensive and satisfying understanding of the story (DH).

FORMALIST CRITICISM: Because a FORMALIST critic is interested in the ways elements of the text work together to create complex unity, s/he might focus on the overall theme of self-discovery. Thus, while the young man, confronted with Caline, finds an element of the new and unknown (or perhaps exotic) in his journey, Caline's brush with him also awakens an inner desire to explore the excitement of the unknown. In fact, imagery emphasizing awakening and enlightenment is used throughout the story, suggesting the theme of self-discovery. In this respect, the final sentence of the tale helps unify the imagery of self-discovery. Caline discovers that it was not the city, nor the journey, nor even the young man himself that she had desired; it was instead the promise of adventure or the exotic which she had sought in her journey, just as it was the exotic that the young man saw in her when he sketched her picture (KB).

PSYCHOANALYTIC CRITICISM: Because a PSYCHOANALYTIC critic is interested in the (sexual) complexity of the human mind in perceiving reality, and in how that complexity affects the ways texts are written and read, s/he might focus on the innocent yet provocative image Chopin creates of Caline in the reader's mind. For example, the reference to her "long brown legs and arms" and to the way she ignored the "bits of straw that clung to her black hair, to her red bodice, and the blue cotonade skirt that did not reach her naked ankles" [1] suggests unconscious sensuality in Caline. When a young man from the train, drawn by her natural beauty, begins to sketch her likeness, Caline stands "motionless, her hands behind her, and her wide eyes fixed earnestly upon him" [6]. Shy, yet evidently pleased by his attention, she casts an earnest gaze that could be interpreted as a voiceless appeal for his affection. Once he is gone, she becomes strangely dissatisfied. Her innate desire to be loved and desired compels her search for the first man who recognized and appreciated the beauty of her body. A PSYCHOANALYTIC critic would seek to reveal the various sexual undertones woven into Caline's behavior (DH).

ARCHETYPAL CRITICISM: Because an ARCHETYPAL critic is interested in certain basic fears, desires, and images that form the way humans perceive reality, he might focus on the first sentence of the story: "The sun was just far enough in the west to send inviting shadows" [1]. Here, the setting sun not only represents the resolution or completion of a day, but it also foreshadows the end of Caline's childhood and girlish innocence. Just as a day passes into night unobtrusively but unremittingly, so Caline's childhood passes quietly and irretrievably into a memory. The inviting aspect of the shadows may symbolize the coming pleasure of womanhood, but the shadows themselves may represent a fear of the unknown future. Thus, an ARCHETYPAL critic would seek to discover the latent symbols and images in a text and reveal their significance to other readers (DH).

Because an ARCHETYPAL critic is interested in the common stories or myths that humans use to structure experience or reality, s/he might focus on how the story reflects an overall journey or quest motif (a common ARCHETYPAL situation). Symbolism suggesting the journey motif is presented throughout the narrative, including the glittering "steel rails" of the railroad [2], the train itself [3], and the traveling passengers (who are on their own journey). Similarly, the opening sentence suggests the journey motif through its reference to a setting "sun" [1], which is often a symbol of exploration in western culture since it implies inviting shadows. Chopin's use of this opening image helps emphasize the story's many symbols of journey, thereby reinforcing the ARCHETYPAL idea that Caline is on a journey of self-discovery (KB).

MARXIST CRITICISM: Because a MARXIST critic is interested in conflicts between economic classes and the way that literature reflects, reinforces, or undermines dominant ideologies, he would definitely focus on the vast gulf between Caline's lifestyle and that of the wealthy travelers on the train. Unaccustomed to country life, the ladies in the party are described as having "walked awkwardly in their high-heeled boots . . . and held up their skirts mincingly" [4], while Caline, on the other hand, barefoot and disheveled after her nap under the haystack, stares unashamedly at the newcomers. A MARXIST critic might also focus on the consequences of Caline's low position in society. All hope of her meeting the "pleasant-faced" young man [6], much less of befriending him, is utterly destroyed because of the inescapable distinction between their economic classes. However, a MARXIST critic might point out that Chopin clearly sympathizes with the poor country girl, and her story tends to produce in the reader a sense of the injustice of separate social and economic classes (DH).

FEMINIST CRITICISM: Because a FEMINIST critic is interested in the various ways that reality is structured in terms of sexual or gender differences, he or she might emphasize Chopin's demeaning description of the ladies from the train as they "laughed immoderately at the funny things which their masculine companions were saying" [4]. A FEMINIST critic would find it intolerable that these women evidently felt obliged to flatter and indulge the men they were with. Such women change their very personalities and opinions to reflect what they believe men desire. FEMINIST critics would seek to persuade readers that women should never be reduced to the degradation of gratifying men's desires in order to achieve a happy and fulfilled life (DH).

STRUCTURALIST CRITICISM: Because a STRUCTURALIST critic is interested in the codes that a text uses to structure the reality reflected in the story, s/he might focus on the repetitive use of the opposing imagery of nature versus city, light versus dark, old versus new/young, and stasis versus journey. All of these oppositions work in a parallel manner to suggest Caline's journey of self-discovery. The opposition of nature and city is a central structural device for the story. Beginning with the initial imagery of Caline sleeping long and soundly in a field, the story suggests that the element of nature is related to Caline's initially naive and innocent condition. Her "naked ankles" [1] represent the natural sensuality of a young girl's innocence and contrast with the social convention of the "Sunday shoes" [11] she wears when she finally leaves for the city. Similarly, the contrast between Caline's father toiling in the field with his "plow" while the passengers disembark from the train [3] also emphasizes the dichotomy of nature and city. Finally, when Caline arrives in the city, she must adjust to the hum of the "French market" city life [13] which she finds to be so different from the quiet of the country.

These kinds of oppositions between nature and city parallel similar oppositions between old and new (or young). While the country and Caline's initial condition are both associated with the old, her awakening is symbolized by many references to things that are new. For example, her parents are old, they speak only their foreign dialect, and they are unaware of what lies beyond their home [9]. Likewise, Caline's father employs the traditional methods of farming—man and mule [3]. Caline stands under an "*old gnarled* mulberry tree" (emphasis added; [3]) with her ankles naked, while the passengers disembark from a modern vehicle wearing stylish "boots" [3]. After the train leaves, Caline looks with "*new and strange interest*" upon the passing trains (emphasis added; [8]).

Meanwhile the opposition of light and dark images more closely parallels Caline's internal awakening. The imagery of emergence from darkness is introduced in the first paragraph. Caline sleeps "in the shade of a haystack" but awakens to a "cloudless" (that is, light) "sky" [1]. Although a dark, "dense wood" surrounds Caline's farm, it is sliced through by "glitter[ing] steel rails" [2] which suggest light and a potential journey. These images, combined with Caline's emergence from the shadow to see the train, reflect both a literal and a figurative enlightenment.

Finally, the opposition of stasis versus journey is anticipated by the previously cited contrasts. Throughout the text, a sense of stability born of stasis is juxtaposed with a sense of adventure resulting from journey. For example, Caline sleeps in the "center of a small field" [1], a fact suggesting her sense of security in her surroundings. She stands beneath an "old" tree [3] that represents stability and longevity. Her "father" is a farmer [3], an occupation which demands patience and tenacity. And, most interestingly, she seeks her information about the travelers from "the old flagman, who stayed down there by the big water tank" [10]. Since trains cannot function without a stable water supply, the flagman represents the stability of staying home and not embarking on journeys. While the previously noted imagery of newness, light, and the city present parallel journey symbols in a positive sense, the contrast between the unknown journey (on the one hand) and the security and stability of staying in one place (on the other) contributes an important element of tension to the story (KB).

READER-RESPONSE CRITICISM: Because a READER-RESPONSE critic emphasizes individual interpretations of the text, s/he might concentrate on the different responses readers might offer of Caline's home. Readers who grew up in remote, rural areas, hidden and sheltered from the world outside, may read about Caline with a twinge of nostalgia as they remember a time when they too looked upon sophisticated, cultured people with wide open eyes of wonder. More urbane readers, however, might pity Caline for growing up uneducated and with no apparent prospects of advancement in society. However, some readers who have been confined to the rush and bustle of city life, and who dream of escaping to the country someday, may in fact envy Caline for growing up on a farm in a simple, natural setting. Thus, a reader-response critic would seek to prove that every reader's impression of Caline's home might be entirely different (DH).

DIALOGICAL CRITICISM: Because a DIALOGICAL critic is interested in the exchange of voices and conflicting viewpoints within the text and between the text and such "external" entities as the audience, s/he might consider the narrator's rendition of the flagman's reply to Caline's questions: "Yes, he knew . . . he knew all about the city" [10]. The narrator imbues the old flagman's words with a subtle touch of smug satisfaction, as though delicately ridiculing the old flagman's idealistic conception of himself as a vast reservoir of knowledge. Because the flagman speaks of the city as a strange, almost foreign place, his knowledge seems quite limited. However, he could be assuming an uncharacteristically simple perspective for Caline's benefit since he knows that she has never experienced city life. Through his effusive advice, the flagman conveys a pleased condescension toward Caline; he seems grateful that someone has sought out his knowledge. Both the old flagman and Caline view themselves very seriously, unlike the narrator, who describes them with a tender but half-amused tone. Thus, a DIALOGICAL critic would endeavor to analyze the continuous dialogue each text supplies within itself and the DIALOGICAL responses it incites among its readers (DH).

DECONSTRUCTIONIST CRITICISM: Because a DECONSTRUCTION-IST critic is interested in the contradictions and insolvable paradoxes inherent in language, s/he might argue that in this story the structural codes associating age with knowledge and associating youth with innocence are by no means unequivocal or clear-cut. For example, when the rich passengers alight from the train, Caline is not the only one who stands gazing in astonishment, for her father "st[ands] staring also, leaning upon his plow" [3]. Similarly, when Caline begins wondering curiously "whence these people came, and whither they were going," "her mother and father could not tell her" [8-9]. Innocence and even ignorance, therefore, are not restricted in this narrative to the young; instead, Chopin implies that parents sometimes know less than their children. A DECONSTRUCTIONIST critic might also point out that by decisively and resolutely departing alone for an unknown city in pursuit of the "pleasant-faced boy" [14] Caline usurps the traditional assertive role of the male in romantic affairs. However, even her aggressive qualities are prone to DECONSTRUCTION, for at the end of the story, Caline dissolves into very vulnerable and stereotypically feminine tears. A DECONSTRUCTIONIST critic would thus seek to reveal the instabilities embedded even in such an apparently simple tale (DH).

NEW HISTORICIST CRITICISM: Because a NEW HISTORICIST critic is interested in power-conflicts not only within the text but also within the text's cultural setting, s/he might focus on Caline's struggle against societal restrictions and her endeavor to break loose from her family's poverty. For instance, after her initial exposure to the affluent and sophisticated travelers, particularly the young man who sketches her likeness, Caline "could not feel the same" again [8]. She seems dissatisfied with her simple impoverished life as a farmer's daughter. Therefore, with a determination and aspiration remarkable for a poor country girl in the late nineteenth century, she sets off alone for the city. By the end of the story, however, Caline seems to realize (or accept) the dismal futility of struggling against her social position and of expecting to befriend a rich young man. Her overpowering disappointment could possibly be associated not only with the consciousness that she will probably never again see the "pleasant-faced boy" [14], but also with the realization that she will probably never break away from the restrictions imposed by her social status. Thus, a NEW HISTORICIST might view the story as an illustration of the ineffectual struggles of the poor to cross the rigid, oppressive line separating them from the rich (DH).

POSTMODERNIST CRITICISM: Because a POSTMODERNIST delights in all forms of self-expression, particularly those that reveal instability or irrationality or irresolution, s/he might value the unresolved ending to Caline's emotional experience. After her seductive encounter with the young man from the train, Caline's dissatisfaction with her former life leads her on a futile search, ending in frustration. She finds no completion to her quest, no satisfaction for her desires, and no profitable denouement to her tears of disappointment. If, in fact, Caline matures from her experiences, it will be because of her perception and acceptance of life 's unpredictability. The very brevity of the story, coupled with the fact that it seems to serve merely as entertainment, might attract POSTMODERNISTS, since they prefer accepting meaninglessness and irresolution rather than imposing false strictures of sense or meaning. A POSTMODERNIST would also value the story's ultimate sense of unfulfillment because such an ending presents a true reflection of reality's incoherence and lack of orderly conclusions (DH).

MULTICULTURAL CRITICISM: Because a MULTICULTURAL critic is interested in the ethnic diversity or other group identities portrayed in a text, he might focus on the unique social classification Caline embodies. For example, Caline's "French patois" [5] not only establishes her as a Creole, but it also suggests that she is illiterate in standard English, a plight most likely irremediable due to her parents' poverty. Her simple attire, consisting of a "red bodice and . . . blue cotonade skirt that did not reach her naked ankles" [1], emphasizes her position as a poor, isolated country girl and helps explains her amazement at the sight of the wealthy travelers and also her initial confusion in the city. Naturally, she is "bewildered" and must "readjust all her preconceptions to fit the reality of it" [13]. However, her naiveté is principally a result of her sequestered upbringing, not of her instinctive simplicity. In fact, coming from such a secluded background, Caline is courageous indeed to brave the strange city alone. A MULTICULTURALIST critic might also suggest that Chopin's use of words distinctive to the New Orleans Creole culture, such as "banquette" [12] and "lagniappe" [13], reflects upon her own Irish/Creole descent, thereby validating the argument that a writer's background and experiences will inevitably affect his or her work. By thus focusing on the important distinctions between various cultures and societies, a MULTICULTURALIST critic seeks to prove that no human being can behave independently of his or her particular group identity (DH)

Kate Chopin's "Caline": Specific Comments from Diverse Critical Perspectives

CONTRIBUTORS: JENNIFER ADGER (JA); JEFF ALEXANDER (JA2); ASHLEY ASHWORTH (AA); MELISSA BAKER (MB); KIMBERLY BARRON (KB); JANIS BLAESING (JB); JENNIFER BROWN (JB2); TANYA BRUMMETT (TB); SHAMEKA CARROLL (SC); ANDREA COOK (AC); JOHN ELDER (JE); ROBERT C. EVANS (RCE); MATT GILMORE (MG); BARBARA HARTIN (BH); SONJANIKA HENDERSON (SH); DEBORAH HILL (DH); MICHAEL HITCH (MH); LAKETA HUDDLESTON (LH); CONNIE JAMES (CJ); STEVEN JONES (SJ); JOHN KELLEY (JK); BARRETT LEE (BL); MONICA FELICIA LEE (MFL); KATHY MAYFIELD (KM); MIKE ODOM (MO); EDWARD PATE (EP); STEPHANIE REED (SR); LORELEI JACKSON SANDERS (LJS); JAY SANSOM (JS); DEBBIE SEALE (DS); DURAND SMITHERMAN (DS2); PATRICK STEELE (PS); MARK STEWART (MS); TERESA STONE (TS); TAMMY TAITE (TT); ERIC THOMASON (ET)

Caline

[1] The sun was just far enough in the west to send inviting shadows. In the centre of a small field, and in the shade of a haystack which was there, a girl lay sleeping. She had slept long and soundly, when something awoke her as suddenly as if it had been a blow. She opened her eyes and stared a moment up in the cloudless sky. She yawned and stretched her long brown legs and arms, lazily. Then she arose, never minding the bits of straw that clung to her black hair, to her red bodice, and the blue cotonade skirt that did not reach her naked ankles.

Because a STRUCTURALIST critic emphasizes binary structures in literature and experience, he might argue that the references to the **sun** and the **shadows** help shape our perception of reality in the story and parallel the similar contrasts between Caline's innocence and her eventual loss of this innocence (JA; TB; BL; MH; DS). In fact, a structuralist critic might see the opposition between innocence and experience as one of the most important oppositions in the whole story (EP). An ARCHETYPAL critic might find the references to the "**sun**" and "**west**" significant because they may already suggest the idea of a beckoning frontier or horizon (MG; BH). The phrase "inviting shadows" adumbrates some of the paradoxical flavor of the story as a whole, since Caline will later feel drawn (or almost invited) to the city but will not find real happiness there. Such paradoxical instability might be of special interest to a DECONSTRUCTIVE critic (BH). The fact that Caline has "**slept long and soundly**" and then is awakened "**suddenly,**" almost as if by a physical "**blow,**" might almost seem to epitomize the action of the entire story:

in the course of this tale, Caline will experience an awakening on many different levels, including an awakening to her own physical desire (MH; DS2). This process might especially interest a PLATONIC critic, who might be troubled by the story's emphasis on physical desire instead of rational thought (DS2). An ARCHETYPAL critic might argue that all humans can relate to the desire for sleep as well as to the fear of having one's sleep suddenly or violently interrupted (TT). A LONGINIAN critic, concerned with the power of literature to elevate the soul, might be intrigued by the description of Caline as she "**open[s] her eyes and stare[s] a moment up in the cloudless sky**," since such language can imply a sense of spiritual transcendence of the physical here-and-now (LH). A FORMALIST might note that as the story opens, Caline's mind is as free of troubles as the sky is free of clouds; by the end of the story, however, her mind and emotions will be figuratively darkened and troubled. The "**cloudless sky**" perhaps symbolizes Caline's relative innocence and inexperience at this point in the story (JA; KM). An ARCHETYPAL critic might argue that at this point Caline is in harmony with her rural physical environment, whereas by the end of the story she will feel alienated from the city to which she travels (KM). A FORMALIST might admire Chopin's skillful use of strong color imagery in the references to "**brown**," "**black**," "**red**," and "**blue**" in the last two sentences of this passage (LH; BL). The fact that Caline is described as having "**yawned and stretched . . . lazily**" perhaps already implies a touch of boredom with her present existence—a boredom that will help explain her later adventurous behavior (SR). A PSYCHOANALYTIC critic might suggest that the description of Caline's "**long brown legs and arms**" already introduces a note of sexuality into this story (MG; SJ; DS2; ET). In fact, Chopin reverses the usual word-order (arms and legs) in a way that emphasizes Caline's sensuous "**legs**" (SJ). The fact that Caline at this point does not "**mind . . . the bits of straw**" that cling to her prepares for two later contrasts: with the ladies from the train, who are quite concerned about their appearance [4], and with Caline herself after she decides to move to the big city and is concerned to dress properly [11] (TB). Note the careful patterning of this opening paragraph, especially its movement from general to specific—from the sun in the sky, then to the whole field, then to a particular haystack, then to Caline as a whole, and finally to particular details of her clothing (ET).

[2] The log cabin in which she dwelt with her parents was just outside the enclosure in which she had been sleeping. Beyond was a small clearing that did duty as a cotton field. All else was dense wood, except the long stretch that curved round the brow of the hill, and in which glittered the steel rails of the Texas and Pacific road.

Because a TRADITIONAL HISTORICAL critic believes that everything reflects the time of its occurrence, he might focus on the description of the railroads here, since such imagery implies the general period in which this story was written and therefore provides clues about the likely reactions of its original readers (BL). Indeed, nearly all the details mentioned in this section would interest a historical critic since those details help locate the story very precisely in a particular historical era (BH). Such a critic would note, for instance, how the reference to the **"log cabin"** immediately helps situate this story in a particular period and also helps locate Caline's family in a particular socio-economic status (MG). A MARXIST might find it significant that the railroad tracks, symbols of the growing capitalist economic system, run so close to the property owned (or perhaps merely rented) by Caline's family (MG). The fact that Caline still lives with her "parents" helps emphasize her youth and inexperience—important themes in a story that is largely about an initiation into psychological maturity (MH). The fact that the rails **"glitter"** helps emphasize how they stand out in—and apart from—the otherwise natural landscape; they are not only artificial but seem almost new in a setting that otherwise seems timeless (ET). At the same time, the "glitter" associated with the rails may make them seem enticing to Caline; they may symbolize new and exciting experiences (MH). The fact that the rails belong to the **"Texas and Pacific road"** helps make them seem representative of the kind of corporate, capitalist culture that was transforming the entire country during this era (RCE). Is it too fanciful to see the **"long stretch"** of the rails as they **"[curve] around the brow** of the hill" as almost suggesting a serpent gliding through a natural landscape? (MH)

[3] When Caline emerged from the shadow she saw a long train of passenger coaches standing in view, where they must have stopped abruptly. It was that sudden stopping which had awakened her; for such a thing had not happened before within her recollection, and she looked stupid, at first, with astonishment. There seemed to be something wrong with the engine; and some of the passengers who dismounted went forward to investigate the trouble. Others came strolling along in the direction of the cabin, where Caline stood under an old gnarled mulberry tree, staring. Her father had halted his mule at the end of the cotton row, and stood staring also, leaning upon his plow.

Significantly, only now does Chopin give her chief character a name—"Caline." Just as she "emerge[s] from the shadow," so her personal name now emerges. In fact, no one else in the story is given this kind of personal identity—a fact that makes it obvious that Caline is the central focus of Chopin's attention (MH). Because a TRADITIONAL HISTORICAL critic is interested in the historical context of a work, s/he might focus on this passage as evidence of a period in which the social structure reflected a large geographic and psychological gap between the urban and rural spheres of society (KB). The description of how "Caline emerged from the shadow" might be seen as part of a larger theme in this story of movement from the familiar to the unknown (MO), just as it might also be seen as part of the story's use of images of light and darkness (KB). Perhaps her movement from out of "the shadow" symbolizes her transition from a private world to a social existence and thus anticipates her later move from the country to the city (MO). The responses of Caline and her father, both stopping their activities and staring at the train, further suggest that the sight of train passengers disembarking was an unfamiliar experience. Since trains pass through the field regularly, it must be the passengers themselves rather than the train that seem unfamiliar (KB). Whereas both Caline and her father seem almost "stupid" with "aston-

ishment" at the sudden stopping of the train, the passengers seem to regard the event with relatively untroubled curiosity. A MULTICULTURAL critic might argue that these different reactions symbolize the different larger cultures to which these different people belong (JB). A MARXIST might note how easily the passengers assume their right to walk across land presumably owned by Caline's father; they never ask his permission or even acknowledge his presence (SJ). Caline's father may be a manual laborer, but he is ignorant of the mechanics of the train engine (KB). The passengers take the sudden stop almost literally in stride—a reaction that perhaps symbolizes their greater sense of power and control over their environment (RCE). Their **"strolling"** may suggest that they feel undisturbed and relaxed (JB; DS2). In contrast, Caline **"stood . . . staring"** (maybe in curiosity or maybe in fear) under the **"old gnarled mulberry tree."** Perhaps the tree represents aspects of Caline's life, implying its vitality but also its geographical rootedness and toughness (JB). Indeed, because ARCHETYPAL critics are often concerned with the natural symbols and images that frequently appear in literature, they might especially focus on the symbolic nature of the **"mulberry tree."** Just as the tree seems natural and beautiful to them, so does Caline (BL). Or perhaps the **"mulberry tree"** suggests Caline's presently sheltered life (MO). It may also symbolize her rural existence, as opposed to the upper-class urbanity of the train's passengers (KB). One can imagine many different theorists giving competing explanations of Caline's initial reticence. A MARXIST might argue that she is intimidated by the stranger's wealth. A Freudian might suggest that she is sexually repressed or inexperienced in dealing with young men. A FEMINIST might contend that she is behaving according to the "shy girl" stereotype imposed on women in her culture. An ARCHETYPAL critic might argue that she is displaying the non-aggressive posture symbolically and traditionally associated with women. A FORMALIST might suggest that her reticence here helps prepare for (and contrast with) with her adventurousness later and thus contributes to the complex unity of the tale. A STRUCTURALIST might assert that her reticence fits into a larger active/passive binary pattern that helps organize the whole story. A DIALOGICAL critic might argue that at present she has no real voice of her own, but such a critic might also suggest that she literally can't speak to the stranger because her language is French while his is English. Finally, a DECONSTRUCTOR might claim that although she speaks no obvious words, she speaks volumes to the curious young man, who will soon, through his drawing, make his own interpretation of what she represents—at least to him (RCE). Meanwhile, because a MARXIST critic emphasizes socio-economic matters, he might be interested in the brief description of Caline's **"father,"** since that description indicates the social class to which she and her family belong. Caline's father is obviously a farmer and (unlike the wealthy passengers on the train) presumably must work hard, long hours of physical labor (MG; BL; MO; DS). The fact that he **"lean[s] upon his plow"** suggests the physically exhausting nature of his work (LH). The fact that Caline has been sleeping while her father works with the plow might suggest, to a FEMINIST, the ways society often links particular kinds of work with particular kinds of gender (BH). The way some members of the group **"stroll"** up the hill toward Caline suggests that she is an oddity to them, almost as if she were a roadside sight along their journey (KB). The references to the **"old gnarled mulberry tree"** and, especially, the **"mule"** and the **"plow,"** when juxtaposed with the image of the train's steam engine, imply psychological distance between the modern industrialization of the urban world and the old-fashioned, animal- and man-powered orientation of the nineteenth-century rural world (KB; MG). Because a MARXIST critic is interested in the ways material and economic conditions affect other aspects of life, s/he might be interested in this passage as a succinct embodiment of the tensions between the poor rural working class and an affluent urban culture (KB; DS).

[4] **There were ladies in the party. They walked awkwardly in their high-heeled boots over the rough, uneven ground, and held up their skirts mincingly. They twirled parasols over their shoulders, and laughed immoderately at the funny things which their masculine companions were saying.**

The fact that the women are called **"ladies"** implies both their economic status and the particular gender roles they have adopted (or have
been encouraged to play [JE; KM]). The word **"ladies"** also distinguishes
them socially and perhaps also in age from Caline, who is more simply
described as a "girl" (AA; JB2; SC; JE). The use of the word **"party,"** rather
than "group," implies that the passengers were not on a serious journey
(KB). Similarly, the image of the women walking **"awkwardly"** over the
"rough . . . ground" (because of their inappropriate shoes) suggests a lack
of preparation to meet the serious challenges of the real, physical world
(KB)—the hard world in which Caline has grown up (JS). Of course, the
women did not anticipate having to walk over **"rough, uneven ground"**
when they originally dressed, but their clothing does not, in any case,
seem especially suited to a long train trip. The fact that these women
feel compelled to dress as they do suggests the degree to which their lives
are dictated by larger cultural codes over which they have little control,
especially since they *are* women (JK; TS). However, just as the **"ladies"**
walk **"awkwardly"** in this rural setting, so Caline will later experience
difficulty in adjusting to life in the city (JA; MO). A FEMINIST critic might
note the typically passive behavior of these women, whose main purpose
in a patriarchal society seems to be to act properly, look pretty, and curry
favor with men (BL; KM). The **"high-heeled boots"** that symbolize their
social status and power in an urban setting make them seem relatively
vulnerable and powerless in a rural setting—a change that emphasizes
that their social status is the product of a highly specific circumstance
and an artificial code (JA). Meanwhile, the references to their **"twirl[ing]
parasols"** and immoderate laughter (or giggling) reinforce an image of
frivolity and vanity (KB; BH), although a PSYCHOANALYTIC critic might
see these gestures as flirtatious and even playfully sexual (TS). A FEMINIST
might find this passage troubling since it could be seen as reinforcing a
stereotype of women as superficial and unintelligent (BH; MO). Chopin
does not portray these women laughing hardily alongside the men or
interjecting their own "funny" anecdotes. Instead, they listen politely and
laugh on cue, thereby maintaining the appropriate social distance and
validating the superior role of the men in their patriarchal society (TS). On

the other hand, a FEMINIST might suggest that Chopin here is implicitly satirizing the behavior and values of these particular women in order to promote social change: by implicitly criticizing these women, she might be attempting to alter and improve the lives of women in general (RCE). A MARXIST might contend, however, that these women are not simply wealthy, pampered females but are symbols of the oppressive capitalist class. Ironically, they might themselves be seen as both the beneficiaries and the victims of their class status: they enjoy the privileges of wealth, but they are also treated (and even view themselves) as material objects. They have no real independent identities because they have "bought into" (or have been born into) a system that treats human beings as commodities. In contrast, although Caline is economically poorer than these urban women, she perhaps has a much stronger sense of independent identity. Although the city women are rich in material goods, Caline is arguably richer in autonomous spirit. The city **"ladies"** walk **"mincingly"** over the ground, but Caline has not "bought into" a system that defines dirty feet as "bad" (RCE; TS). A FORMALIST or ARCHETYPAL critic might contrast the **"parasols"** of these ladies with the "brown," presumably sun-tanned, "legs and arms" of Caline mentioned in section 1: Caline shows the impact of nature, whereas the ladies are insulated from it (SJ). MULTICULTURALIST and MARXIST critics would both find this entire passage interesting since it symbolizes the distinctions between urban (and upper-class) and rural (and lower-class) cultures (TS).

[5] They tried to talk to Caline, but could not understand the French patois with which she answered them.

Because a MULTICULTURAL critic emphasizes such differences as those of age, sex, race, and gender, he might focus on how the failure of communication here results from differences of language and culture, which in turn help to shape the similar differences in character and emotion between Caline and the travellers (TB; CJ; BL). A MULTICULTURAL critic might focus on this passage as an example of an interaction or interface between two different cultural groups. Since the passengers cannot understand Caline, they are obviously from a different cultural group than she is (KB) and are probably also even from a different section of the country (ET). Because these ladies possess the social skills and self-confidence necessary to interact with other people, including strangers, it is they who approach Caline (CJ). Chopin's use of the word "patois" might interest a DIALOGICAL critic since the story thereby includes a bit of the very dialect it mentions (MFL). However, cultural differences go beyond even the distinction in language, as the tourists are of a different class altogether. In addition, the tourists have money, but Caline is poor; the tourists have experience beyond a certain locality by virtue of travel, whereas Caline has none; the tourists are educated, but Caline is not; the women tourists wear nice dresses, but Caline has only her provincial clothing ; one tourist [see 6] is even artistic enough to draw her picture, while Caline has no instruction in the arts. The tourists are urban, but Caline is rural. Thus a wide MULTICULTURAL chasm separates Caline and the tourists (BH).

[6] One of the men—a pleasant-faced youngster—drew a sketch book from his pocket and began to make a picture of the girl. She stayed motionless, her hands behind her, and her wide eyes fixed earnestly upon him.

A FEMINIST critic might be bothered by the fact that the male "youngster" never thinks to seek Caline's permission to sketch her; instead, he assumes he has a right to do so, in part because he is male and is therefore used to taking the initiative when dealing with females (AC). In light of all the differences between Caline and the travellers, the young man's response to her suggests a curiosity about the unknown. In his "sketch," he is perhaps attempting to capture part of the exotic experience of his journey (JA; KB). Ironically, his attempt to capture Caline on paper just as she is will result in changing her in practically every way: as a result of this encounter, she will later leave her parents, move to the city, and then experience feelings she has never felt before (SH). A HORATIAN or READER-RESPONSE critic might argue that young people, in particular, would find this story of interest because it emphasizes the experiences of persons like themselves, who are learning about new aspects of the world (LH). A MULTICULTURALIST critic might find this particular moment especially interesting, not only because the young man and Caline represent two distinct cultures but also because the young man makes Caline the object of his study. The fact that the young man is privileged enough to have studied art, and that he comes equipped with the necessary materials, might also interest such a critic; certainly these facts would also be of interest to a MARXIST critic (MG). The fact that Caline has "**wide eyes**" might intrigue a FORMALIST critic, who might see such phrasing as implying her childlike innocence and curiosity (MS). Perhaps the image also implies that from this point forward, Caline will see her whole life much differently than she has seen it up till now (JS). A FEMINIST might argue that by "**mak[ing] a picture of the girl**," the young man tries to impose a kind of control over her; he tries to make her "his" and inevitably sees her from his own limited perspective (MS). The fact that Caline is "**motionless**" and that her eyes are "**fixed**" might interest a THEMATIC critic, who might see these traits as typifying her relatively passive character throughout the story. Ironically, her later decision to take the initiative and move to the city seems to violate this pattern, but by the very end of the story she is passive and unmoving once again (JK). Her passivity here might also interest a FEMINIST critic (AC; TT), while the contrast between his activity and her "**motionless**" state might also interest a STRUCTURALIST critic, who might argue that this kind of difference symbolizes larger differences in the typical roles of men and women in Caline's culture: the young man is the active observer, while Caline is the passive object of observation (TT). By sketching her, he imposes a kind of control over her (DS). On the other hand, the fact that Caline's eyes are "**fixed earnestly**" on the young man suggests that she is observing him at least as intently as he is observing her (JB2). Presumably Caline feels important because she is the object of this young man's attention, whereas a FEMINIST critic might argue that Caline should not need such male attention in order to feel significant (AC). A FORMALIST critic, however, might appreciate the way the single word "**motionless**" effectively epitomizes Caline's sense of the importance of this moment, especially her desire not to ruin the picture by moving (AC).

[7] Before he had finished there was a summons from the train; and all went scampering hurriedly away. The engine screeched, it sent a few lazy puffs into the still air, and in another moment or two had vanished, bearing its human cargo with it.

Perhaps the fact that the boy does not **"finish"** sketching Caline resembles the fact that Caline is not quite finished herself. She is not quite grown up, and has not had enough worldly experiences to help her along in this process. Caline really knows no other world than her own, which is isolated from all other people except her parents. The fact that the boy does not complete his sketching of Caline may also imply that he may not be finished with Caline yet. Perhaps Chopin hints—as Caline later hopes—that the two will meet again and have some sort of a relationship. Certainly this is how a more conventionally romantic story would end (AC). The fact that the passengers are described as **"scampering away"** may suggest a freedom of movement and freedom of mind that Caline will soon find very appealing (SR). Or perhaps such **"scampering"** ironically suggests the ways in which their lives are regimented and controlled by the technology originally invented to serve them (SH). The word may also imply their desire to return to the comfort of the train (JS). The **"lazy puffs"** and **"still air"** contribute to our sense of the inactiveness of Caline's environment, while the fact that the train has soon **"vanished"** shows that it disappears as quickly as it had stopped (JB). The **"puffs"** of smoke also darken the "cloudless sky" mentioned in the first paragraph of the story, just as Caline's encounter with the passengers from the train will later darken her own initially innocent and inexperienced outlook on life (JA; DS). Meanwhile, the reference to the passengers as **"human cargo"** paradoxically makes them seem inhuman, impersonal, and also separate from Caline's reality (AA; JB; MS). This phrase may imply the degree to which the industrial revolution had begun to transform human beings into mere things (JK; LJS). The words **"human cargo"** constitute a kind of oxymoron as well as a particularly concentrated bit of irony (RCE), while the fact that the passengers are described as **"scampering"** back to the train may suggest the degree to which their behavior has become conditioned (JK).

[8] **Caline could not feel the same after that. She looked with new and strange interest upon the trains of cars that passed so swiftly back and forth across her vision, each day; and wondered whence these people came, and whither they were going.**

A FORMALIST might suggest that the succinct statement that "Caline could not feel the same after that" is typical of Chopin's skillful economy with words. It is interesting that Chopin uses the words "could not feel" instead of "would not feel." Chopin's phrasing indicates that Caline is incapable of remaining the same, whereas if the author had chosen "would not feel," she would suggest that Caline makes a definite choice not to feel the same (CJ). A STRUCTURALIST critic, concerned with the ways cultural codes shape our comprehension of reality, might be interested in the contrast between the narrator's polished English diction (**"whence . . . whither"**) and the "French patois" [5] spoken by Caline and her parents (SR). For a STRUCTURALIST, this contrast would be part of a larger *system* of oppositions that help organize the story—such as the opposition between rich and poor, urban and rural, etc. (RCE).

[9] **Her mother and father could not tell her, except to say that they came from "loin là bas," and were going "Djieu sait é où."**

The fact that Caline's parents speak in French dialect, and that Chopin actually quotes them doing so, would immensely interest a DIALOGICAL critic, since Chopin thus includes at least two very distinct kinds of voices in her text—the standard English of the narrator and the French "patois" of these two characters. Because these differences in speech imply even larger differences in culture, they would also be of great interest in MULTICULTURAL critics (MFL).

[10] One day she walked miles down the track to talk with the old flagman, who stayed down there by the big water tank. Yes, he knew. Those people came from the great cities in the north, and were going to the city in the south. He knew all about the city; it was a grand place. He had lived there once. His sister lived there now; and she would be glad enough to have so fine a girl as Caline to help her cook and scrub, and tend the babies. And he thought Caline might earn as much as five dollars a month, in the city.

The fact that the **"flagman"** is **"old"** immediately associates him with archetypes of wisdom and experience (MS). Because a STRUCTURALIST is interested in patterns that reveal themselves in binaries, he might not only contrast the flagman's age with Caline's youth (RCE) but might also focus on the fact that the people on the trains were coming **"from the great cities in the north"** and were headed toward **"the city in the south,"** since such phrasing implies a larger structure of distinctions between two vastly different cultures (SR). It is interesting , for instance, that there are many **"*great* cities in the north"** (emphasis added) while there is only *one* "city in the south." This single contrast implies a great deal about the relative urbanization of the two regions (SR). Notice, too, that Chopin never mentions New Orleans by name but relies instead on the reader's historical knowledge of the social structure at that time to suggest which **"city"** she means (SR). By describing the city as a **"grand place"** before he mentions the money Caline might make, the flagman, whether deliberately or not, appeals to her romantic dreams rather than emphasizing the pragmatic facts of her life there. Perhaps he instinctively realizes that Caline is less interested in money than in more "lofty" matters—the kinds of matters that would interest a LONGINIAN critic (LJS). A FEMINIST critic would note how automatically the **"old flag*man*"** (emphasis added) assumes that he knows which traditionally female jobs will best suit this young woman: her tasks will be to **"cook and scrub, and tend the babies"** (JA; JA2; LH; SH; SR; MS). Both the flagman and Caline are influenced in their thinking by traditional stereotypes of a woman's proper role (JA). A TRADITIONAL HISTORICAL critic would obviously be greatly interested in determining precisely how much purchasing power **"five dollars a month"** would represent in today's economy (MO). Only during the period when Chopin was writing would one tuly understand whether **"five dollars"** was a genuinely great or small amount (JB). A MARXIST would note that Caline's ability to move to the city and live there is determined entirely by her ability to sell her labor; she lacks the relative freedom to travel enjoyed by the wealthy people on the train (SH; MFL; KM). A MARXIST critic might also note that although the flagman himself is a member of the working class, he probably makes more money than Caline and, in this case, acts as a kind of employment broker for his sister (LJS).

[11] So she went; in a new cotonade, and her Sunday shoes; with a sacredly guarded scrawl that the flagman sent to his sister.

An ARCHETYPAL critic might argue that the desire to seek new experiences by journeying to a new place is one of the most basic of human desires (TB; SR). Such a critic might also interpret Caline's journey to the city as part of the necessary process of individuation—of Caline becoming a distinct and mature person, even though the growth of her maturity may also involve the experience of psychological pain (JA). A READER-RESPONSE critic might suggest that different readers would react differently to Caline's decision to travel to the city: readers attracted to large cities themselves would sympathize with her choice, while those attracted to rural life might find her decision unfortunate. Readers of the latter sort might even see the old flagman as a figure representing misguided temptation (LJS). A TRADITIONAL HISTORICAL critic might see Caline's journey as typifying the more general migration that was occurring during this time from country areas to urban centers (LJS). The adornment implied by the **"new"** skirt and the **"Sunday shoes"** (worn by a poor rural girl) suggests the monumental significance of the occasion, as does the reference to the flagman's note being **"sacredly guarded"** (KB). The **"new cotonade"** is appropriate to the new experiences

Caline will now undergo in her new environment (JS). A STRUCTURAL-
IST would note that "**Sunday shoes**" derive their significance from the
fact that they are part of a larger structural system in which such shoes
contrast with normal or everyday shoes (JB). A FEMINIST, meanwhile,
might note that Caline's change of clothes implies her need not only to
make herself more conventionally attractive to men but also to dress in
a way that seems culturally appropriate to other women; her change of
clothes reflects her need to conform to cultural expectations (MG). Does
the reference to the "**sacredly guarded scrawl**" imply that Caline herself
is illiterate? If so, this fact would be of interest both to MULTICULTURAL-
IST and MARXIST critics, since her relative lack of education would not
only help determine the way she experienced life but also the ways she
would be treated by others, including her need to depend on selling her
manual labor (LJS).

[12] **The woman lived in a tiny, stuccoed house, with green blinds,
and three wooden steps leading down to the banquette. There seemed
to be hundreds like it along the street. Over the house tops loomed the
tall masts of ships, and the hum of the French market could be heard
on a still morning.**

Interestingly, the female who lives in this house is described as a
"**woman**," so that she is already distinguished from the upper-class "ladies" mentioned earlier (AA). Meanwhile, the fact that she is said simply
to "[**live**] **in**" the house may suggest that she does not own it but merely
rents it (RCE). The fact that the house is "**stuccoed**" might interest a
FORMALIST critic as an example of Chopin's artistic skill: she chooses a
single word that immediately implies a kind of architecture associated
with warm climates (TT). The fact that there are "**hundreds**" of similar
houses might intrigue a THEMATIC critic since this detail can be seen
as a symbol of the anonymity and lack of individuality associated with
life in a big city. Just as there are hundreds of rather indistinguishable
houses in the city, so Caline herself will later feel threatened with a sense
of alienation and loss of individuality (MS; PS). The "**tiny**" size of the

woman's house might imply, to a MARXIST critic, that the woman herself is far from wealthy and would suggest the extent to which social status is tied to income (JK). Ironically, this **"tiny . . . house"** is probably not much bigger than the log cabin Caline inhabited in the country; she has changed locales but has not really changed her status in any significant way (MH). The **"tiny"** size of the **"hundreds"** of houses might also suggest to a MARXIST that these homes were constructed both quickly and cheaply to provide housing rapidly for the suddenly expanding size of the urban lower-middle class (JA). A MARXIST might also argue, however, that although Caline's employer is by no means rich, she nonetheless is encouraged by the nature of the economic system to use the labor of someone even less wealthy than herself (JA). Meanwhile, the fact that the employer is a woman might interest FEMINIST critics, either because the woman might be seen as taking advantage of Caline, or because she might be seen as assisting another female. The fact that Caline lives in the home of a woman, moreover, would have made her situation less suspect to some readers than it might have seemed if Caline were employed by a single male (RCE). A FORMALIST might note how effectively the single verb **"loomed"** implies the size of the **"ships"** (JB). Both the **"house tops"** and the **"tall masts"** imply a physical environment that is literally "built up" and civilized, unlike the relatively flat rural landscape with which Caline is most familiar (BH). A READER-RESPONSE critic might suggest that a seasoned sailor would probably not even notice or be impressed by the **"tall masts"** that catch the inexperienced Caline's attention, just as a veteran worker in the "French market" might almost ignore the **"hum"** that makes such a strong impression on Caline (RCE). A FORMALIST would note how the word "hum" helps personify the market, making it seem almost a distinct living thing (MS) and perhaps suggesting a sense of calm purposefulness (BH). Ironically, this sense of calm will soon be disrupted in much the same way as Caline's rest was disrupted at the very beginning of the story. Thus the two halves of the work can be seen as forming a kind of symmetrical structure (RCE).

[13] **Caline was at first bewildered. She had to readjust all her pre-**

conceptions to fit the reality of it. The flagman's sister was a kind and gentle task-mistress. At the end of a week or two she wanted to know how the girl liked it all. Caline liked it very well, for it was pleasant, on Sunday afternoons, to stroll with the children under the great, solemn sugar sheds; or to sit upon the compressed cotton bales, watching the stately steamers, the graceful boats, and noisy little tugs that plied the waters of the Mississippi. And it filled her with agreeable excitement to go to the French market, where the handsome Gascon butchers were eager to present their compliments and little Sunday bouquets to the pretty Acadian girl; and to throw fistfuls of lagniappe into her basket.

Caline's need to "**readjust all her preconceptions to fit** [a new] **reality**" would seem especially interesting to a THEMATIC critic, since this need is one of the central motifs of the entire story (MS). Meanwhile, a NEW HISTORICIST critic might find the description of Caline's "**kind and gentle task-mistress**" particularly interesting since it implies that although this woman enjoys power over Caline, she exercises that power with an unusually benign thoughtfulness (LJS). A FEMINIST might suggest that the woman behaves this way because she sympathizes with a fellow female; a MARXIST might suggest that she she treats her employee well either because she is a worker herself [see section 10] or because she realizes that such treatment will help her retain Caline's services (RCE). By emphasizing Caline's comfortable relationships with her employer and other urban-dwellers, Chopin prepares for her later focus on the *internal* struggle Caline experiences in the city (LJS). A FORMALIST critic, interested in every detail of the story's precise phrasing, might suggest that the word "**stroll**" implies relaxation and calm (and thus prepares, ironically, for the turmoil Caline will soon feel), while the word "**stately**" implies both the beauty and the usefulness of the steamers. A FORMALIST might also note how effectively Chopin juxtaposes the large "**steamers**" and the small "**tugs**," just as she earlier juxtposes the "**sugar sheds**" and the "**cotton bales**." Such diverse details quickly convey a sense of the large, complicated world Caline now inhabits. The verb "**plied**," meanwhile, is effectively precise: it implies a regular, routine, purposeful motion (MB;

RCE). Just as Caline's father had to plow his fields, so the tugs must ply the waters of the river so their operators can earn a living (MH; PS). A MARXIST critic, in fact, might note the class distinctions implied in the contrasts between the **"stately steamers"** and the **"noisy little tugs"** (SJ). Because an ARISTOTELIAN critic is interested in the text as a highly crafted complex unity and in the author's poetic skill, he might focus on the ways Chopin creates the relaxed, langorous rhythm of this sentence simulating a lazy Sunday afternoon. One of the skillful techniques Chopin uses here is the alliteration of such phrases as **"solemn sugar shed," "compressed cotton,"** and **"stately steamers"** (MB; BH; SJ; SR). Chopin forces the reader to slow down and notice small details in much the same way as Caline does (SJ). The reference to the **"compressed cotton bales"** reminds us that Caline's father grows cotton, but the bales represent the end-stage of the commercial process—the change of the cotton from crop to commodity (MG). Once Caline moves to the city, images of journey continue in the references to the various kinds of ships and in the very strong ARCHETYPAL image of the **"Mississippi"** River, all of which suggest that Caline's personal journey has not yet been completed or fulfilled (KB). Because a MULTICULTURAL critic emphasizes differences of age, sex, race, and gender, he might focus on how the final sentence of this passage is full of words implying different cultural identities: the references to the **"French market,"** the **"Gascon butchers,"** the **"Acadian girl,"** and **"lagniappe"** all suggest different cultures (BL; KM). The market (a capitalist institution) is the place where these diverse cultures come together and mix (MG). A MULTICULTURALIST might admire Caline's interest in (and openness to) experience of other cultures (LH), while a MARXIST might note how relatively privileged she seems at this moment in the story: she is now able to **"stroll"** while others work (like the wealthy passengers mentioned earlier [3]), although she will soon discover just how different her life actually is from the lives lived by those privileged travellers (SH). Meanwhile, a PSYCHOANALYTIC critic might find the action of the male butchers—who **"throw fistfuls of lagniappe"** into her **"basket"**—sexually suggestive (JA; MS). A MULTICULTURALIST might note that the actions of these males are more stereotypically masculine and assertive than those of the sensitive young man who had paid tribute to Caline's beauty by sketching her (RCE). A FEMINIST might point out, however, that in the cases of both the young man and the butchers, males take the initiative in making overtures to the more passive female (MB; ET). The fact that these men are not only **"handsome"** but are also **"butchers"** associates them with carnality and the flesh, while the fact that they are **"Gascon"** associates them with the unusual or exotic. Meanwhile, their physicality implicitly contrasts with the artistic qualities associated with the "pleasant-faced boy" whose attentions prompted Caline's visit to the city (RCE). On the other hand, both the **"butchers"** and the boy are presumably attracted to Caline almost entirely because of her physical beauty, not because of any deeper qualities of her character or personality (JA). Both the butchers and the artist have a special interest in the quality of flesh (RCE). Meanwhile, a HORATIAN or READER-RESPONSE critic might appreciate this entire passage because it demonstrates Chopin's ability to capture the essence of urban life as skillfully as she had already sketched the countryside, so that her story would appeal to readers interested in both kinds of locale (JK).

[14] **When the woman asked her again after another week if she were still pleased, she was not so sure. And again when she questioned Caline the girl turned away, and went to sit behind the big, yellow cistern, to cry unobserved. For she knew now that it was not the great city and its crowds of people she had so eagerly sought; but the pleasant-faced boy, who had made her picture that day under the mulberry tree.**

An ARCHETYPAL critic, who emphasizes the importance of basic human desires and fears, might argue that at first the city had appealed to Caline's strong desire for novelty, but that now it awakens her instinctive fear of loneliness and the unknown. Meanwhile, her journey to a strange place is precisely the kind of typical symbolic story on which ARCHETYPAL critics place great stress (RCE). An ARCHETYPAL critic might also suggest that her response to disappointment is utterly typical of the feelings most humans would experience in a similar situation (AC; JK). A NEW HIS-

TORICIST critic, who is interested in how power affects human life, might focus on Caline's action of "**cry[ing] unobserved**." Presumably she fears being glimpsed in her moment of pain. The fact that she sheds tears near a water-filled "**cistern**" seems appropriate, and perhaps the "**yellow**" color of the cistern befits the weakness she now feels (BH; EP). Or perhaps the bright "**yellow**" coloring of the cistern provides an ironic contrast with the melancholy that now sweeps over Caline (RCE; EP). The mere fact that the cistern is painted a bright color suggests that it has some aesthetic function and is not completely utilitarian (EP). The "cistern" may also remind us (and/or Caline herself) of the big "water tank" [see section 10] not far from her home, where she began her journey to this unfamiliar city (RCE; PS), or it may be meant to contrast, in its metallic hardness, with the appealing rural haystack with which the story opened (LSJ). In any case, clearly Caline feels relatively powerless at this point in the story (MO). The fact that she feels the need to cry "**unobserved**" might suggest that she feels that a *public* display of weakness would make her feel (and be treated) as even weaker than she already is (RCE). A Freudian PSYCHOANALYTIC critic might argue that although Caline tries to control her emotions and even seems ashamed of expressing them publicly (since she cries "**unobserved**"), her id is too powerful for either her ego or her superego to dominate, and so it expresses itself in tears. These tears, a Freudian might note, are also strongly linked to her repressed (or even previously unconscious) erotic desires (RCE). In any case, a PSYCHOANALYTIC critic would certainly suggest that Caline's tears are the product, at least on one level, of sexual desire and frustration (LH). A HORATIAN or READER-RESPONSE critic might suggest that Caline's reaction here would provoke a sympathetic reaction in any reader who had ever faced a similar disappointment (MFL; MO). A PLATONIC critic, who favors objective, rational approaches to reality, might find it appropriate that Caline faces disappointment after giving in to her merely emotional impulse to move to the big city (MO). A postmodern critic, attuned to the flux and complexity of experience, might caution against any rigid, single, or specific interpretation of Caline's crying (MO). A FEMINIST critic might find Caline's tearful response unfortunately typical of the reaction of many women who have felt that relationships with men are essential to their happiness (AC; SH; MFL). A FEMINIST might lament that Caline responds to her feelings in such a stereotypically "feminine" way (SH). A FORMALIST critic, attuned to the ways artists impose shape and unity on their works, might notice how skillfully Chopin returns us, in the final words of this tale, to the "**mulberry tree**" which, in its rootedness and naturalness, had already seemed [3] such a significant symbol of Caline's earlier life (SR). Earlier the "**mulberry tree**" had been called "**old and gnarled**" [3], perhaps suggesting that at that point in the story Caline was growing tired of her surroundings. Here, however, it is referred to simply as "**the mulberry tree**," suggesting, perhaps, that Caline is remembering her old environment more fondly now that she is missing it (SR). A DECONSTRUCTOR might note that the story ends on a note of irresolution; it leaves us in a kind of limbo; it does not clearly indicate how Caline should be feeling at this moment or how she should or will respond to what she *is* feeling. In a sense, the story leaves us in the same kind of limbo as it leaves Caline (MG; EP). A DECONSTRUCTIVE critic might add that "innocence" of the sort initially associated with Caline is a privileged concept in Western culture and, thus, is given a preferred status over "experience," which is seen as the corrupter of "innocence." Caline's "lessons of experience" in the city overturn this hierarchy and put these constructs into freeplay. By the end of the story, Caline is no longer an "Acadian girl" but a woman of adult experience. Consequently, Caline's tears may have as much to do with her transitional feelings between the states of "innocence" and "experience" as they do with her feelings of disappointed love (EP). An ARISTOTELIAN or FORMALIST critic might be interested in the ways that the conclusion of the story relates to its opening. In the first paragraph, Caline experienced a literal, physical awakening, whereas in the concluding paragraph she comes to a different, inner sort of realization—of her yearning for the young man who drew her picture. Her first awakening was not unpleasant; her later one is far more painful (LH; LJS). A LONGINIAN critic might be interested in Caline's desire for love since it may symbolize her desire for transcendance and elevation, her yearning to be moved and transported beyond the common, mundane world that now surrounds her (JA; MFL; KM). A PSYCHOANALYTIC critic, who strongly emphasizes the importance of the unconscious, would find Caline's sudden realization extremely fascinating since it shows the degree to which human behavior can be motivated by impulses we only dimly understand. Caline, after all, has changed her entire life by moving to the city in pursuit of a dream she only now begins to consciously comprehend (JK). A THEMATIC critic might argue that Caline cries partly because she realizes not only that she is unlikely ever to meet the **"pleasant-faced boy"** again, but also because she understands now that even if they ever did meet again, the cultural and economic differences between them would make any relationship extremely improbable (BH). Ironically, this realization, although painful, may also benefit Caline in the long run (LJS). An ARCHETYPAL critic might argue that by the end of the story, Caline has undergone a process of maturation, initiation, and individuation: by suffering pain, she has become a different person than she had been when the story opens, and she now understands her relationship with the **"boy"** in a more mature (if also more painful) way than she had understood it earlier (JA).

Kate Chopin's "La Belle Zoraïde": Specific Comments from Diverse Critical Perspectives

CONTRIBUTORS: Jennifer Adger (JA); Debbie Altman (DA); Benjamin Beard (BB); Janis Blaesing (JB); Curtis Bowden (CB); Nataliya Bowden (NB); Lee Bridges (LB), Spencer Brothers (SB); Sonja Brown (SB2); Roger Burdette (RB); Melissa Crane (MC); Ree Ann Clark (RAC); Timothy D. Crowley (TDC); Shannon Dean (SD); Foster Dickson (FD); Paul Duke (PD) Kathleen Durrer (KD); Heather Edwards (HE); Robert C. Evans (RCE); Matt Gilmore (MG); Jacques Grant (JG); Shelly Green (SG); Kenneth W. Griffin (KG); Drayton Hamilton (DH); Barbara Hartin (BH); Phyllis Hedrick (PH); Charlotte Henderson (CH); Sonjanika Henderson (SH); Deborah Hill (DH2); Angelisa LaVan (AL); Barrett Lee (BL); Christy Myers (CM); Katie Magaw (KM); KM2 (Kathy Mayfield); Kevin Nutt (KN); Kurt R. Niland (KRN); Pat Norman (PN); Ann O'Clair (AMO); Michael Odom (MO); Margo Paraska (MP); Edward Pate (EP); Lane Powell (LP); Neil Probst (NP); Stephanie Reed (SR); Terri Richburg (TR); Denean Rivera (DR); Melissa Roth (MR); Marie Robinson (MR2); Claire Skowronski (CS); Julie D. Sellers (JDS); Angela Soulé (AS); Frances Stewart (FS); Mark Stewart (MS); Randy C. Stone (RCS); Tammy Taite (TT); Ondra Thomas-Krouse (OT-K); Peter Walden (PW); Gwendolyn Warde (GW); Kristi Widner (KW); Claudia Wilsch (CW); Jonathan Wright (JW); Carolyn Young (CY).

La Belle Zoraïde

[1] The summer night was hot and still; not a ripple of air swept over the *marais* [marsh]. Yonder, across Bayou St. John, lights twinkled here and there in the darkness, and in the dark sky above a few stars were blinking. A lugger that had come out of the lake was moving with slow, lazy motion down the bayou. A man in the boat was singing a song.

The "**hot**," "**summer**" setting already suggests a sultry, lusty, lazy, and languorous atmosphere (JDS), and summer is also a season associated with the prime of life (FD, PD). Both points are relevant to this story's themes and central character, especially since we will see Zoraïde's life destroyed (FD). An ARCHETYPAL critic might argue that the story begins by emphasizing feminine elements of darkness, water, and heat (TR). The calm "**still[ness]**" with which the story opens perhaps implies that something latent or hidden might lie beneath the surface of the immediate surroundings or one's impressions of them (PD). Certainly such stillness contrasts with the turmoil emphasized later in the work, especially near its end (AL). To reinforce the languid nature of the setting, Chopin uses very simple sentences. Complex sentences might have worked against her intention of developing a sense of the "**still**," oppressive evening heat (DA). The word "*marais*," meanwhile, might interest a STRUCTURALIST critic, who might see this French word in an English text as indicative of the many significant pairings and contrasts embedded into this story: black and white, reality and fantasy, paradise and perdition, and (very shortly) a story within a story. The linguistic duality signaled by a word such as "*marais*" is strongly reinforced at the end of the story, where

Chopin gives us both English and French versions of the same remarks (LB). Included within her simple sentence structure are many long, rounded vowel sounds (in words such as **"yonder," "bayou," "John," "lugger," "come," "out," "of," "moving," "slow," "motion, "down," "bayou," "boat," and "song"**) that again help create a sense of the still air and unrelenting heat (DA). Heavy and unhurried, the long vowel sounds almost force the reader to pronounce each word in the phrase as slowly and deliberately as the movements of the boat itself (DH2). The sparkling lights give the opening scene almost a fairy-tale prettiness (DR), but this story will soon prove no fairy tale. The lights against the darkness also presage the story's preoccupation with relations between the races (DR). Chopin uses the commonplace adjectives **"twinkl[ing]"** and **"blinking"** in a very unconventional way, perhaps to convey how uncanny even the most ordinary objects can appear at night. For example, most people might say, "lights **blink[ed]** here and there in the darkness" and "above a few stars were **twinkl[ing]**." Chopin, however, by switching the verbs, turns the dark night upside-down, so that the lights seem to be **twinkl[ing]** while the stars are **blinking**. A FORMALIST critic might even suggest that this reversed description foreshadows Zoraïde's disoriented view of her world at the end of the story (DH2). A FORMALIST critic would take great interest in the complexity created by the description of the lights and the stars: several layers are kept separate and, at the same time, are fused through similarities in (and repetition of) sounds. Thus with **"bayou"** and **"sky,"** the "y" sound is shared but is also slightly altered within each word. In addition, both depth (in the bayou) and height (in the sky) are suggested, but these contrasts are further unified by the words **"twinkled"** and **"blinking."** By describing the lights below as **"twink[ling]"** and the stars above as **"blinking,"** Chopin fuses the two planes by using similar sounds while keeping them physically separate (MP). The final word (**"song"**) introduces a literal note of lyricism into the story, but the lyricism will soon be submerged into an ugly brutality (RCE). A STRUCTURALIST critic might note how the story's language, even in this first paragraph, already implies various complicated codes. Words such as *"marais,"* **"yonder," "bayou," and "lugger,"** for instance, already suggest a definite place and time (nineteenth-century Louisi-ana), and properly interpreting the story will therefore depend on some familiarity with the interrelated "codes" of this complex culture (HE). The mere use of a word such as **"lugger"** helps create confidence in the author's knowledge of the remote locale she is about to describe (DA). A TRADITIONAL HISTORICAL critic might report that a **"lugger"** was a nauti-cal term for a small boat used for fishing, sailing, or coasting and having two or three masts, each with a lugsail (DH2). The narrator's off-hand reference to a specific locality suggests the reader's familiarity with the territory described—a tactic that already lends the narrative tone a sense of intimacy and authority (LP).

[2] **The notes of the song came faintly to the ears of old Manna-Loulou, herself as black as the night, who had gone out upon the gallery to open the shutters wide.**

Note how efficiently yet clearly Manna-Loulou is introduced: in a few words Chopin creates a vivid picture of her age, her appearance, her circumstances, and her social role (LP). Manna-Loulou's **"old"** age may suggest her wisdom and depth of experience (SB). In a different kind of story, Manna-Loulou's **"black[ness]"** might suggest that she is an evil personality, but in Chopin's tale she in fact emerges as one of the most attractive of all the characters (PW). A THEMATIC critic might notice how the reference to Manna-Loulou's **"black[ness]"** enhances the motif of darkness and blackness that is so important in this tale. As will later become obvious, this theme of darkness is relevant not only to the use of colors in the story but also to its ultimate focus on injustice, despair, and insanity (DH2). Meanwhile, the word **"gallery"** already suggests a large, grand home (DA). By opening the shutters Manna-Loulou exposes the house to a wider world and a larger reality (KD, MC). In bayou country, however, shutters are traditionally kept closed at night to ward off dangers and troubles (especially infection); the act of opening them therefore seems ironic (FD). Perhaps the shutters are opened to help improve circulation of the air; the fact that this is necessary suggests that the night may be particularly warm and stifling (SD). The fact that Manna-Loulou hears the music only faintly is possibly relevant to the story's theme of beauty and happiness being out of reach (PN). Note how this single sentence implies three of the five senses—hearing (**"notes of the song"**), sight (**"black as the night"**) and touch (**"open the shutters wide"** [LP]).

[3] Something in the refrain reminded the woman of an old, half-forgotten Creole romance, and she began to sing it low to herself while she threw the shutters open:

The word "**romance**" not only foreshadows an important theme of the story (JDS) but also seems ironic in a work that deals with the actual destruction of a romance (DR). This "**half-forgotten**" romance seems relevant to the story that is about to be remembered and revived by Manna-Loulou (OT-K); the phrase "**half-forgotten**" also seems ironic in view of the story's final emphasis on memory and its loss (RCE). Within the space of only a few sentences, Chopin has moved the reader from a most general subject (the weather) to one that is quite specific (this woman's personal memory [DA]). Manna-Loulou's action of throwing "**open the shutters wide**" is perhaps symbolically appropriate, since she is about to unlock a storehouse of memories and allow them to escape (AMO).

> [4]"Lisett' to kité la plaine.
> Ma perdi bunhair a moué;
> Ziés à moué semblé fontaine,
> Dépi no pa miré toué."
>
> [Lizette, {since} you have left the plain
> I have lost my happiness;
> My eyes are like a fountain,
> Since I cannot look at you.]

Significantly, the song deals with lost contact, with lost happiness, with weeping, and with an inability to see, just as Zoraïde will later lose her lover, her baby, her mind (JDS), and finally even her identity (JW). Significantly, too, Zoraïde will never actually see her baby after it is born (DR).

A POSTMODERNIST critic might note that Chopin apparently has no qualms about including a "popular" text, this Creole ballad, within a piece of serious "literature" (KN).

[5] And then this old song, a lover's lament for the loss of his mistress, floating into her memory, brought with it the story she would tell to Madame, who lay in her sumptuous mahogany bed, waiting to be fanned and put to sleep to the sound of one of Manna-Loulou's stories.

Note the continued emphasis on age: the elderly Manna-Loulou recalls an "old, half-forgotten Creole romance," here called more simply **"an old song."** An ARCHETYPAL critic might suggest that the ancientness stressed so far implies the permanent human significance of the emotions and insights that the song (like Manna-Loulou's own later story) embodies. Even the focus on a **"lover"** and **"his mistress"** implies a concern with one of the most basic and ARCHETYPAL of all human relationships (RCE). A FORMALIST critic would admire the skillful alliteration of such a phrase as **"a lover's lament for the loss of his mistress"** (LP). However, the fact that the lover laments the loss of a **"mistress"** (rather than of a "wife" or "beloved" or "sweetheart") perhaps already suggests a note of illicit passion—a theme that is later very relevant (MC). Once again the theme of loss is emphasized here—thus foreshadowing the story's subsequent key events (JDS). The fact that the song **"floats"** into her memory is typical of the languid, unhurried motion of the whole narrative up to this point. Eventually, though, the pace will significantly quicken (JW). Chopin slowly brings the setting of the story from across the lake, onto the gallery, and then into the Madame's room, almost in the manner of a languid uninterrupted tracking shot in a film, thus underscoring the smooth unity of the opening passage (KN). Added to the setting's external sensuality is the shift of focus to the interior of the house, specifically to a bedroom that bears a **"sumptuous . . . bed"** (TR). A MARXIST critic might note the fact that the bed is made of **"mahogany"**—a detail that already implies unusual wealth (KM2). Is the phrase **"put to sleep"** in any way foreboding or ominous? (OT-K) Or is the gentleness suggested by the phrase ironic, since the story will prove to be so disturbing and disquieting? Later, the story will specifically be described as having inhibited sleep (RCE). Madame waits to be soothed physically (by being **"fanned"**) and psychologically (by being told a story). Yet the story she hears will not prove entirely soothing (RCE). Ironically, it is the voice of Manna-Loulou that her mistress wants to hear rather than the specific content of the old woman's story. Such comparative inattention suggests how relatively unimportant Manna-Loulou really is, as a person, to the woman who "owns" her (AMO).

[6] **The old negress had already bathed her mistress's pretty white feet and kissed them lovingly, one, then the other. She had brushed her mistress's beautiful hair, that was as soft and shining as satin, and was the color of Madame's wedding-ring. Now, when she reentered the room, she moved softly toward the bed, and seating herself there began gently to fan Madame Delisle.**

A MULTICULTURAL critic might suggest that in some ways Manna-Loulou fits the racial stereotype of a large black female slave who adopts a maternal attitude toward her white owners and their children. In this sense she can be seen as an "Aunt Jemima" or "mammy" figure (BH). A TRADITIONAL HISTORICAL critic might note that the term **"old negress"** alone, an expression that would now be considered offensive and insulting, is enough to designate the slave culture of the Old South in which this story is immersed (DH2). An ARCHETYPAL critic might argue that the description of Manna- Loulou as **"old"** already implies her wisdom (RCE). Because a STRUCTURALIST critic is concerned with the binary nature of language, s/he might focus on the dualities present in this passage (and throughout the story). These include old and young, black and white, beauty and ugliness, and subservience and power (MP). Indeed, note how the reference to Madame Delisle's **"pretty white feet"** contrasts explicitly with the earlier description of Manna-Loulou as being "black as the night." The black/white contrast, of course, is an image pattern crucial to the entire story (LB). The simple fact that so much time and detail are devoted to describing Madame Delisle's appearance, in contrast to the relatively sparse description of Manna-Loulou, already suggests the white woman's social and economic superiority (DA). Indeed, Manna-Loulou's attentions to her mistress appear almost worshipful (DH2). Chopin's use of such words as **"soft," "softly," "gently"** and **"sleep,"** combined with the alliteration of such phrases as **"soft and shining as satin,"** helps reinforce the relaxed, relaxing mood so far established—a mood the rest of the story will later disrupt (CB). Significantly (especially in light of the ensuing tale), the relationship between Manna-Loulou and the mistress seems similar to that between a mother and a child (DR, FD). Although technically the mistress enjoys greater power, in some respects she seems passive and dependent in her relationship on Manna-Loulou (DR, MC). It seems ironic that the woman who possesses the most power in this situation is also the one who seems least mature (AMO). A DECONSTRUCTIVE critic might suggest, however, that in some respects Manna-Loulou, although technically the "inferior" party in this relationship, actually enjoys a position of superiority, at least in a moral sense (CB). Despite Madame Delisle's physical attractiveness, isn't it in fact Manna-Loulou who eventually seems the more beautiful (in character) of the two? (CB) Might a MARXIST critic suggest, however, that Manna-Loulou's soft and gentle treatment of her mistress is the result of years of conditioning bred partly from fear of the mistress's domination? (CB) Alternatively, is there perhaps even a hint of eroticism in their relationship? If so, such a hint would provide still another link between this prologue and the tale Manna-Loulou is about to report (FD). Is there any allusion, in the reference to Manna-Loulou **"bath[ing]"** Madame Delisle's feet, to Jesus' washing of the disciples' feet (CB) or to Mary Magdalene washing the feet of Jesus? (PD). In either case, such a possibility would prepare for the even more explicit religious allusions later in the story (RCE). Is Manna-Loulou thereby linked with the Biblical ARCHETYPE of the Good Servant?

(CB) Is there also perhaps, in the imagery of Manna-Loulou "**kiss[ing]**" the mistress's feet, a subtle allusion to Mary humbly prostrating herself before Jesus? (JW; PD)   Perhaps Chopin means to imply that Madame Delisle, as a false Christ, is an unfit mistress to Manna-Loulou, as an ironic Saint Mary Magdalene (PD). Perhaps the "kiss[ing]" indicates Manna-Loulou's genuine gratitude for being permitted to serve as a house slave rather than being made to work in the fields (KM2). In any case, is the mistress living vicariously through Manna-Loulou's tales? (OT-K) The pleasures Madame Delisle experiences here are ones (an ARCHETYPAL critic might argue) that most readers might also find appealing (CB), but is our ability to empathize with Madame Delisle's yearning for comfort undercut by our recognition that her pleasure depends on her exploitation of Manna-Loulou? (RCE). Ironically, Manna-Loulou's effort to relieve her mistress of the oppressiveness of the evening heat symbolizes her own social oppression (DH). In any case, the emphasis on comfort here contrasts powerfully with the story's later emphasis on both physical and emotional misery (RCE). Similarly, the reference to Madame Delisle's "**wedding ring**" subtly introduces the theme of marriage—an important motif of the later story (CB). At the same time, a MARXIST critic might observe how the reference to the "**wedding ring**" implies that Madame Delisle's hair is golden and therefore further links her to wealth and materialism (MS). A FEMINIST critic might note how casually it is assumed that a woman will (or must) have a husband (BH). Is the mistress's husband dead, or is he merely absent? (MC) If he is dead (as is in fact implied in Chopin's accompanying story "A Lady of Bayou St. John"), then the tale of lost love she is about to hear would be particularly fitting (RCE). The suggested sensuality of the "**sumptuous mahogany bed**" (another image implying darkness [DH]) seems somewhat ironic, since Madame Delisle apparently does not often (if at all) share her bed with her husband (TR). He is obliquely alluded to only in the description of Madame Delisle's hair as being "the color of [her] wedding ring." It also appears that Madame Delisle is childless. Interestingly, the absence of a husband and childlessness are two characteristics Madame Delisle shares with Madame Delariviére, a main character in Manna-Loulou's ensuing story (TR). These traits are also ones later shared by Zoraïde herself (RCE).

[7] **Manna-Loulou was not always ready with her story, for Madame would hear none but those that were true. But tonight the story was all there in Manna-Loulou's head—the story of la belle Zoraïde—and she told it to her mistress in the soft Creole patois whose music and charm no English words can convey.**

A DIALOGICAL critic might suggest that Manna-Loulou's tale, like any other story told orally, changes slightly with each telling. Each storyteller invariably adds his or her own inflections and fabrications in order to emphasize what he or she deems most important (DH2). Interested in the ways each detail of a text contributes to its complex unity, a FORMALIST critic might notice the intricacy Chopin creates by telling a story within a story. A FORMALIST might also notice how Chopin's detailed descriptions encourage the reader to compare and contrast the inner story with the outer narrative. For example, Zoraïde and Manna-Loulou, both being favorite slaves, provide diversion and amusement for their mistresses— Manna-Loulou by her storytelling and Zoraïde by her happiness, beauty, and charm. However, while Zoraïde is young and "dainty as the finest lady of la rue Royale," Manna-Loulou is old and "black as the night"; while Zoraïde is expected to do nothing but sit prettily "at her mistress's side," Manna-Loulou is expected to attend to her mistress's every need; and, while Zoraïde eventually disobeys her mistress, Manna-Loulou remains submissive. The characters of Madame Delariviére and Madame Delisle also provide interesting points of comparison. For example, they are both wealthy women accustomed to the pampered, coddled lifestyle of slave owners. However, the similarities end there, for, whereas Madame Delariviére exhibits cruelty and indifference, Madame Delisle exhibits compassion and concern; whereas Madame Delariviére induces defiance and disobedience in Zoraïde, Madame Delisle induces love and tenderness in Manna-Loulou; and whereas Madame Delariviére eventually loses Zoraïde's attendance, Madame Delisle succeeds in keeping Manna-

Loulou's devoted services. A FORMALIST might also point out that while the differences between these two sets of characters provide the story with a heightened degree of complexity, the similarities provide a sense of congruity and balance (DH2). Further similarities and contrasts also link the inner and outer tales. For example, in the outer story the slave woman is older than her mistress, while in the inner story the reverse is true. In both stories the slaves are favorites of their mistresses, but whereas Manna-Loulou is shown to be a hard worker, Zoraïde at first leads a life of relative privilege. Both slaves, however, are expected to please their mistresses (SR).

By mentioning Manna-Loulou's **"soft Creole patois,"** the narrator suddenly emphasizes a language barrier that further complicates a tale that had seemed to begin so simply. In fact, the nonchalant inclusion of the word **"patois"** is itself a specific instance of the linguistic complexity of the story (TDC). The reference to the **"music and charm"** of Manna-Loulou's tale seems to imply, ironically, that the tale will end happily or will be soothing; instead, of course, it ends in tragedy and is disturbing (JDS). Chopin contrasts the richly exotic and mellifluous tones of Manna-Loulou's story-telling with the indifferent brutality of the story she tells, and perhaps this contrast is also relevant to the apparently loving relationship between Manna-Loulou and her mistress and the more complicated feelings Manna-Loulou really experiences toward her mistress (JG). Note, for instance, the sense of command and assumed superiority implied by the simple phrase **"Madame would hear none but those that were true"**—words suggesting that Madame Delisle's desires are all-important (RCE). By using the device of the story-within-a-story, Chopin can play with the notion of the opposition between written and "oral" texts—an opposition likely to be of particular interest to POST-MODERN critics, who are intrigued by the mixing and transgression of conventional genres (KN).

[8] **"La belle Zoraïde had eyes that were so dusky, so beautiful, that any man who gazed too long into their depths was sure to lose**

his head, and even his heart sometimes. Her soft, smooth skin was the color of *café-au-lait*. As for her elegant manners, her svelte and graceful figure, they were the envy of half the ladies who visited her mistress, Madame Delariviére.

A FEMINIST might note the heavy emphasis here on Zoraïde's merely physical beauty (BL). The opening sentence here suggests that although any man might first feel lust (**"lose his head"**) for Zoraïde because of the beauty of her eyes, in some cases such lust might metamorphose into a deeper kind of genuine love (**"lose . . . his heart sometimes"**). Such a metamorphosis is, of course, exactly the sort that le beau Mézor experiences when he later meets Zoraïde (LP). The opening emphasis on the youthful beauty of Zoraïde's eyes prepares, ironically, for her later appearance as a **"sad-eyed"** woman (RCE). Indeed, **eye** imagery will be used significantly and repeatedly throughout the story (DH). Perhaps Manna-Loulou begins by stressing Zoraïde's beauty in order to help interest Madame Delisle (who is also beautiful) in the slave's story: by emphasizing Zoraïde's beauty, Manna-Loulou perhaps encourages Madame Delisle to view her almost as an equal rather than as just an inferior (SB; CH). The phrase **"lose his head"** is at this point merely hyperbolic; in retrospect, however, it seems ominous, not only because literally it implies death (JDS) but also because later Zoraïde herself will figuratively lose both her head and her heart (DR). Zoraïde's **"dusky"** color helps continue Chopin's emphasis on images of light and darkness (OT- K) and also gives her a quality of mystery (KD), while the reference to the **"depths"** of her eyes already suggests the complexity of her character (DR). An ARCHETYPAL critic might note, in fact, that a person's **"eyes"** are traditionally considered the windows into a person's soul (RCE). A FEMINIST critic might suggest, however, that even though Zoraïde in some ways seems an exotic figure, in other ways Chopin's description of her fits various common female stereotypes (HE). In certain respects she fits the correct, culturally prescribed image of a "proper" woman, especially in her softness, grace, and elegance (HE). The fact that **"any"** man might find her attractive suggests, significantly, that her beauty transcends artificial distinctions of race or class, although these distinctions will subsequently prove all-important (JW). The description of her skin appeals simultaneously (and synaesthetically) to the senses of sight, touch, and taste (MC), while the reference to "*cafe-au-lait*" already subtly symbolizes the mixing of colors and flavors that Zoraïde herself (a mulatto) embodies (JW). The fact that the dark-black Manna-Loulou so carefully describes the skin color of Zoraïde subtly suggests how important race is in her society and therefore also in her own consciousness (PP). Yet by stressing the beauty of Zoraïde's skin, Chopin implicitly challenges the artificial distinctions between "white beauty" and "black ugliness" on which the systems of slavery and racism depended (KRN). The emphasis on Zoraïde's manners, her figure, and the reaction she provokes from "**ladies**" already suggests that she occupies an unusual position for a woman of color in her society (FD). Not until the last three words of the cited passage do we discover that she is indeed a servant; only later do we discover that she is in fact a slave (RCE). Until those final three words, all the emphasis thus far has been on her own independent attractions and powers—an ironic emphasis in a story that will later stress how much she is subject to the power of others (RCE). Zoraïde arouses the "**envy**" of "**half the ladies who visited her mistress**" not only because of her physical beauty but because such beauty reflects well on the woman who owns her: Zoraïde is a prize possession, and the other women are probably at least as envious of the good fortune of Madame Delariviére in possessing her as they are of the slave's own beauty. They perceive only her outer, physical and social attractions and care little for her inner character or personal needs. Ironically, by the end of the story, physical charms are among the few traits Zoraïde still possesses after her character and emotions have been ravaged (AMO). The fact that Manna-Loulou claims that only "**half**" the ladies envied Zoraïde not only recalls the earlier statement that "**any**" man would fall in love with her, but it also makes her latter claim seem more credible. Perhaps Manna-Loulou is also implying that the response of the men is more natural and thus more absolute than the superficial envy of the women (TDC).

[9] "No wonder Zoraïde was as charming and as dainty as the finest lady of la rue Royale: from a toddling thing she had been brought up at her mistress's side; her fingers had never done rougher work than sewing a fine muslin seam; and she even had her own little black servant to wait upon her. Madame, who was her godmother as well as her mistress, would often say to her: —

This initial description of Zoraïde makes her sound not much different from the pampered Madame DeLisle, especially in the emphasis on her lack of work and in the reference to her being attended by a black servant. Later, of course, the experiences of Zoraïde and Madame Delisle will diverge dramatically. A STRUCTURALIST critic might even see Zoraïde as ultimately a reverse image of Madame Delisle—the white woman luxuriating in a serene paradise, the black woman spiraling downward into madness (LB). The reference to Zoraïde as a "**toddling**" child is perhaps a bit of ironic foreshadowing, since the same word will later be used to describe Zoraïde's own daughter (DR). Also ironic is Madame Delariviére's role as godmother, since a godparent not only has responsibilities for a child's religious and spiritual instruction (DR) but also is obliged to raise a child in the event of the parent's death (JA). Later, of course, Madame Delariviére will behave in ways that seem anything but Christian, and she will also play a very ironic role in raising Zoraïde's daughter. Is there any possibility, in fact, that Manna-Loulou is the now-grown "**little black servant**" of Zoraïde? This possibility would help to explain her intimate knowledge of Zoraïde's story (AL). Similarly, is it at all possible that Zoraïde (who is, after all, a mulatto) is herself a daughter of Madame Delariviére? (FD). This possibility might help explain not only Madame Delariviére's solicitous care for the young Zoraïde but also her later vehement reaction when Zoraïde plans to marry a black man (FD).

[10] "'Remember, Zoraïde, when you are ready to marry, it must be in a way to do honor to your bringing up.

Her opening word—"**Remember**"—implies that this is not the first time she has announced these plans (JW). The word also already implies that in Madame Delariviére's opinion, Zoraïde also needs to be carefully guided and controlled (PP, OT-K). Finally, in retrospect it seems extremely ironic that the first word we hear Madame Delariviére speak to Zoraïde is "**remember**," since by the end of the story Zoraïde's memory (and even identity) will be destroyed largely as a result of Madame Delariviére's conduct (PN). Although the word "**ready**" may simply imply being of a proper age (MR), it may also suggest freedom of choice (CM)—a suggestion immediately and ironically undercut by the next clauses, especially by the word "**must**" (RCE). Madame Delariviére's reference to "**honor**" seems extremely ironic in light of her later dishonorable conduct—although that conduct (even more ironically) is motivated by a very peculiar sense of what is *socially* honorable (JDS). The mistress speaks of Zoraïde's need to "**honor**" her obligations, thereby de-emphasizing the mistress's own obligations to the young woman who has served her so loyally (AMO).

[11] "'It will be at the Cathedral. Your wedding gown, your corbeille [hope chest], all will be of the best; I shall see to that myself. You know, M'sieur Ambroise is ready whenever you say the word, and his master is willing to do as much for him as I shall do for you. It is a union that will please me in every way.'

The details mentioned here reinforce our sense of Madame Delariviére's wealth and status (CH), while the reference to the "**cathedral**" again associates her, ironically, with Christianity. However, the fact that she mentions a cathedral rather than simply mentioning a "church" makes clear, as well, her interest in social distinctions and social display (RCE). The "**cathedral**" represents the center of both the religious and political power of Madame's patriarchal faith (TR). Madame enjoys power and does not mind wielding it, and as a widow, wealthy in her own right, she appears in many respects more masculine than conventionally feminine (TR). She imagines the marriage as a public ceremony, not as an intimate union (TR), and she treats Zoraïde, in fact, as an item on display

(KD), so that her kindness, paradoxically, is essentially selfish (RCE). Thus, although Madame Delariviére has showered Zoraïde with material gifts, at the same time she denies the girl any truly independent sense of hope (JW). The reference to the **"hope chest"** is therefore ironic (JW), especially since a hope chest is normally associated with the establishment of an independent home and, with it, an autonomous identity—the very possessions Zoraïde will later be denied (DR). In fact, Zoraïde's entire situation as a favored servant is fundamentally ambiguous and inherently contradictory (FD). Madame Delariviére's closing reference to her own pleasure underscores her essential self-interest (JW); and eventually, of course, she will be anything but pleased, either in her initial response to Zoraïde's plans to marry or with the final outcome of the events she sets in motion (RCE). Her promise that **"I shall see to that myself"** seems especially ironic in light of subsequent events, since her later direct intervention in Zoraïde's life will cause Zoraïde endless pain. Although Zoraïde is allowed the illusion that she has power not only over her own life but also over the life of M'sieur Ambroise (who is **"ready whenever you say the word"**), in fact it is the mistress and master of these two slaves who really control their fates, as subsequent events will show. By the end of the story, indeed, it will be M'sieur Ambroise (presumably with his master's approval) who will ultimately reject Zoraïde rather than Zoraïde who will have the power to accept Ambroise. Zoraïde will thus be denied even the small measure of control she is explicitly promised here (RCE).

[12] **"Monsieur Ambroise was then the body servant of Doctor Langle. La belle Zoraïde detested the little mulatto, with his shining whiskers like a white man's, and his small eyes, that were cruel and false as a snake's. She would cast down her own mischievous eyes, and say:**

The name **"Ambroise"** is extremely ironic, since "ambrosia" is the food of the gods and (by extension) anything pleasing to taste or smell (FD). Obviously Zoraïde regards the servant as anything but appealing (FD); the word **"little"** implies weakness, pettiness, inferiority, and lack of respect (DR), while the fact that he is Doctor Langle's "**body servant**," although in one sense an indication of a prestigious position analogous to Zoraïde's (TR), in another sense insinuates powerlessness, servility, dependence, and perhaps even effeminacy (DR). He is a kind of living adjunct to the "body politic" of the white plantation system (TR). His "**shining whiskers**" may imply that he is significantly older than Zoraïde and therefore unappealing to her partly for that reason (LB). His "**small eyes**" (which contrast with the "beautiful" eyes mentioned earlier [8] as belonging to Zoraïde and the "fierce" eyes mentioned later [15] as belonging to his rival, le beau Mézor [RCE]) make him sound almost reptilian or rodent-like (DR). An ARCHETYPAL critic might argue that Chopin here plays on a natural human fear or dislike of reptiles (MG). "**Snake[s]**," in fact, are of course conventional symbols of evil and deception (PD). Is there any irony in the fact that Zoraïde detests Ambroise in part because of his appearance? (JDS) She herself, after all, is judged largely on the basis of her own appearance, and this concern with appearances will later help determine her own fate (JDS). Does her reaction to the "**little mulatto**" reflect any confusion or essential ambivalence concerning her own identity? (DR, OT-K) Perhaps, subconsciously, she desires either one clear racial identity or another (DR); perhaps her vehement rejection of Ambroise indicates her underlying unhappiness with her own status as a mulatto (OT-K). The reference to her perception of Ambroise's moral traits—his cruelty and falseness—suggests that her rejection is based not entirely on his appearance; her assessment encourages us to pay attention to his later conduct to determine whether he deserves to be described in these ways (RCE). Ironically, whereas the whites of Zoraïde's day would regard blackness as an undesirable trait, Zoraïde is repelled by Ambroise partly because he resembles a white man (RCE). By marrying Ambroise, the servant of a master who desires to marry Zoraïde's own mistress, Zoraïde would be even more tightly tied into a position of dominance and control than is already the case. The projected relationship between these four people might even seem almost incestuously interconnected (RCE). Because a NEW HISTORICIST critic is partly concerned with the play of power between individuals within a social class, s/he might focus on the tension between Zoraïde and Ambroise. Despite the fact that they share similar social conditions, an uncomfortable exchange of energy occurs between them: Ambroise is vying for a wife over whom he might have control, while Zoraïde views him as a threat to her present position. Both are bound in servitude to their masters—a condition they cannot change—but both are also struggling to maintain or enhance what little freedom of self they possess (MP). The reference to Zoraïde's **"mischievous eyes"** is the first subtle clue that the young woman has a mind and will of her own and will not necessarily follow Madame's plans (CH). The word **"mischievous"** seems to imply, ironically, that Zoraïde is at fault for lying, whereas such deception is her only defense against further misery (AMO). Her willingness to defy her mistress slightly here through such **"mischievous"** conduct foreshadows her much more serious defiance later (RCE).

[13] **"'Ah, Nénaine [Godmother], I am so happy, so contented here at your side just as I am. I don't want to marry now; next year, perhaps, or the next.' And Madame would smile indulgently and remind Zoraïde that a woman's charms are not everlasting.**

Chopin's skillful use of dialogue throughout this short tale helps individualize the characters; each of them has a distinctive voice and therefore each of them seems more convincingly real (HE). Zoraïde's reply shows how skillfully she can use language and play on her mistress's vanity (CM), particularly in a situation in which she has, in fact, no real choice (JW). Although she uses a term of affection (**"Nénaine"**), her subservient diplomacy clearly indicates that she is not comfortable enough with Madame Delariviére simply to tell her the truth. The fact that Madame **"smile[s] indulgently"** at Zoraïde's stated reluctance to marry shows her smug assumption that she has total control over all aspects of Zoraïde's life (GW). Meanwhile, the claim that **"a woman's charms are not everlasting"** is clearly ironic in light of Zoraïde's later horrible fate (DR; PW). A FEMINIST critic might claim that Madame Delariviére's final statement here shows that, despite her apparent power and authority, she herself is subtly aware of being trapped in a patriarchal situation in which her value, like Zoraïde's, is defined by her appearance (AS). Just as Zoraïde is subjugated by a racist society, so is Madame herself subjugated by a society dominated by men (AS). Such patriarchal power affects a privileged white woman as well as a literal slave (BH). Madame Delariviére is constantly "**remind[ing]**" Zoraïde and urging her to "**remember**"—phrasing that suggests the constant indoctrination and social conditioning to which Zoraïde has already been exposed (RCE). At the same time (a FEMINIST critic might suggest), Madame Delariviére's preoccupation with her slave's prospective wedding suggests the shallowness and emptiness of her own life: she apparently has little else to occupy her thinking or her energies (BH).

[14] **"But the truth of the matter was, Zoraïde had seen la beau Mézor dance the Bamboula in Congo Square. That was a sight to hold one rooted to the ground. Mézor was as straight as a cypress tree and as proud looking as a king. His body, bare to the waist, was like a column of ebony and it glistened like oil.**

The reference to "**Congo Square**" already associates Mézor with black Africa (FD); in this and other respects (especially physically) he is the opposite of the small, half-white Ambroise (RCE). Note that **Mézor**, unlike Ambroise, has no "M'sieur" attached to his name—a fact that suggests his relative freedom from social control (DH). The adjective that identifies him—"**le beau**"—refers to his personal appearance, not to his social standing (RCE). Even the definite article "**le**" ("the") may imply that Mézor is a unique, special individual; he is not "just another slave" (CS). Mézor has the same kind of stunning impact on Zoraïde that she was earlier said to have on men (JDS; DR): by noting that the sight of him could "**hold one rooted to the ground**," Chopin uses language that carries connotations of earthiness, nature (FD), stability (RCE), and fecundity (TR). Zoraïde's vision of Mézor puts her in touch, in a sense, with her own ethnic and cultural roots (CS). The fact that he is "**straight**" suggests strength, sturdiness (DR), and self-assurance (PD), while his association with the cyprus and ebony trees links him with life, vitality (DR), and exotic richness (PD). (An ARCHETYPAL critic might even argue that trees are traditionally linked to the ARCHETYPE of the Great Mother, since their roots go deep into the earth [TR]). Perhaps Zoraïde's interest in Mézor also implies her interest in her black roots—an interest already suggested by her rejection of Ambroise (PH). Mézor seems to represent the natural, self-assured culture and identity for which Zoraïde longs. Her roots appear to be important to her, and Mézor epitomizes the blackness that contrasts with her half-white lifestyle (SG). When Zoraïde sees Mézor dancing, she becomes like him: she is now more aware of her position in nature. The two of them seem perfectly matched, not only in the similar adjectives attached to their names but also by the similarity of the names themselves—"**Zoraïde**" and "**Mézor**" (FS). Mézor's natural royalty (he is "**as proud looking as a king**") belies his social status as a slave (RAC; KG), and from this point forward Zoraïde will become a social rebel as she offers allegiance to this new "**king**" (RCE). A FEMINIST critic, however, might be troubled by this depiction of Zoraïde as a creature so easily controlled by sexual desire. Is she simply sacrificing one kind of domination for another? (AS) Is her feeling for Mézor truly love or is it mere physical lust? (RB) If it *is* merely lust, perhaps this superficial attitude has been paradoxically encouraged by being raised in a society that places so much emphasis on mere physical appearance (RB). Clearly the description of Mézor's body as a "**straight . . . column**," "**glisten[ing] like oil**," has sexual (FD), even phallic (CY) overtones, suggesting his strength and implying the potency he later demonstrates (RCE). The "**glisten[ing]**" of the "**column of ebony**" once again reinforces the story's image pattern of light counterpoised by darkness. Zoraïde sees the physicality of Mézor in sexual terms, but Mézor's master undoubtedly sees the slave's strength as an aspect of his monetary value (AMO). Although Mézor is strong, however, he is also graceful and is thus a fitting partner for the beautiful Zoraïde herself (MC). His skill at "**dance**" associates him with festivity, freedom from care, and harmony of body and soul, but his dancing is also ironically associated with a liberty he will later lose (RCE). His skill at dancing, and his devotion to it and delight in it, may reflect its status as one of his few outlets of true self-expression (AMO). Zoraïde's first glimpse of Mézor is also our first glimpse of him: he appears as unexpectedly to us as to her, and he appears in a vision that associates him with the strength and independence he will later be denied (RCE). A Longinian critic might admire Chopin's use of elevated, exalted language when describing Mézor, since such language helps associate him with sublimity or elevation (CW). Does this language—which is technically the language of Manna-Loulou, the storyteller—reflect Manna-Loulou's own desire for a loving relationship with a strong black man? After all, the only relationship of hers that we know about is her relation with her young white mistress. No husband or children of Manna-Loulou are ever mentioned (RB). Perhaps Manna-Loulou, in this sense, empathizes with the loneliness and isolation later felt by Zoraïde (RCE).

[15] **"Poor Zoraïde's heart grew sick in her bosom with love for le beau Mézor from the moment that she saw the fierce gleam of his eye, lighted by the inspiring strains of the Bamboula, and beheld the stately movements of his splendid body swaying and quivering through the figures of the dance.**

Here the claim that Zoraïde's **"heart grew sick"** is partly hyperbolic, but by the end of the story, of course, she will be plunged into a literal mental and emotional sickness from which she will never recover (SB). Her metaphorical **"sick[ness]"** here is associated with a kind of pleasure; later, her true sickness will be far more literally painful (RCE). Chopin seems to play here with the standard stereotype of both male and female slaves as controlled mainly by their passions; perhaps she alludes to this stereotype in order to show later how shallow it is (BH). A feminist critic might suggest that Chopin here invokes the unfortunate stereotype of women as passionate creatures who cannot control their emotions (SH). On the other hand, both a psychoanalytic and an archetypal critic might suggest that Zoraïde is merely manifesting the enormously powerful and primal effects of sexual longing. For both kinds of critics, such longing would be simply a part of human nature (KM2). Perhaps the reference to Zoraïde's **"bosom"** already prepares us for the story's later very heavy emphasis on motherhood (SB). Once again Chopin effectively uses imagery of light in such words as **"gleam," "lighted,"** and **"splendid"** (FD), and once again Mézor combines opposites by seeming both **"fierce"** and **"stately,"** his graceful self-control making him an appropriate match for Zoraïde (MC). The **"fierce gleam"** of Mézor's eye contrasts sharply with the earlier description [12] of M'sieur Ambroise's **"small eyes, that were cruel and false as a snake's"** (DR). Mézor's eyes almost associate him with an impressive beast, such as a lion or tiger, so that he seems a natural creature rather than a product of corrupt human society (DR). Although Zoraïde seems almost possessed by the sight of Mézor, neither of them, ironically, can possess either each other or even themselves; Mézor's power is emphasized here, only to be brutally denied later (JW). This emphasis on ecstatic possession, coupled with the references to **"the inspiring strains of the Bamboula"** and Mézor's **"stately movements,"** would greatly interest LONGINIAN critics, who tend to focus on irresistibly sublime or elevated passions (RCE).

[16] **"But when she knew him later, and he came near to her to speak with her, all the fierceness was gone out of his eyes, and she saw only kindness in them and heard only gentleness in his voice, for love had taken possession of him also, and Zoraïde was more distracted than ever. When Mézor was not dancing Bamboula in Congo Square, he was hoeing sugar cane, barefooted and half-naked, in his master's field outside of the city. Doctor Langle was his master as well as M'sieur Ambroise's.**

The **"kindness"** of Mézor's eyes and the **"gentleness"** of his voice contrast effectively with the earlier description [12] of Ambroise's **"small eyes, that were cruel and false as a snake's"** (KD). Earlier Zoraïde had been attracted mainly by Mézor's physique; now she perceives the beauty of his character or soul (SB). He seems to embody a **"kindness"** which, unlike that of Madame Delariviére, is not manipulative or selfish (SB). Mézor's dignified self-respect and self-assurance are implied by his willing-

ness to approach Zoraïde and speak to her, even though he is black and
she is a mulatto and even though he is a manual laborer and she has led
a life of relative privilege (RCE). Although earlier Mézor had seemed to
possess Zoraïde, now their "**possession**" seems mutual; this relationship
between equals is ironic in a story that so much emphasizes slavery, just
as this relationship rooted in "**love**" is ironic in a story that so much
stresses relationships of power (JW). The imagery of Mézor "**hoeing
sugar-cane, bare-footed and half-naked**" is ambiguous: on the one hand
it suggests poverty (KD) and primitiveness (OT-K) and thus contrasts
with our earlier visions of him, when he had enjoyed freedom from labor.
On the other hand, it emphasizes once more his strength and even his
sensuality, his closeness to the earth (RCE). An ARCHETYPAL critic might
even suggest that Mézor is linked with the feminine earth and depicted
as an agent of growth and fecundity; unlike M'sieur Ambroise, Doctor
Langle's "body servant," Mézor is connected not so much with a human
master as with the forces of nature (TR).

[17] "**One day, when Zoraïde kneeled before her mistress, drawing
on Madame's silken stockings, that were of the finest, she said:**
  "'**Nénaine, you have spoken to me often of marrying. Now, at last,
I have chosen a husband, but it is not M'sieur Ambroise, it is le beau
Mézor that I want and no other.' And Zoraïde hid her face in her hands
when she said that, for she guessed, rightly enough, that her mistress
would be very angry.**

Zoraïde's "**kneel[ing]**" before her mistress is functional since she is
performing a service, but it also symbolically suggests submission (KD),
almost as if the mistress possesses the power of a god—as indeed she does
in some respects (JDS). A FORMALIST critic, interested in connections between the diverse parts of the work, might note how Zoraïde's posture and
conduct recall Manna-Loulou's attention to the feet of her own mistress
[6] earlier in the story (SR). Perhaps this posture is even meant to suggest
a perversion of religious imagery, as if Madame Delariviére occupies a
position of superiority to which she is unentitled (BB). In any case, the

implied religious imagery here is part of a larger pattern in this story of religious language and allusions (BB). Ironically, the woman who wears such beautiful silk stockings will soon reveal her inner ugliness (AMO). There seems a nice contrast between Zoraïde's submissive posture and her matter-of-fact, assertive language: she does not make a request but instead announces a choice, even though she correctly anticipates the response (MC). A DIALOGICAL critic, concerned with the negotiation of different voices within a work, might focus on the subtle changes in tone and control of Zoraïde's speech. Zoraïde begins by addressing her mistress as "**Nénaine**," a soft, placating word, so that her voice at first seems childlike and unthreatening. However, she soon mentions how she has been "**spoken to**" (not "spoken with"), so that the subtle use of a single preposition implies her mistress's superiority or condescension rather than any conversational equality between the two women. In her next sentence, however, Zoraïde undermines her previously subservient tone by stating, "**I have chosen**"—phrasing that implies a certain strength and power of will, although even here the suggestion is somewhat muted (MP). Zoraïde's claim to have "**chosen**" is ironic, because the only "choice" her mistress will permit is the "choice" of when to acknowledge the mistress's choice *for* her of Ambroise. Zoraïde's use of the verb "**want**" when referring to Mézor also reminds us that her choice is simultaneously an expression of will (PP), possessiveness (MC), and sexual desire (O-TK). The word "**want**" also reminds us that although all of Zoraïde's material needs have been taken care of, she is the only person in a position to know what she truly desires (PN). The contrast between the fine beauty of the mistress's clothing ("**silken stockings, that were of the finest**") and the ugly anger of her reply will soon be apparent (JDS). Does the fact that Zoraïde hides her face imply that she anticipates a potentially violent reaction, or does it suggest that witnessing the mistress's anger would be too psychologically painful? (SG, RCE) Might it even suggest an element of shame? (SG)

[18] "**And indeed, Madame Delariviére was at first speechless with rage. When she finally spoke it was only to gasp out, exasperated:**

"'That Negro! that Negro! Bon Dieu Seigneur [Good Lord God],
but this is too much!'

Ironically, the religious Madame Delariviére, who serves as Zoraïde's
godmother and looks forward to a wedding at the cathedral, instinctively
takes God's name in vain: a small but effective symbol of her larger
hypocrisy (CH). She not only indicates her frustration that her own
long-held plans have been threatened (FD) but also suggests, perhaps, a
condescending assumption that this threat will pose no final problem:
she seems "**exasperated**" in the way one might be with a misbehaving
child, yet still seems confident of eventually exerting her authority (KD).
As with any idealized object, Zoraïde is quickly plunged from pedestal to
pit in her mistress's eyes (PP). It seems both ironic and appropriate that
Madame Delariviére invokes "**God**" when expressing her racism—ironic
because from a modern point of view her attitude seems to contradict
her religion and her role as Zoraïde's godmother, but appropriate because
from Madame Delariviére's point of view Zoraïde seeks to violate the
God-given, natural order of things. By invoking God, especially in the
exact terms that she uses, Madame Delariviére indicates her acceptance
of a hierarchical power structure, which Zoraïde seems about to violate
(RCE). Later Manna-Loulou herself will mention the phrase "good God"
in a way that may communicate a subtle irony (PW).

[19]"'Am I white, nénaine?' pleaded Zoraïde.
"'You white! *Malheureuse!* [Miserable one!] You deserve to have
the lash laid upon you like any other slave; you have proven yourself
no better than the worst.'
"'I am not white,' persisted Zoraïde, respectfully and gently. 'Doctor
Langle gives me his slave to marry, but he would not give me his son.
Then, since I am not white, let me have from out of my own race the
one whom my heart has chosen.'

The fact that Zoraïde addresses Madame Delariviére as "**Nénaine**"
("godmother") makes the mistress's brutal anger seem all the more ironic,

and perhaps Zoraïde's use of the term is even slyly calculated (RCE). By asking whether she is white, Zoraïde not only tries to make her mistress acknowledge reality (PP) but also subtly uses the mistress's own logic against her; Zoraïde thus demonstrates her mental agility and resourcefulness (MC; RB). At this point Zoraïde is described as "plead[ing]," but, with typical balance, Chopin will later describe her as "persist[ing]." Once again, then, Chopin suggests the complexity of Zoraïde's character (MC)—a complexity neatly underlined by the shift from the question "Am I white" to the statement "I am not white" (HE). When Madame Delariviére exclaims, "You white!", is she expressing stinging sarcasm (KD) or is she indicating that to her it seems absurd to link the two words? (MC) Her exclamation here recalls her earlier reference [18] to Mézor as "That Negro!" (RCE) It seems ironic that the mistress calls Zoraïde "miserable," not only because it is the mistress who is responsible for the slave's misery but also because Zoraïde's true misery is only just beginning, and Madame Delariviére will also be responsible for it, as well (AMO). It seems ironic that the mistress claims Zoraïde has "proven" herself so awful, because as yet Zoraïde has done nothing more than merely announce her choice (PP). Ironically, too, it will soon be Madame Delariviére who will actually prove herself "no better than the worst" (RCE). Since Zoraïde's identity has been clouded by her upbringing, it seems significant that she speaks of choosing "from out of [her] own race"; is she here attempting to claim or regain her identity as well as naming a lover? (KD) A READER-RESPONSE critic might argue that nearly all readers could empathize with Zoraïde's desire to choose her own mate (SG). An ARCHETYPAL critic might even argue that such desire for self-determination is deeply rooted in human nature (KM2).

[20] "However, you may well believe that Madame would not hear to that. Zoraïde was forbidden to speak to Mézor, and Mézor was cautioned against seeing Zoraïde again. But you know how the Negroes are, Ma'zélle Titite," added Manna-Loulou, smiling a little sadly. "There is no mistress, no master, no king nor priest who can hinder them from loving when they will. And these two found ways and means.

Is there, perhaps, any touch of irony in the phrase **"you may well believe,"** especially since these words are addressed by Manna-Loulou to her own mistress? Does she perhaps (unconsciously?) suggest that the woman who dominates her own life will naturally be able to understand the perspective of the woman who owns Zoraïde? (SB) A FEMINIST critic might note that whereas Zoraïde is **"forbidden"** to speak to Mézor, the latter is only **"cautioned"** against seeing Zoraïde again. Perhaps such phrasing implies the extent to which female slaves were regarded as weaker than their male counterparts (SR). Although Manna-Loulou claims that erotic self-assertion is a behavior specific to blacks, it is actually universal (PH, FD) and partly involves the attraction of anything that is forbidden (MC). Manna-Loulou tells the story in the way she expects her mistress will want to hear it, which partly explains why she speaks of blacks as if she were not one herself (FD). Yet this odd expression of apparently racist sentiment is also counter-balanced by a tone of admiration at the determination and will of Zoraïde and Mézor (MC). What might have seemed a statement reflecting racial self-hatred can thus be seen as reflect- ing a sense of strength—an assertion that although blacks may have been physically enslaved, no one could subjugate their hearts (SG). Manna- Loulou seems almost defiant but is sly enough to appear to agree with her mistress's point of view about the behavior of blacks (FS). The old woman is described as **"smiling a little sadly,"** partly because she knows the unfortunate outcome of their meetings—the defeat that will result from this apparent success (KD). Perhaps this phrase also suggests that Manna-Loulou can identify and sympathize with the kind of emotion she now describes (TDC). Does Manna-Loulou's final statement here reflect at all on her own relations with her own mistress? (FD) Does she here imply the limits of her own loyalty? (RCE) Does her list of authority figures—**mistress, master, king, and priest**—subconsciously reflect the patriarchal hierarchy that controls her culture, with religion as the chief instrument of patriarchal control? (AS) Perhaps the list also helps mitigate any suggestion that Manna-Loulou is specifically challenging the system of slavery in particular; perhaps she instead implies that literally no power could thwart the intentions of determined black lovers (DH).

[21] "When months had passed by, Zoraïde, who had grown unlike herself—sober and preoccupied—said again to her mistress: —

"'Nénaine, you would not let me have Mézor for my husband; but I have disobeyed you, I have sinned. Kill me if you wish, Nénaine; forgive me if you will; but when I heard le beau Mézor say to me, "Zoraïde, mo l'aime toi [I love you]," I could have died, but I could not have helped loving him.'"

Ironically, Zoraïde addresses her mistress almost as if the latter were a deity: "I have disobeyed you, I have sinned" (PH). In fact, the phrase "I have sinned" is used by Catholics in making confession (KD). This confession puts Madame Delariviére in the god-like position of being able to choose to respond either with mercy or with punishment (SG). Surely Zoraïde does not truly believe that she has "sinned" by loving Mézor, but she knows her actions and beliefs are morally reprehensible to her mistress. Zoraïde's own moral code seems to involve doing what is right according to her own heart and soul (KG). If, on the other hand, Zoraïde *does* genuinely believe that she has in some sense "sinned," then her phrasing suggests how much she has indeed internalized the values of the larger culture (RCE). Alternatively, in confessing to her mistress, is Zoraïde perhaps motivated by knowledge that she is already pregnant? (PH) Would she confess otherwise? Or is she motivated to confess by her fundamental honesty? (FD) Her two references here to potential death are examples of ironic foreshadowing, since in a very real sense she does die as a result of her love (JS). Emotionally and mentally (if not quite literally), Madame Delariviére does indeed help "kill" Zoraïde: by the end of the story the young woman is alive but lifeless (SB). Paradoxically, although Zoraïde can (at least temporarily) accept the love of le beau Mézor, she will never have the opportunity to show any love to the child that will be born of this union (AL). Perhaps part of the reason that Zoraïde finds Mézor's appeal so irresistible is that she has never (because of her status) really felt truly loved and has never, perhaps, been told before that she was loved (MC). Indeed, an ARCHETYPAL critic might argue that **"loving"** and being loved are two of the most primal of all human emotions (TT; MS). A LONGINIAN critic might find her final statement here an excellent example of a sublime emotion—the overpowering force of **love** (SB2).

[22] **"This time Madame Delariviére was so actually pained, so wounded at hearing Zoraïde's confession, that there was no place left in her heart for anger. She could only utter confused reproaches. But she was a woman of action rather than of words, and she acted promptly. Her first step was to induce Doctor Langle to sell Mézor.**

Madame's feelings of being **"pained"** and **"wounded"** seem obviously ironic in light of the much deeper pain and suffering she later inflicts on Zoraïde (SB). Does Madame Delariviére's lack of anger paradoxically reflect her lack of fundamental love for Zoraïde? (MC). Or does the mistress understand Zoraïde's feelings but act as she feels she must? (AL) Or, alternatively, does she express her anger through her swift actions rather than through words? (PP) The fact that she is described as **"hearing Zoraïde's confession"** contributes to the pattern of ironic religious imagery that runs throughout the story. A priest who heard a confession would be obliged not only to show some compassion to the sinner but also to keep the confession private. A priest would also seek to reconcile the sinner to God and the community by imposing an appropriate penance. In contrast to all these ideal responses, Madame Delariviére is full of rage, immediately reveals her knowledge to her accomplice, Dr. Langle, and imposes a punishment that seems to exceed by far the "sin" committed (PD). The word **"promptly"** implies the mistress' succinct efficiency (FD); she is calculating and methodical in her vindictiveness (MR). She doesn't take time to sulk; she simply acts (PP). The mistress here cannot speak clearly but does have complete control of her will; in contrast, by the end of the story Zoraïde will still be able to speak but will lack true self-control because of her radical emotional disturbance and deterioration of intellect (PD). Although at first Chopin might seem to suggest that the mistress had decided to relent (she lacks anger; she seems confused), this momentary possibility only emphasizes the suddenness of her cruelty (KD). Although the word **"induce"** might suggest that she had to convince or persuade the doctor to sell Mézor, we soon discover that he was only too eager to act (RCE). The fact that he is a doctor, and thus professionally committed to the alleviation of pain and suffering, makes his callousness seem all the more ironic (RCE).

[23] **"Doctor Langlé, who was a widower, had long wanted to marry Madame Delariviére, and he would willingly have walked on all fours at noon through the Place d'Armes if she wanted him to. Naturally he lost no time in disposing of le beau Mézor, who was sold away into Georgia, or the Carolinas, or one of those distant countries far away, where he could no longer hear his Creole tongue spoken, nor dance Calinda, nor hold la belle Zoraïde in his arms.**

Paradoxically, Madame Delariviére exploits Doctor Langle's affection in order to destroy Zoraïde's own chances for love (JA). A FEMINIST critic might note the irony of a strong woman using her social power to destroy another woman (SB2). A FEMINIST might also note how Madame Delariviére takes advantage of the power she enjoys as a single woman and potential wife (SR). Although Langle acts on own his desires, he thereby prevents Zoraïde from acting on hers (MR). Although slaves were theoretically inferior to their masters and were often considered subhuman, Manna-Loulou describes Langle as if he were a ridiculous animal; his professional degree apparently does not enhance his wisdom (RCE). The black narrator is obviously contemptuous of her white "superior" (MC), and Madame Delariviére treats the doctor with the same kind of condescension (as if he were a child) she had earlier displayed toward Zoraïde (PN). Ironically, however, although the reference to Doctor Langle "[**walking**] **on all fours**" is merely a bit of sarcastic hyperbole in the case of a white professional, such demeaning behavior could actually have been commanded of a slave such as Mézor or Manna-Loulou (MR2). The idea that he might behave like an animal is simply a joke, but in reality he treats other human beings as if they were truly animals

(SR). Contrast Doctor Langle's presumed willingness here to make a public fool of himself with the dignified, manly public display Mézor had made of *him*self when earlier dancing the Bamboula (RCE). Langle is presumably willing to debase himself to win the woman he desires, whereas Mézor treats Zoraïde as a worthy equal (SB). The word "[n] **aturally**" is powerfully ironic, since Langle's behavior is so completely un-natural and inhuman (FD), while the word "**disposing**" suggests a quick, efficient, emotionless (FD) use of power (PP). The word implies that inconvenient people can literally be thrown away (PP). Manna-Loulou's contempt for Doctor Langle is perhaps one of many subtle reflections of the pervasive feminine point-of-view of this entire story: the tale is told by a woman, to a woman, and about a woman, and Chopin's own audience would presumably consist mostly of women (FD). Note how the description of Mézor's fate directly echoes details mentioned earlier, such as his dancing, his speech, and his physical contact with Zoraïde (BB). Does Mézor's banishment to a land where his Creole tongue will not be understood recall, in any respect, the confusion of tongues that resulted from the Biblical Tower of Babel? (OT-K) The indefiniteness of Mézor's new location ("**one of those distant countries far away**") implies how impossible it would be for Zoraïde ever to find him, even if she were somehow able to try (FD). The very word "**countries**" emphasizes the cultural gulf and sense of geographical distance between Louisiana and other states (TDC). From this point forward, Mézor effectively vanishes not only from Zoraïde's experience but from ours as readers (RCE). Certainly Mézor is in some sense a victim (DR), particularly since he was originally Zoraïde's choice. The final three phrases of this passage emphasize his complete isolation—his alienation from his familiar tongue, from his favorite activity, and also (most important) from the person he loves—the mother of his child. Ironically, not even Mézor's "**Creole tongue**" is even really "**his**": instead, it is the language he has learned from his owners and is the language of their culture. Yet it is also the only language he knows (RCE). Although Mézor may bitterly lament his separation from Zoraïde, at least his sale removes him to a new location in which he may build a new life, while his opportunity for mobility may help him cope psychologically. Zoraïde, in contrast, remains forever rooted to the locale where she first found love and then lost it (GW). For her there is neither geographical nor mental escape (RCE).

[24] "The poor thing was heartbroken when Mézor was sent away from her, but she took comfort and hope in the thought of her baby that she would soon be able to clasp to her breast.

"La belle Zoraïde's sorrows had now begun in earnest. Not only sorrows but sufferings, and with the anguish of maternity came the shadow of death. But there is no agony that a mother will not forget when she holds her first-born to her heart, and presses her lips upon the baby flesh that is her own, yet far more precious than her own.

Zoraïde is aptly described as a "**poor thing**" not only because Manna-Loulou (unlike others) pities her (AMO) but also because it is partly her literal poverty that allows her to be treated as a "**thing**" rather than as a full human being (SB; NB). If the word "**heartbroken**" seems a cliché, it is nonetheless exactly the kind of language one might expect from an unpretentious narrator such as Manna-Loulou (RCE). The word also echoes the earlier claim that when Zoraïde first saw Mézor, "her heart grew sick in her bosom" [15]; now her heart is not merely sick but shattered (SB). Typically, the innocuous passive voice is used in the description of how Mézor "**was sent away**" (NB, AO). Note Zoraïde's desire to clasp "**her baby**" to "**her breast**": the alliteration and repetition of the personal pronoun "her" (TR) imply her intense yearning to feel that she owns at least one thing that belongs personally to her (NB), while the verb "**clasp**" is much more forceful than another word (such as "hold") might have been (LP). The word "**clasp**" suggests that Zoraïde feels a need to cling to her baby, whereas usually it is a baby who clings to its mother (AMO). Calling Zoraïde "**la belle**" at this point simply highlights the ugly circumstances in which her daughter is taken from her (KW). Note how this whole passage oscillates between positives and negatives: from negative ("**heartbroken**") to positive ("**comfort and hope**") in the first sentence, then from negative (psychological "**sorrows**") to even more

negative (physical **"sufferings"**) at the beginning of the second, then to
even more intense pain (**"anguish"**) followed immediately by the prospect of at once forgetting such anguish in anticipation of the pleasure of
physical and emotional contact with one's newborn (RCE). This kind of
oscillation is typical of Chopin's style and helps her stories achieve a great
deal of moment-by-moment complexity and suspense (RCE). Even the
last clause of this passage is typical of this oscillating pattern: Chopin first
makes what seems to be a definitive statement (**"flesh that is her own"**)
and then immediately modifies and complicates it (**"yet far more precious
than her own"**) (RCE). The reference to the **"shadow of death"** not only
explicitly recalls the famous language of Psalm 23 [22 in the Catholic
Bible] (SD) but also contributes to the story's larger focus on imagery of
darkness (MC). However, while the psalm traditionally lends comfort
and support to those facing death or any other great obstacle, here the
allusion starkly emphasizes the fact that Zoraïde can find no comfort
and can never regain her former self (NP). Although the word **"shadow"**
seems to imply an agony that is merely temporary and passing, Zoraïde
in a sense will never emerge from the mental anguish she now suffers,
even though her physical pain will cease (KM). Paradoxically, Zoraïde
is literally close to death as she brings new life into the world (OT-K).
A LONGINIAN critic might regard Zoraïde's powerful motherly instincts
as sublime yearnings that supposedly lie deep within human nature—a
point of view with which an ARCHETYPAL critic might well agree (TT).
FEMINIST critics, on the other hand, might object to any claim that all
women feel such maternal yearnings (RCE). The reference to a mother's
"first-born" seems ironic not only because Zoraïde, so far as we know,
will never have another child (RCE) but also because she is deprived of
her first and only child in the same way that she was deprived of her
first and only love (KM). The phrase suggests a hope for the future that
seems especially ironic since Zoraïde's future will hold such little hope
(NB). Although a mother may indeed forget all agony when she holds
her first child, Zoraïde will never have even this opportunity for happiness (KW). The anticipated baby seems **"precious"** to Zoraïde because
it will be one of the few things in life that will seem truly her **"own,"** yet

it seems **"far more precious than her own"** partly because it is also the product of her union with the now-banished Mézor (SB). Ironically, of course, because Zoraïde is a slave even her child does not truly belong to her or its father (KM): it immediately becomes the property of Madame Delariviére (SB). The **"flesh"** of Zoraïde's flesh—her baby—is not her own any more than Zoraïde's body is her own, except perhaps during the passionate encounters when she gave herself to Mézor (CS).

[25]**"So, instinctively, when Zoraïde came out of the awful shadow she gazed questioningly about her and felt with her trembling hands upon either side of her. 'Oú li, mo piti a moin? Where is my little one?' she asked imploringly. Madame who was there and the nurse who was there both told her in turn, 'To piti á toi, li mouri' ('Your little one is dead'), which was a wicked falsehood that must have caused the angels in heaven to weep. For the baby was living and well and strong. It had at once been removed from its mother's side, to be sent away to Madame's plantation, far up the coast. Zoraïde could only moan in reply, 'Li mouri, li mouri,' and she turned her face to the wall.**

The word **"instinctively"** not only implies natural conduct that contrasts with the unnatural behavior of Madame Delariviére and Doctor Langle (KW), but it also suggests that Zoraïde, unlike so many other characters in this story, innately tends to care about others: her immediate impulse is to reach out in love, which makes the treatment she herself suffers seem all the more ironic (SB). **"Instinctively"** also immediately suggests that Zoraïde intuitively senses that something dreadful has happened (KM), and it additionally seems an appropriate word since Zoraïde, from this point forward, will largely be a creature of instincts who will lose her ability to reason (AMO). The word **"trembling,"** meanwhile, suggests physical frailty and sickness that bitterly foreshadow the mental breakdown Zoraïde will shortly suffer (KM). She comes out of the temporary or physical **"shadow"** of childbirth, but she is never able to overcome the permanent or psychological shadow of being a slave and being deprived of her child (BH). The reiteration (**"Madame**

who was there and the nurse who was there") perhaps makes the lies of
the attending women seem all the more brazen and heartless: both had
seen Zoraïde give birth, both had seen her anguish, both had seen her
"**imploring**" quest for her child, but both denied Zoraïde her joy, and
the repetition stresses the deliberate nature of their crime (KW). Such
conduct seems ironic enough for two women but especially ironic in a
"**nurse**" (TR). Of course, a MARXIST might argue that the nurse merely
acquiesces to Madame Delariviére's greater economic power (RCE). Once
more Madame Delariviére shows her perversion of her role as Zoraïde's
godmother (TR). Being apparently childless herself, she shows no understanding or concern for the psychological bond that Zoraïde had already
established with the baby as she carried it (TR). The cold-hearted way in
which Madame disposes of both Mézor and the baby raises the matter
of another missing person in the story. Where is Zoraïde's mother? It
certainly appears that at some point the absent mother must have shared
a close bond with Madame in order for Madame to serve as godmother
to her child. Yet she is never mentioned. Did she die within a year or so
of Zoraïde's birth? Or is her absence more ominous? Did it foreshadow
the later "disappearances" from which Zoraïde suffers? Did Madame covet
Zoraïde enough to wrest her from her mother's arms? (TR)

The adjective "**wicked**" greatly intensifies the noun "**falsehood**"
(AMO); although some falsehoods can be motivated by good intentions,
Manna-Loulou wants there to be no doubt that this one is evil (MC).
The weeping "**angels**" seem strangely passive and ineffective (BB)—an
ironic touch since "**angels**" are usually depicted not only as constantly
rejoicing (BH) but as agents who intervene to promote human good
(CH). Here, however, they seem impotent (CH), just as later God will
be described as almost sanctioning Zoraïde's earthly suffering (BB). The
speculation that the angels "**must**" have wept accentuates the ironic reality
that on earth no one sympathizes with Zoraïde except for Mézor, whom
she now has also lost (NB).

The baby's life and strength emphasize, by contrast, Zoraïde's mental
and physical weakness (JDS). Note the progressive strengthening of the
adjectives: "**living . . . well . . . strong**" (RCE). Of course, in spite of

these positive terms, the baby is nonetheless still condemned to slavery (AMO). Note the antiseptic, passive verb **"was removed,"** which de-emphasizes any sense of personal responsibility or blame (AO; NB). Although Zoraïde accepts the explanation that her baby is dead, that acceptance marks the beginning, in a sense, of her *own* demise—her own mental death (MC). By turning her face to the presumably blank and empty **"wall"** (SB), Zoraïde in a sense turns her back on life (AL), hope, and the future (NB); this is just the first stage in a slow process of withdrawal (RCE). An ARCHETYPAL critic might argue that Chopin here plays on two of the most powerful and basic of all human instincts: the desire to have children and the fear of losing them (JB).

[26]"**Madame had hoped, in thus depriving Zoraïde of her child, to have her young waiting-maid again at her side free, happy, and beautiful as of old. But there was a more powerful will than Madame's at work—the will of the good God, who had already designed that Zoraïde should grieve with a sorrow that was never more to be lifted in this world.**

A TRADITIONAL HISTORICAL critic might note that Madame Delariviére acts in accordance with the accepted norms of her culture and that the reaction of her contemporaries to her behavior would have been far less outraged than our own is likely to be (JB). How ironic that Madame Delariviére wishes Zoraïde to be **"free"** as before: not only will Zoraïde from this point *never* be free, but even in the past she was never truly free (FD; NP; KM). Ironically, there is a sense in which Madame Delariviére, by denying Zoraïde access to (and knowledge of) the child, is trying to get back her *own* child—Zoraïde (PP). Is there any resemblance between Zoraïde and the Virgin Mary, both of whom had children taken away from them and thus became famously grieving mothers? (PN) Fittingly, Madame Delariviére's attempt to deny Zoraïde what the young woman herself desires will result in the mistress being denied her own desires as well (MC; NB). Is Zoraïde, from one perspective, rightly punished for her sin of illicit sex? (MO; SB; NB; AS) Or is there a sense in which

Zoraïde exemplifies the Jansenist idea that those chosen by God must suffer in this world? (FD) Chopin's phrasing seems to imply that only the "**will**" of "**God**" can undermine the determined and forceful will of Madame Delariviére—as if the latter were herself a kind of deity (KM). Earlier, it was Madame Delariviére herself who had invoked the name of the "good God" (PW). Note, however, the powerfully ironic syntax of the final cited sentence here: at first Chopin seems to suggest that the evil of Madame Delariviére will be thwarted by "**the will of the good God**," but then the apparent direction of the sentence seems thrown into reverse when it is revealed "**that Zoraïde should grieve with a sorrow that was never more to be lifted.**" Such reversals are typical of Chopin's style, even at the level of individual sentences (RCE). The crucial phrase in the final sentence, of course, is "**in this world**": it implies that Zoraïde will no longer suffer in the next world, and it may imply that she will be compensated there for her sufferings here (PH; NP; MO). Does the phrase perhaps also suggest a less comforting eternal fate for Madame Delariviére? (RCE)

[27] "**La belle Zoraïde was no more. In her stead was a sad-eyed woman who mourned night and day for her baby. 'Li mouri, li mouri' she would sigh over and over again to those about her, and to herself when others grew weary of her complaint.**

"**Yet, in spite of all, M'sieur Ambroise was still in the notion to marry her. A sad wife or a merry one was all the same to him so long as that wife was Zoraïde. And she seemed to consent, or rather to submit, to the approaching marriage as though nothing mattered any longer in this world.**

An important theme of Chopin's story may be the importance of freedom: the story may be designed to show what human beings would be like if they exercised no choice or control in their daily lives (MO). Significantly, from this point forward Zoraïde is never again called "**la belle**" by Manna-Loulou, the narrator (KW). She continues to exist physically, as the same body, but she is now no longer the same person.

The young girl whose eyes had earlier been one of her greatest charms is now merely a **"sad-eyed woman"** constantly mourning for the loss of her baby—mourning that probably also reflects a continued mourning for the loss of Mézor (RCE). This woman who has already been shown so little pity is now shown even less: **"others grew weary of her complaint"** (SB)—with perhaps the word "complaint" even suggesting that they regard her as a weak, self-indulgent whiner (AMO). M'sieur Ambroise, however, continues to regard her (at least for the time being) as a kind of trophy who is still worth acquiring (TR), perhaps as a means of cementing his link with the powerful Madame Delariviére (and thus winning the regard of his own master, Doctor Langle) or perhaps as a desirable physical object whom he can sexually exploit and whose mindlessness is therefore, in some sense, advantageous. A FEMINIST critic might argue that his attitude epitomizes the ways in which women are so often objectified—that is, regarded as mere objects or possessions (SH; MS). It seems doubtful that the **"approaching marriage"** would still have been the once-anticipated grand celebration planned for the cathedral (RCE).

[28]**"One day, a black servant entered a little noisily the room in which Zoraïde sat sewing. With a look of strange and vacuous happiness upon her face, Zoraïde arose hastily. 'Hush, hush,' she whispered, lifting a warning finger, 'my little one is asleep; you must not awaken her.'**

"Upon the bed was a senseless bundle of rags shaped like an infant in swaddling clothes. Over this dummy the woman had drawn the mosquito bar, and she was sitting contentedly beside it. In short, from that day Zoraïde was demented. Night nor day did she lose sight of the doll that lay in her bed or in her arms.

Despite her loss of mental power and psychological self-command, Zoraïde, as a mulatto owned by Madame Delariviére, still apparently enjoys greater power than the **"black servant"** who now enters to attend to her needs (RCE). The fact that Zoraïde is described as sitting and **"sewing"** suggests both her physical passivity and her lack of mental engagement: her movements are mechanical and repetitive, and her focus seems at first entirely on her work. As it happens, however, her focus is less on the cloth she sews than on the rag baby she now considers the center of her universe (RCE). Although her "**happiness**" is described as "**vacuous**," this is an external judgment: Zoraïde herself knows why she is happy (AMO). And, typically, her happiness seems rooted mainly in love: once more her instinctive reaction is concern for another's comfort, even if the object of her attention can never return that affection (SB). Ironically, the "**black servant**" to whom Zoraïde lifts a "warning finger" is one of the few other humans over whom she now exercises any control: even a mindless Zoraïde is still higher in the racial hierarchy than the pure black maid (RCE). Despite her mental breakdown, however, Zoraïde still has command over her language: she speaks in coherent sentences and in ways that would make perfect sense in a different context (PD). Part of the poignancy of her condition, in fact, is that she seems so rational in her irrationality (PD; RCE).

Contrast the plain "**bed**" on which Zoraïde and her "baby" lie with the "sumptuous mahogany bed" [5] in which Madame Delisle now listens to this tale (DR). The word "**rags**" suggests the tattered, discarded ruins of Zoraïde's former life and hopes (RCE). Ironically, Zoraïde, who was herself raised almost as if she were a precious doll on display, now herself mothers a considerably less attractive doll of her own (DR). While earlier the real baby had been referred to as "it," Zoraïde now imagines the rag-baby as "**her,**" once again reinforcing the feminine emphasis of the entire story (FD). By attributing her own sex to the baby, perhaps Zoraïde subconsciously treats it as an alter-ego, giving it the nurturing and genuine love she herself never received (MR). As always, though, her instinct is to love and protect another (AO; SB). Because the rag baby is "senseless," it ironically resembles Zoraïde, its now-demented "mother" (DR). Perhaps, by using the word "shaped," Chopin implies Zoraïde's active attempt to shape, construct, or resurrect her substitute child. Ironically, though, she lacks any real power to shape her own life except by removing herself from the world (DR). Clearly the reference to "**swaddling clothes**" alludes to the story of the infant Jesus, but this rag-baby (unlike the infant savior) has no power to redeem or undo or even share in Zoraïde's suffering (BB). Paradoxically, Zoraïde both loses (RCE) and gains (DR) freedom through her madness. Perhaps Chopin refers to Zoraïde as "**the woman**" to suggest the universality of her maternal instincts (DR), but perhaps the phrase also suggests that she is no longer the seemingly happy, carefree girl on whom the story at first focused (RCE). The phrase "**in short**" seems somewhat ironic, since the evolution of the demented Zoraïde was anything but short. It required years to confuse Zoraïde about her place in society, yet only a few short and thoughtless decisions by Madame were required to trigger Zoraïde's madness (DR). Chopin mentions "**night**" and "**day**" as if there were no difference between them, and for Zoraïde there *is* no difference. Since she no longer allows the outside world into her mind, light and dark are largely irrelevant (DR). Having lost sight of her lover, her living child, and her earlier dreams, Zoraïde will now not allow herself to lose sight of the rag doll, which has become her world (DR). From the perspective of the outside world, she seems unfocused; from her own perspective, however, she is now totally focused on the only thing that matters (RCE).

[29] "**And now was Madame stung with sorrow and remorse at seeing this terrible affliction that had befallen her dear Zoraïde. Consulting with Doctor Langlé, they decided to bring back to the mother the real baby of flesh and blood that was now toddling about, and kicking its heels in the dust yonder upon the plantation.**

Does the word "**stung**" suggest, perhaps, merely a small prick of pain? (AMO). Certainly Madame's "**sorrow and remorse**" are nothing compared to Zoraïde's suffering (RCE). Ironically, Madame Delariviére feels that she has lost Zoraïde in much the same way that Zoraïde feels she has lost her own daughter (BB). Note again the passive phrasing "**affliction that had befallen**": once more Madame accepts no obvious personal responsibility (MR2), and perhaps the passive voice is even somewhat appropriate, since it is largely the social system that gives people like Madame power that is responsible for the "**affliction**" of people like Zoraïde (AMO). Even Madame's decision to reverse course does not express an impulsive or instinctive concern for another (of the sort that Zoraïde so often demonstrates [SB]). Instead, she reaches the decision only after first "**consulting**" with Doctor Langle (NB).

Ironically, the word "**toddling**" had earlier been used to describe Zoraïde herself as an infant (FD). When the baby was born it had been described as an "**it**," as a mere thing or abstraction [25]; now, suddenly, it is a "**real baby of flesh and blood**" (KD). Nevertheless, it is still never referred to by name—a fact that indicates its relative unimportance to the people who control it (MO). The fact that the baby possesses much of the liveliness once associated with its mother makes their separation, and Zoraïde's present condition, seem all the more pathetic (OT-K). Does the reference to the infant "**kicking its heels**" also remind us of its father's passion for dancing? (RCE). Because it has been born a slave, however, the child's freedom and joy can only be temporary and ephemeral (SB).

[30] "**It was Madame herself who led the pretty, tiny little "griffe" girl to her mother. Zoraïde was sitting on a stone bench in the courtyard, listening to the soft splashing of the fountain, and watching the fitful shadows of the palm leaves upon the broad, white flagging.**

The sentence beginning "[i]t **was Madame herself**" may at first seem to imply that her act is honorable (RCS), but it may also suggest an attitude of pride and self-important condescension (BH): she engages in a typically grand gesture (MR2). Even her decision to return the child manifests her power (SR). Nevertheless, we don't easily forget that "**it was Madame herself**," after all, who first removed the girl from Zoraïde (RCS). A TRADITIONAL HISTORICAL critic would note that a "**griffe**" was the child of a black and a mulatto (SG). The fact that such a word even existed in Zoraïde's culture suggests again that culture's obsession with minutely detailed racial classification, and because the infant girl is a "**griffe**" rather than a mulatto, she will enjoy even less freedom and even fewer opportunities than her mother (RCE). On the other hand, it is (ironically) precisely because Zoraïde's position was once so favored that she is now so afflicted: perhaps if she had been born a mere black slave and had attracted no special attention, she would have been free to choose her own mate and raise her own child (RCE).

Ironically, when Madame finally shows compassion, it is too late: Zoraïde, like the lifeless "**stone**" she passively sits on (NB), has already lost all feeling and sense (NP); like the stone, she now seems cold, hard, stiff, and inert (SH). Sadly, there is no indication of thought, no indication that Zoraïde is *contemplating* her surroundings or her circumstances. She seems nearly catatonic, perceiving the world merely through the senses of sound and sight, perhaps choosing the comfort of these senses over the pain of remembrance and contemplation (RCS). Also, Chopin's description of the "**shadows . . . upon the broad, white flagging**" seems to symbolize the state of affairs between the black slaves and the white slave owners. Such phrasing seems to suggest that the slaves are in a way not real, not tangible, but are mere silhouettes against a broad white world (RCS). Interestingly, the only other "**fountain**" previously mentioned in this story [4] had been mentioned as part of the song of sorrow with which the story opened (RCE). Even the water seems lifeless and controlled in this artificial, man-made environment (TR). Perhaps as a final irony, the tree that towers over Zoraïde is a "**palm**," the tree sacred to the Roman Catholic Church, the tree of Christian triumph (TR). Yet such a tree is also, of course, appropriate to the setting in Louisiana (RCE).

[31]"'Here,' said Madame, approaching, 'here, my poor dear Zora-ïde, is your own little child. Keep her; she is yours. No one will ever take her from you again.'

"Zoraïde looked with sullen suspicion upon her mistress and the child before her. Reaching out a hand she thrust the little one mistrust-fully away from her. With the other hand she clasped the rag bundle fiercely to her breast; for she suspected a plot to deprive her of it.

Here again Madame presumes to present herself as a source of wise and beneficent power. By claiming that "**no one**" will take the child again, perhaps she subsconsciously tries to relieve herself of responsibility for her own part in the initial taking of the child: she speaks as if someone else had been responsible. The phrase **"keep her; she is yours"** diminishes the very act it describes: Madame still disposes of people as if they were her personal property (RCS), and in the very act of granting Zoraïde possession of her own child, Madame shows who is still in control (SR). Ironically, no one *will* **"ever take"** the child from Zoraïde again, but only because Zoraïde herself will refuse to accept the infant (RCE).

It hardly seems surprising that Zoraïde is suspicious. After all, she has been led to believe that her child was dead, and it would be perfectly in keeping with Madame Delariviére's manipulative personality to try to deceive Zoraïde into accepting a false substitute (RCS; RCE). The very suspiciousness that thus seems to confirm Zoraïde's insanity is also, paradoxically, in some ways perfectly rational (RCE). Even so, the following sentence has an amazing effect. For an instant, we see Zoraïde **"reaching out a hand,"** and we hope that she will accept her child into her arms. Just as instantly, however, she **"thrust[s] the little one away from her."** We now know that there is no hope for a reunion. We also know from Zoraïde's behavior that she has now truly lost her mind (RCS). Ironically, this is one of the few moments in the story when the usually passive Zoraïde is both angry and active, but the target of her hostility is her own child (TR).

[32]**"Nor could she ever be induced to let her own child approach her; and finally the little one was sent back to the plantation, where she was never to know the love of mother or father.**

Here the irony is stinging. For once, Zoraïde is given the opportunity to take what is rightfully hers. We know, however, that she is fated for unhappiness, so we are not surprised that she doesn't accept her child. We are saddened, further, knowing that her inability to reason was, in the first place, caused by the pain of losing her child, and that it is this very inability to reason that now prevents her from realizing that her child is being offered back to her (RCS). Paradoxically, Zoraïde's real child will know her place in the world much more clearly than her mother did. She will be raised as a slave and will have no expectations that can be trampled on by white masters (DR). It seems ironic that it is now said that the little girl is **"never to know the love of mother or father,"** since this, after all, had been Madame Delariviére's original plan for her (AMO).

[33] "And now this is the end of Zoraïde's story. She was never known again as la belle Zoraïde, but ever after as Zoraïde la folle, whom no one ever wanted to marry—not even M'sieur Ambroise. She lived to be an old woman, whom some people pitied and others laughed at—always clasping at her bundle of rags—her 'piti.'

The opening sentence here serves two very important purposes. First, it literally announces the conclusion of Manna-Loulou's telling of Zoraïde's story; secondly, it implies, figuratively, the end of Zoraïde's life as a beautiful, intelligent, passionate woman—la belle Zoraïde (RCS). Yet the statement that **"this is the end of Zoraïde's story"** is also powerfully ironic, since this is not really the "end" of her story but merely the end of our knowledge of it (CH). Zoraïde's life will continue for a long while (SB): she is not allowed even the relief of death (FS), and she has even lost one of her chief values to society—her value as a potential wife (AMO). She is no longer attractive even to M'sieur Ambroise, who had earlier seemed easy to satisfy (RCE). Is there perhaps a note of increased empathy on Manna-Loulou's part toward Zoraïde, who is now described as an "old woman" (thus resembling Manna-Loulou herself [RCE])? As before in her life, Zoraïde now receives little real sympathy, and perhaps she is **"laughed at"** (ironically) even by some of her fellow slaves (MO). Whereas earlier Zoraïde had longed to "clasp" her own child, now she is left merely **"clasping at her bundle of rags,"** and perhaps the words **"clasping at"** even suggest a sense of fear, desperation, and anticipated loss (RCE). Ironically, her real, true child will never receive this kind of attentive concern (NP)—concern which contrasts sharply with the kind of meanness Zoraïde herself is shown by others (SB). Might a POSTMODERNIST critic, however, find Zoraïde's transformation too abrupt and the tragic ending too neat—too much a concession to the audience's desire for a tidy, pat conclusion? (CY)

[34]"Are you asleep, Ma'zélle Titite?"

"No, I am not asleep; I was thinking. Ah, the poor little one, Man Loulou, the poor little one! better had she died!"

A FORMALIST critic might admire the fact that Chopin's story ends where it began: with Manna-Loulou and Madame Delisle in the latter's bedroom (KN). The story moves from the present to the past and then back to the present (KN), and it begins and ends on the same note of languor (DH). Paradoxically, a story that was presumably intended to promote sleep has apparently inhibited it (RCE). Note the intimacy apparently implied by the diminutive phrase **"Ma'zélle Titite."** On the other hand, Manna-Loulou may be employing a childhood term in order to appease or placate her mistress in the event that the latter's silence indicates not intimacy but instead anger at a slave who may be perceived as attempting to manipulate her mistress's emotions by telling a tale that reflects so poorly on the behavior of whites (EP). A NEW HISTORICIST critic, interested in the complexities of power relations, might suggest that it would be cognitively difficult for Manna-Loulou to be outraged by what happens to Zoraïde without also being outraged by her own oppression. Since emotional rebellion would cost her too much, she acquiesces (DH). Does the phrase **"I was thinking"** raise the hope that Madame Delisle has learned a profitable lesson by hearing the story? (RCE) Ironically, however, Madame Delisle's final statement, if it refers to the baby, seems to suggest that *she* would have responded not much differently than Zoraïde's mistress in the same situation (RCS). Given the moral complexity of "La Belle Zoraïde," the realization that nobody in Manna-Loulou's tale except the child seems to have stirred Madame Delisle's sympathy even strikes the reader as horrific (CS). Ironically, Madame Delisle seems to miss the whole point of Manna-Loulou's story, perhaps deliberately failing to realize that Zoraïde's problems are caused by the system and by those, such as Madame Deleriviere, Doctor Langle, and even Madame Delisle herself, who unthinkingly represent that system (FS; BH).

Even for an avowed storyteller, Manna-Loulou's knowledge of the details of Zoraïde's life, from infancy through old age, seems surprising. Manna-Loulou seems most affected after she recounts Madame Delariviére's derision of Mézor as "'That Negro! that Negro!'" [18] It is then that she looks sad. Unlike Zoraïde, the "*café-au-lait*" mulatress [8], Manna-Loulou is "herself as black as the night" [2]. Similarly, Mézor's skin was "ebony" [14]. Zoraïde's child is described as "'a pretty, tiny little "griffe" girl" [30]. A griffe is the offspring of a Negro and a mulatto. Presumably, then, Zoraïde's child was dark-skinned. Could Manna-Loulou in fact be Zoraïde's lost daughter? If so, such a relationship with Zoraïde would add ironic significance to the last exchange in the story. (TR)

Madame Delisle shows compassion, but she misses the point by thinking that Zoraïde's child would be better off dead. This view disregards the value of the child's individual life and the ultimate value of maternity, both of which appear to be important themes in the story. Manna-Loulou nurtures Madame Delisle. In this she represents the story's strongest abiding feminine principle. In this respect she may be the story's literal "manna," that which feeds and promotes life (TR).

[35]But this is the way Madame Delisle and Manna-Loulou really talked to each other:

"Vou pré droumi, Ma'zélle Titite?"

"Non, pa pré droumi; mo yapré zongler. Ah, la pauv' piti, Man Loulou. La pauv' piti! Mieux li mouri!"

The resounding "But" with which this passage begins, along with the abrupt lapse into Creole dialect, seems purposely designed to remove the average American reader from sharing Manna-Loulou's and Madame Delisle's conversation and sentiments, yet this very strategy paradoxically engages the reader's attention even more intensely (TDC). In one sense this final re-emphasis on linguistic differences seems to imply that what the reader has just read would really be incomprehensible to the common English-speaking American. However, the tactic may also be intended to convey just the opposite implication: that we have just been

given a true glimpse into the life of Louisiana Creole culture (TDC).
Manna-Loulou's tale ends simultaneously with the ending of Chopin's
story (CS). An ARISTOTELIAN critic or a FORMALIST might argue that this
over-all structure, which is that of a story-within-a-story, contributes to
the complex unity of the piece: for an ARISTOTELIAN or FORMALIST, not
only does mentioning Manna-Loulou and Madame Delisle before and
after the story of Zoraïde unify Chopin's work, but this structural device
also emphasizes how the tale functions as a moral parable from which
its readers can learn a lesson (CW). The inter-related stories of the two
mistresses and two servants might definitely provoke a STRUCTURALIST
critic, meanwhile, to explore the similarities and differences between
the two codes (or sign-systems) embodied in the two stories. For instance, might analogies be drawn between Zoraïde and Manna-Loulou?
A LONGINIAN critic, meanwhile, might argue that Madame Delisle's
sympathetic reaction implies that Zoraïde's fate arouses a response that
transcends artificial divisions of race and class (CW). The repetition of
the ending in two different languages arguably makes its meaning all the
more emphatically heart-breaking. Metaphorically, the two women (slave
and mistress) in each story do not really speak each other's language. This
lack of true communication is ironically underscored by the repetition of
the final dialogue between Madame Delisle and Manna-Loulou. A rigidly
hierarchical society separates the two sets of women, and no "common"
spoken word can bridge the gap between them (CS; JG).

Frank O'Connor's "Guests of the Nation" and "The Bridal Night": General Comments from Diverse Critical Perspectives

Kathleen B. Durrer, Katie Magaw, Scott Johnson, and Claire Skowronski

Although Frank O'Connor is generally regarded as a master of the modern short story, his fiction has not received as much critical attention as might have been expected. Perhaps because much of his work seems relatively uncomplicated and straightforward, it has been discussed (when discussed at all) mainly in thematic terms. In other words, critics tend to have been as interested in what O'Connor writes *about* (such as the theme of loneliness) as in *how* he writes. O'Connor, therefore, is an author ripe for critical re-evaluation, and his work invites attention from a wide variety of interpretive perspectives. Among the ancient and modern theories that might prove useful in reading his writings are the following: Platonic, Aristotelian, Horatian, and Longinian criticism; thematic, historical, formalist, and archetypal criticism; psychoanalytic, Marxist, feminist, and structuralist criticism; and (to name just a few more examples) dialogical, deconstructive, postmodern, reader-response, multicultural, and new historicist criticism.

Readers unfamiliar with these various theories will have an easier time making sense of them if they recall M.H. Abrams' famous argument that any literary theory that tries to be complete must account for four basic aspects of literature: the author, the text, the audience, and the universe

(or "reality").[1] Abrams' list can be usefully supplemented by adding a
fifth category: the role or function of the critic herself. Any reasonably
well developed theory, in other words, will be a theory about all these
factors and the relations among them. The assumptions a theorist makes
about the author, for example, will inevitably affect (and be affected by)
the assumptions he makes about the text, the audience, "reality," and the
purposes of criticism. Indeed, Abrams argues that each theory will tend
to emphasize *one* of these aspects as crucial or most important. Plato, for
instance, tends to emphasize the importance of accurately understanding
reality, and his entire theory of literature seems affected by this central
emphasis. He thus assumes that because neither the author nor the literary text can help us understand reality, and because most members of
the audience do not seek such understanding, literature has little value.
Plato's views of the critic derive directly from this conclusion: for him the
critic functions as a kind of philosophical traffic cop, admitting certain
"useful" kinds of literature to the republic but banishing the rest.

In attempting to suggest some ways in which two of Frank O'Connor's
best stories ("The Bridal Night" and "Guests of the Nation") might be
approached from a variety of theoretical perspectives, it may be worthwhile
to review quickly the basic assumptions these theories make concerning
the categories just mentioned. These assumptions are summarized (by
Robert Evans) in the barest terms in the following list, and then some
brief possible applications of the approaches to the two stories are immediately provided.—RCE

PLATONIC CRITICISM: Because Plato prizes an accurate, objective
understanding of "*reality*," he sees "creative" writers and "literary" texts
as potential distractions: they may lead the already-emotional audience
to neglect the proper pursuit of philosophical truth, which the critic

---

[1] For a fuller explanation of Abrams' views and of the theories already mentioned,
see the lengthy introduction to *Short Fiction: A Critical Companion*, ed. Robert C. Evans,
Anne C. Little, and Barbara Wiedemann (West Cornwall, CT: Locust Hill Press, 1997),
xv-lxxvi. The word "reality" will be placed within quotation remarks to emphasize that
it is a fundamentally contested concept.

should seek, explain, and defend by using logic and reason.

"The Bridal Night": Plato probably would view this story (as he viewed most literature) as trivial and potentially dangerous, if only because the repeated references to loneliness and wildness obviously appeal to the reader's emotions. The passion-driven action of the story seems to encourage irrationality. Plato might feel vindicated by the fact that Denis ends up in an asylum, safely purged from society. Nevertheless, because Denis is presented sympathetically, the reader may finally empathize with a character who has abandoned all reason. Plato might therefore ultimately attack the story for contributing almost nothing to the reasonable pursuit of truth.—**Scott Johnson**

Although the old woman obviously feels sympathy when she describes her son crying (21-23),[2] Plato would condemn such an emotional outburst (especially in an adult human male, who has a particular obligation to be rational) because such behavior both expresses and reinforces enslavement to the passions.—**Katie Magaw**

"Guests of the Nation": Since Plato prizes a person's ability and willingness to subjugate any sense of individuality in favor of the good of the "whole," a Platonic critic might fault the Irish soldiers for allowing their private emotions to conflict with the dictates of their public responsibilities. Such a critic might similarly blame Hawkins for his willingness to abandon loyalty to his country in order to save his own life. On the other hand, a Platonic critic might also conceivably argue that the Irishmen, by participating in killings they consider unreasonable and unjust, fail in their responsibilities to a higher truth. In either case, Plato would most probably be interested in whether the story encourages or discourages reasonable conduct and a proper appreciation of transcendent truths.

---

[2] The text of "The Bridal Night" used throughout this section is the version published in O'Connor's *Collected Stories* (New York: Knopf, 1981), 19-25. Citations will be given parenthetically, preceded by the abbreviation "*CS.*" The text of "Guests" used here will be the revised version, available (for instance) in *Stories by Frank O'Connor* (New York: Vintage Books, 1956), 3-16.

The story would be praised if it promoted reason and morality and condemned if it did not.—**Claire Skowronski**

ARISTOTELIAN CRITICISM: Because Aristotle values the *text* as a highly crafted complex unity, he tends to see the author as a craftsman, the audience as capable of appreciating such craftsmanship, the text as a potentially valuable means of understanding the complexity of "reality," and the critic as a specialist conversant with all aspects of the poetic craft.

"The Bridal Night": Aristotle would probably praise "The Bridal Night" since every aspect of the story contributes to its overall effect. He might especially note, for example, the ways the end of the story mirrors its beginning. Moreover, O'Connor's subtle, unobtrusive repetition of words and images not only unifies the work but also helps propel it toward its logical and inevitable conclusion. Aristotle valued this sense of inevitability because it implied that every part of a work was tightly linked to every other part. In the story's first paragraph, for instance, the narrator mentions seeing "one light only"—a phrase that anticipates the old woman's reference, a few sentences later, to her "'one son only'" (*CS* 19). Such echoes help unify the work, in part by underscoring its basic mood and theme of human loneliness. Throughout the story, O'Connor uses similar techniques to ensure that the story achieves a complex unity.—**Scott Johnson**

"Guests of the Nation": Aristotle considered skill in the use of genres (i.e., different forms of writing) crucial to the writer's craft. In the genre of the short story, for instance, Aristotle's insistence on complex unity can seem especially crucial, since the short story form is so restricted in length. "Guests," however, may be viewed not only as an exemplary model of the short story form but also as a perfect illustration of Aristotle's criterion of complex unity. By repeating various activities, settings, and phrases (the significant word "chum," for instance, recurs more than twenty times), O'Connor gives his story a highly unified structure. Yet he also gives the story (as Aristotle recommended for tragedy) a clear beginning, middle, and end, while the story's conclusion provides both the "reversal" (of fortune) and the "recognition" (sudden new insight) Aristotle prized in an effective tragic work. In addition, like a good Aristotelian tragedy, "Guests" evokes both pity and fear, particularly since it involves good but flawed men harming persons close to them. Finally, the reversal and recognition nearly coincide (as Aristotle recommended). In all these ways, then, O'Connor has created a work that is both highly complex and tightly unified.—**Kathleen B. Durrer**

HORATIAN CRITICISM: Because Horace emphasizes the need to satisfy a diverse *audience*, he tends to see the author as attempting to please and/or teach them, the text as embodying principles of custom and moderation (so as to please the widest possible audience), "reality" as understood in traditional or conventional terms, and the critic as a fatherly advisor who tries to prevent the author from making a fool of himself.

"The Bridal Night": Horace might have admired both the effectiveness and the restraint and moderation of O'Connor's story. Certainly he would have admired its unity—a unity that is neither too complex nor too obvious but rather one that conforms to the moral and artistic expectations of a broad-based audience. For example, the language of the characters conforms to such expectations, for the woman, in her own lonesome cadence, uses the kind of colloquial diction one would imagine an old Irish woman using to convey her heartfelt emotions. Moreover, Horace probably would have admired O'Connor's ability to create a story that is both pleasing and implicitly enlightening since it depicts the beauty and necessity of human attachment and compassion. Although Denis's madness might easily have seemed inexplicable or ridiculous if depicted by a less talented writer, O'Connor manages to create characters and situations that are both credible and affecting.—**Katie Magaw**

"Guests of the Nation": O'Connor's use of language in this story exemplifies Horace's criteria of moderation and decorum. The four men speak as one would expect simple soldiers to do, and O'Connor avoids any extreme use of language, even when using such language might have seemed appropriate. Hawkins' "deplorable tongue" (5), for instance, is never allowed to interrupt the narrative flow. Even at the end of the story (when, shortly before the killings, profanity might have seemed justifiable), Bonaparte simply reports that Hawkins "let out a cold-blooded remark that even shocked me" (13). O'Connor also practices moderation in describing the Englishmen's deaths. No blood or violent images are mentioned; instead, Hawkins falls to his knees and lies "flat at Noble's feet, slowly and as quiet as a kid falling asleep" (13). Belcher falls over "like a sack of meal" (15)—a powerful image, but not one that might cause an audience to reject the work as too violent. While the reader's mind imagines the horror, the actual narration is a model of Horatian moderation. O'Connor, however, does not sacrifice his artistic or ethical principles to satisfy his audience. His story challenges conventional views of war as heroic and just, but he does so by implication and thus again exercises moderation.—**Kathleen B. Durrer**

LONGINIAN CRITICISM: Because "Longinus" (whose real identity is unknown) stresses the ideally elevated nature of the sublime *author*, he tends to view the text as an expression of the author's power, the audience as desiring the ecstasy a great author can induce, social "reality" as rooted in a basic human nature that everywhere and always has a yearning for elevation, and the critic as (among other things) a moral and spiritual advisor who encourages the highest aspirations of readers and writers alike.

"The Bridal Night": Longinus might have admired O'Connor's ability to create a work that appeals to one of the loftiest capacities of humanity by portraying the beauty and dignity of human love and attachment. Indeed, Longinus might emphasize how Miss Regan's final act of selfless, genuine kindness exemplifies the human potential for moral and spiritual elevation. Her selfless act suggests how humans can counteract the despair of loneliness and behave nobly and generously in an often brutal world.— **Katie Magaw**

"Guests of the Nation": Although O'Connor's generally plain, straightforward style of writing may seem remote from the "sublimity" or elevation Longinus endorses, the story's evocative final paragraph—with its intense imagery, haunting rhythms, and deeply serious content—deliberately transcends the more colloquial tone of the rest of the work. By memorably expressing and eliciting powerful emotions that all people can share, the final paragraph strikes the reader with what Longinus might characteristically term the force of a lightning bolt. If any part of the story qualifies as "sublime," this is it.—**Kathleen B. Durrer**

TRADITIONAL HISTORICAL CRITICISM: Because traditional historical critics tend to emphasize the ways social *"realities"* influence the writer, the writer's creation of a text, and audiences' reactions to it, they stress the critic's obligation to study the past as thoroughly and objectively as possible to determine how the text might have been understood by its original readers.

"The Bridal Night": Near the beginning of the story the narrator asks the old woman about her son and then explains his own question: "'Is it in America he is?' I asked. (It is to America all the boys of the locality go when they leave home. [*CS* 19])." A traditional historical critic would probably contend that this brief passage tacitly reflects the social and economic conditions of Ireland during the period in which the story takes place. Such a critic might emphasize the tumultuous social and economic displacement that resulted in the mass emigration of many members of the lower classes to America. Indeed, a historical critic might contend that Denis' mental depression can be explained, at least in part, by the general depression (the economic hardship and despair) common during this period of Ireland's history.—**Katie Magaw**

"Guests of the Nation": A traditional historical critic would obviously want to explore the actual details of typical relations between English and Irish soldiers during this particular conflict. Such a critic might want to examine the plausibility of O'Connor's depiction of the men's friendship and might be especially interested in knowing whether the story reflected any specific facts or genuine incidents (as apparently it did). A historical critic might also want to know how O'Connor's own experiences with war may have affected his writing of this tale.—**Claire Skowronski**

THEMATIC CRITICISM: Because thematic critics stress the importance of ideas in shaping social and psychological "*reality*," they generally look for the ways those ideas are expressed by (and affect) the texts that writers create. They assume that audiences turn to texts for enlightenment as well as entertainment and that writers either express the same basic ideas repeatedly or that the evolution of their thinking can be traced in different works.

"The Bridal Night": A thematic critic might assert that the basic theme of this work is human loneliness, and that life's greatest moments occur when a person penetrates another's insularity, however briefly. Everyone in this story seems isolated to some extent. Mrs. Sullivan has "'the one son only'" (*CS* 19), and her husband is absent for one reason or another. Denis goes mad from loneliness after he is unable to win the woman he loves. Winnie is always either alone or with her students and thus seems disconnected from the rest of the village. The language of the story reinforces the theme of loneliness, partly through the repetition of such words as "lonesome" and "stranger." In fact, the characters are basically strangers to one another. Although they occasionally alleviate each other's loneliness, none of these instances suggests a permanent union. When Winnie lies down with Denis, he is soothed (but only temporarily) by her presence. Even the narrator is lonely, as his first spoken words ("'Tis a lonesome place'" [*CS* 19]) make clear.—**Scott Johnson**

"Guests of the Nation": A thematic critic might emphasize how this story blends such themes as intellect versus emotion, duty versus friendship, and isolation versus communion. Donovan, for instance, expects his fellow soldiers, Bonaparte and Noble, to respond intellectually and carry out the executions without emotion. The old woman, on the other hand, seems to embody a more intuitively emotional response to life. Bonaparte and Noble are thus torn between the expectation that they should listen to "reason" and the temptation to follow their hearts. Similarly, Bonaparte and Noble also feel torn between duty to their cause and friendship for the English soldiers, a friendship Donovan does not share. As the story proceeds, the early feelings of communion are lost and all the men become increasingly isolated from each other and, eventually, from themselves. At the end, one wonders whether Noble is praying for the dead British soldiers or for his own soul. In any case, Bonaparte leaves him and goes outside to face his own demons—alone. A thematic critic, then, would show how the story wrestles with some of the most important ideas and problems any human can confront.—**Claire Skowronski**

FORMALISM: Because formalists value the *text* as a complex unity in which all the parts contribute to a rich and resonant effect, they usually offer highly detailed ("close") readings intended to show how the work achieves a powerful, compelling artistic form. Formalist critics help audiences appreciate how a work's subtle nuances contribute to its total effect.

"The Bridal Night": A formalist critic might approach this story by emphasizing how the patterns of imagery succinctly contribute to the harmonious and unified complexity of the work. For example, such a critic might note how the story begins and ends with patterns of imagery associated with light and darkness. In fact, a formalist critic might argue that such images—including the single light in the beginning and the blanket of darkness at the end—underscore the themes of loneliness and despair that help unify this text. A formalist might note how other aspects of the work (including the old woman's lonesome voice and the pining cries of the wild birds) also contribute to the work's artistic unity.—**Scott Johnson**

"Guests of the Nation": A formalist critic might choose to focus on the pattern of repetition and subtle variation apparent in the first three sections of the story, culminating in an abrupt shift of tone at the opening of section four. Initially, the soldiers settle into a pleasant, predictable routine. The first paragraph in each of the first three sections opens "at dusk." The work day is over, and the soldiers—both Irish and English—play cards to relax and wile away the hours before retiring for the evening. Each time, Donovan joins them. In the first section, however, Donovan "supervises" the game, and the reader knows that he is both "above" and "outside" the camaraderie shared by the other men. In the similar opening paragraph in section two, the reader learns that the four friendly soldiers enjoy "tea" together before Donovan comes in, a fact that further emphasizes their "civil" relations—relations not shared by Donovan. In fact, at this point Bonaparte senses that Donovan feels "no great love" for the English soldiers. At the start of section three the routine begins to repeat itself, but this time Donovan is literally associated with a "dark presentiment." As darkness inevitably follows dusk, the opening paragraph of section four cycles into a night rather than another routine and predictable day. The men—and the reader—all know the terrible act ahead of them, and nothing remains *but* Donovan's darkness—a darkness that swallows the faint "light" of possibility that someone can prevent the deaths.—**Claire Skowronski**

PSYCHOANALYTIC CRITICISM: Freudian or psychoanalytic critics emphasize the key role of the human mind in perceiving and shaping *"reality"* and believe that the minds of writers, audiences, and critics are highly complex and often highly conflicted (especially in sexual terms, and particularly in terms of the rational ego and the irrational "id"). They therefore argue that such complexity inevitably affects the ways texts are written and read. The critic, therefore, should analyze the psychological patterns that affect the ways texts are created and received.

"The Bridal Night": A Freudian psychoanalytic critic might approach "The Bridal Night" by focusing on how the complex psychological manifestations of such latent impulses as sexuality and desire resonate throughout the story. Perhaps such a critic would begin by juxtaposing the ways in which Denis and Miss Regan respond to these latent sexual impulses, particularly the ways in which their actions reflect the three fundamental realms of the psyche—the id, the ego, and the superego. For example, such a critic might conjecture that Denis' imploring request to have Miss Regan spend the night with him is significantly motivated by the instincts of the id (the primal component of the human psyche that is dominated by bodily impulses and desires). Perhaps a Freudian critic would suggest that because Denis' mental incapacity enables him to exist apart (or at least detached) from the oppressive precepts of society, he is not constricted by the mandates of either the super-ego (the realm of the psyche that strives for perfect social conformity and obedience) or the ego (the component of the mind that mediates between the desires of the id and the demands of the superego). Miss Regan, however, does operate within society and therefore acknowledges societal expectations. Her awareness is reflected in her "worried" but determined desire to fulfill Denis's earnest wish (*CS* 24). Indeed, a Freudian critic might contend that the very fact that she is concerned about the social consequences of her actions represents the influence of the superego. Conversely, her determination to fulfill Denis' request might reflect the inevitable emergence of the ego, for perhaps her complex conduct is motivated both by her own primal desires and by her attempts to repress these desires and thereby conform to societal conventions.—**Katie Magaw**

"Guests of the Nation": A psychoanalytic critic, focusing on the story's setting, might contrast the associations of the bright interior of the house with the exterior darkness. The cottage, with its comforting fires and the domestic influence of the motherly old woman, might be seen as representing social and moral order and might therefore be interpreted as symbolizing the tempering influence of civilization on the uncivilized impulses of the unconscious. When inside the house, the men treat each other as equals, and disagreements (such as the ideological differences of Hawkins and Noble) are settled through discourse rather than through physical aggression. In contrast, the exterior darkness might be seen as representing the untamed unconscious. Only under the cover of darkness is the full extent of human aggression revealed. Furthermore, a psychoanalytic critic might have many interesting things to say about the ostensibly rational Jeremiah Donovan, who ironically seems unable to control his emotions. He blushes when addressed, rocks back and forth when speaking, quickly loses his temper with the old woman, and shakes with excitement when anticipating the killings. Perhaps he feels a desperate need to assert power. Although Bonaparte and Noble eventually return to the house and re-light the lamp, Donovan remains literally and figuratively in the outer darkness.—**Kathleen B. Durrer**

ARCHETYPAL OR "MYTH" CRITICISM: Because archetypal critics believe that humans experience "*reality*" in terms of certain basic fears, desires, images (symbols), and stories (myths), they assume that writers will inevitably employ such patterns; that audiences will react to them forcefully and almost automatically; and that critics should therefore study the ways such patterns affect writers, texts, and readers.

"The Bridal Night": An archetypal critic influenced by the theories of Carl Jung might claim that in this story, Denis journeys into his unconscious. The first part of this journey ends in madness, just as Oedipus' similar journey in Sophocles' *Oedipus Rex* ends in blindness and exile. An important part of Denis' journey involves initiation into femininity—an initiation completed when Winnie, his "anima" or female aspect, lies down beside him. The two halves of his psyche are temporarily reconciled in this brief "bridal" union. By ending with the same imagery with which it began, the story appropriately achieves an almost circular structure, since circles often function as archetypal symbols suggesting completion and unity.—**Scott Johnson**

"Guests of the Nation": An archetypal critic might comment on the heavy use of the symbolism of darkness in this work. The story opens with the words "at dusk"—immediately suggesting the setting sun and the end of life. Such imagery then continues throughout the work. Each of the first three sections opens at dusk, and the entire story takes place in the evening, with only candles, lanterns, and firelight available to hold off the darkness (thereby suggesting the uncertainty of life, which is easily extinguished). As death draws nearer, the significance of darkness intensifies. Bonaparte, for example, extinguishes the candle before he reveals to Noble that they may have to kill their English friends (8). Later, when the Irishmen enter the cottage to remove the Englishmen, the house is "pitch-dark," but at first no one even thinks of lighting a lamp (15). Ultimately, although the men walk toward the lantern light in the dark bog (12), this light will bring only death (not life or hope). At the site of the killings, Noble holds the lantern between his legs, as if to hide in the darkness. Finally, when Noble returns to the cottage after the killings and attempts to light the lamp, the old woman's question ("'What did ye do with them?'" [16]) startles him so that the match dies in his hand. By using such strong symbolic imagery (an archetypal critic might claim), O'Connor evokes some of our most basic human fears and thus helps give his story an almost automatic power.—**Kathleen B. Durrer**

MARXIST CRITICISM: Because Marxist critics assume that conflicts between economic classes inevitably shape social "*reality*," they emphasize the ways these struggles affect writers, audiences, and texts. They assume that literature will either reflect, reinforce, or undermine (or some combination of these) the dominant ideologies (or patterns of thought) that help structure social relations. Marxist critics study the relations between literature and society, ideally seeking to promote social progress.

"The Bridal Night": A Marxist critic might argue that Denis' madness is linked directly to his poverty. Although he lacks even "'the price of an ounce of 'baccy,'" he is obsessed with a woman who has "'money to her name in the bank'" (*CS* 21). Indeed, the text implies that she is considerably wealthy. The references to Denis' and Winnie's contrasting economic classes appear, in fact, in the same paragraph that first mentions Denis' madness. Moreover, although at the end of the story Winnie is no worse off than before and is not even subject to public criticism (facts explicable in terms of her superior social status), the impoverished Denis ends up in an asylum—a fate a richer person might have escaped.—**Scott Johnson**

"Guests of the Nation": A Marxist critic might emphasize how this story illustrates the artificial divisions nationalism can create between men who are not only friends but who also are members of the same social class.—**Kathleen B. Durrer**

A Marxist critic might respond to the story by arguing that Hawkins is right: war is a tool that capitalists manipulate in order to protect their own selfish interests. Soldiers in the field are simply pawns, willingly sacrificed by higher-ranking officers in order to protect the men who make decisions in relative safety and comfort at a distance from the fighting. In the end, the Irish soldiers epitomize the operations of the capitalist system. Unable to bring about their own small "revolution" to save their British friends, Bonaparte and Noble symbolize the oppressed lower class, forced to carry out blindly the orders of their superiors, while Donovan willingly embraces the status quo and, without conflict or hesitation, shoots the British soldiers. A Marxist critic might argue, however, that Donovan is also a victim of a capitalistic war machine since he did not personally make the decision to murder the soldiers but was simply following a superior's orders. Another Marxist critic might suggest that the story fails as a political statement because, in the end, the system seems inevitably to "win," and no social progress occurs. Still another Marxist critic might argue, though, that the story succeeds as a political statement because Bonaparte and Noble refuse to shoot the soldiers themselves, even though Donovan might easily have ordered them to do it. The reader thus sees, at least to some extent, that solidarity and listening to one's conscience can supersede blind obedience to duty.—**Claire Skowronski**

STRUCTURALIST CRITICISM: Because structuralist critics assume that humans structure (or make sense of) "*reality*" by imposing patterns of meaning on it, and because they assume that these structures can only be interpreted in terms of the codes the structures embody, they believe that writers will inevitably rely on such codes to create meaning, that texts will inevitably embody such codes, and that audiences will inevitably use such codes to interpret texts. To understand a text, the critic must be familiar with the systematic codes that shape it; he must master the system(s) inherent in the text.

"The Bridal Night": A structuralist might note that this story is organized by a series of paired opposites such as youth/age, light/dark, land/sea, and isolation/community. Land, for instance, symbolizes safety, sanity, and nurturing, whereas the sea symbolizes the unknown, instability, and madness. Thus when Denis' madness begins to worsen, Mrs. Sullivan says that "'he could hardly sleep'" and could be heard "'groaning as loud as the sea on the rocks'" (*CS* 21). This dichotomy between land and sea is often very important to the structure of human narratives. In myth, a return to land is almost always joyous, while travels at sea are conventionally filled with peril. This land/sea pairing, then, is one of the codes by which this story achieves its meaning.—**Scott Johnson**

"Guests of the Nation": A structuralist critic might focus on the many patterns of oppositions within this text and might then examine the ways they contribute to the story's meanings. In fact, the story itself is a study in oppositions—not only between nations but between religion and atheism, war and peace, life and death, rural and urban, light and dark, warmth and cold, noise and silence, male and female, joy and guilt, and many other paired opposites. By studying how O'Connor employs such patterns, a structuralist critic would help map the "codes" by which the story achieves and conveys significance.—**Kathleen B. Durrer**

FEMINIST CRITICISM: Because feminist critics assume that our experience of "*reality*" is inevitably affected by categories of sex and gender (such as divisions between male and female, heterosexual and homosexual, etc.), and because they assume that (heterosexual) males have long enjoyed dominant social power, they tend to assume that writers, texts, and audiences will all be affected (usually negatively) by "patriarchal" forces. The critic's job will be to study (and even attempt to counter-act) the impact of patriarchy.

"The Bridal Night": Near the beginning of the story, the narrator asks the old woman, "'Your own flock are gone from you, I suppose?'" (*CS* 19). A feminist critic might note how explicitly this question implies a fundamental, perhaps even rigid, definition of a woman as a mother. Indeed, such a critic might stress how O'Connor's use of the word "flock" emphasizes this prescribed role, for it accentuates the primitive perception of a woman as a breeder who is defined by her capacity to nurture, sustain, and fulfill the needs of her children. Certainly a feminist critic would reject this implication, since it fails to value the woman's full individuality. Such a critic might also note how the question anticipates the elderly woman's enveloping sense of barrenness, for after tragically losing her only son to a mental illness, she seems to lack any substantial purpose and thus succumbs to a sense of aimless despair and emptiness.—**Katie Magaw**

"Guests of the Nation": A feminist critic might see O'Connor's story as typifying the male-dominated literary and social worlds of the early 1920s. The story has only one female character, "the old woman of the house where we [the male soldiers and prisoners] were staying." Although the house presumably belongs to her, her ownership does not alter her subservient position. She labors to keep the household running—chopping sticks, carrying water, or hauling turf for the fire. Her resignation to her solitary labor is so strong that Belcher's offer of assistance renders her literally speechless. In addition to playing a subservient role, she is also portrayed as mentally inferior to the male characters. When the argumentative Hawkins tries to get her to complain of the drought she responds with confused pagan folklore, and when she rebukes Hawkins for blaming the capitalists for starting World War I, she is portrayed as a woman with only a vague, confused, inaccurate idea of world events.

Nowhere is her insignificance in the male-dominated events of the story more vividly portrayed than when Donovan silences her protests when the prisoners are being removed. Obviously (a feminist might contend) this is a society in which men make the rules and women serve without question.—**Kathleen B. Durrer**

DECONSTRUCTION: Because deconstructive critics assume that "reality" cannot be experienced except through language, and because they believe that language is inevitably full of contradictions, gaps, and dead-ends, they believe that no writer, text, audience, or critic can ever escape from the insoluble paradoxes language embodies. Deconstruction therefore undercuts the hierarchical assumptions of any other critical system (such as structuralism, formalism, Marxism, etc.) that seeks to offer an "objective," "neutral," or "scientific" perspective on literature.

"The Bridal Night": A deconstructor might approach this story by noting the inherent instability and inconsistency embedded in the male/female pairing, in which the male is usually privileged over the female. Such a critic might begin the process of subverting this hierarchical arrangement by illustrating how the text (which is itself intrinsically unstable) contradicts the supposed stability of this pairing. Perhaps a deconstructor would begin by noting, for instance, that Miss Regan fills a more elevated and privileged social role than Denis despite the fact that he is male, while Denis himself, incapacitated by his mental illness, plays a less important role. Furthermore, such a critic might contend that Denis, in his fervent longing for Miss Regan, ultimately relinquishes himself to her control and power. Nevertheless, while seemingly at a disadvantage, Denis, as an embodiment of a male-dominated society, is still able to exert influence over Miss Regan by convincing her to submit to his impulsive demands. Indeed, a deconstructor might also emphasize the freedom that is paradoxically inherent in Denis' insanity, for he is no longer bound by severe societal dictates that mandate proper behavior, and therefore his excessive request is attributed merely to his "madness." Miss Regan, on the other hand, is constrained by these social values, for she ultimately risks losing her reputation by fulfilling Denis' desires. A deconstructor might show, therefore, that in this story the standard male/female hierarchy is highly unstable and full of contradictions.—**Katie Magaw**

"Guests of the Nation": A deconstructive critic might note that a trained soldier's duty requires demonstrating loyalty to the state, requiring the soldier to subjugate his will and his private morality to the appropriate chain of command. A soldier's duty, then, implies a hierarchy of the state over the individual. A deconstructor might subvert this assumed hierarchy, however, and suggest that a soldier is first a member of a moral society that condemns cold-blooded murder; therefore, his duty as a human being conflicts with his military training and inevitably leads to an unstable tension. The story shows how difficult it can be to follow one's duty (*which* duty?) and how tightly entangled "public" and "private" morality can be. Further, a deconstructor might argue that war inevitably establishes a binary opposition of "us" versus "them" in which whoever is "us" is superior to "them." Yet O'Connor shows how difficult it can be to preserve this distinction, as well as how easily such other opposites as "winner/loser," "victory/defeat," "life/death," and "free/imprisoned" can collapse. By the end of the story, the nominal victors feel defeated: although technically free, they are now imprisoned in a kind of perpetual living death. Similarly, the nominal losers have in a sense triumphed: they now enjoy a sort of freedom from the pain of life while still living quite intensely in the minds of the men who helped kill them.—**Claire Skowronski**

READER-RESPONSE CRITICISM: Because reader-response critics assume that literary texts are inevitably interpreted by individual members of the *audience* and that these individuals react to texts in ways that are sometimes shared, sometimes highly personal, and sometimes both at once, they believe that writers exert much less control over texts than we sometimes suppose, and that critics must never ignore the crucial role of audience response(s).

"The Bridal Night": Early in the story the old mother responds to a question from the narrator, who then comments on her response: "'I never had but the one,' she replied, 'the one son only,' and I knew because she did not add a prayer for his soul that he was still alive" (*CS* 19). One type of reader-response critic might approach this passage by focusing on how O'Connor uses it to encourage a particular experience or interpretation in the minds of diverse readers. Such a critic might focus on the underlying pathos embedded in such phrases as "'but the one'" and "'the one son only.'" A reader-response critic might contend that these phrases powerfully evoke sympathy for the old woman and therefore elicit a positive response to O'Connor's underlying theme of the despair of human loneliness. However, another reader-response critic might argue that various interpretations of this passage are inevitable since ultimately the individual experiences of particular readers dictate the "meanings" of texts. For instance, readers who have endured the traumatic loss of a child might be especially inclined to empathize with the old woman and perhaps even be able to find a consoling expression of their own sorrow in the woman's despairing words. Conversely, it may be difficult for a reader who has never been a parent and experienced intense attachment to a child to be strongly affected by the woman's resounding grief as she mourns the loss of her only son.—**Katie Magaw**

"Guests of the Nation": A reader-response critic would probably be interested in the diverse interpretations the story has elicited from different kinds of readers. Readers with personal experience of the long-standing Irish/English conflict, for example, might react indignantly at the portrayal of certain characters. Thus a patriotic Englishman (or a committed leftist) might find Hawkins unsympathetic since he seems to have little loyalty either to his country or to his ideology. Similarly, a committed Irish nationalist might respond negatively to Bonaparte and Noble (who find it difficult to justify retaliating against the English army's murder of Irish soldiers). On the other hand, to a Christian reader Hawkins' atheism might intensify the tragedy of his death because he dies with no hope of redemption. Readers with military experience might empathize with the responses of Bonaparte and Noble to the requirements of duty, while pacifists might use the story to illustrate the senseless results of war. Clearly, the list of such possible responses could easily be extended.— **Kathleen B. Durrer**

DIALOGICAL CRITICISM: Because dialogical critics assume that the (worthy) *text* almost inevitably embodies divergent points of view, they believe that elements within a text engage in a constant dialogue or give-and-take with other elements, both within and outside the text itself. The writer, too, is almost inevitably engaged in a complex dialogue, through the text, with his potential audience(s), and the sensitive critic must be alert to the multitude of voices a text expresses or implies.

"The Bridal Night": A dialogical critic might emphasize the differences in the voices of the narrator and Mrs. Sullivan. The narrator's more sophisticated voice seems consciously literary. Mrs. Sullivan speaks in the vernacular, and her telling of the story has a conversational feel. The narrator, apparently an outsider, refers to Mrs. Sullivan as one of "[t]hese lonesome people in the wild places" (*CS* 20), suggesting that he is from a more civilized place. The text therefore includes voices representing two distinct social classes. Interestingly, Mrs. Sullivan does most of the talking: O'Connor allows the lower-class character to express herself freely, rather than have the narrator impose a monological view. The narrator, in fact, is part of the audience, a fact that further detaches him from the text and allows the different voices in the story free rein to express their varied perspectives.—**Scott Johnson**

"Guests of the Nation": A dialogical critic might first choose to focus on the "voice" (Bonaparte) telling the story, because he speaks for everyone. Through both Bonaparte's conversations with the other characters and his dialogue with the reader as the story's narrator, the reader hears (perhaps more clearly than Bonaparte himself) the conflicting voices he articulates. Another dialogical critic might suggest that Bonaparte unfairly colors Donovan's personal character, since the reader perceives Donovan only from Bonaparte's point of view, which is not sympathetic to the possibility that Donovan is acting honorably in his role as a soldier. A reader looking at events from Donovan's perspective might even suggest that Bonaparte and Noble, not Donovan, act inappropriately by befriending enemy soldiers during a war. Finally, still another dialogical critic might choose to focus on the colloquial speech that moves the men (and invites the reader to come along) through the comfortable routine of their days together, particularly since the casual speech changes abruptly in the fourth section of the story. At that point, there is suddenly no conversation among all four friends. In fact, Bonaparte and Noble fail to speak at all until the British soldiers are dead and buried. The seemingly emotionless Donovan now speaks for the Irish soldiers, and his suddenly animated but "cold" and "excited" tone is anything but conversational. The previously silent Belcher suddenly speaks up, while Donovan shoots down the always-loquacious Hawkins in mid-speech. The silence of Bonaparte and Noble speaks of the inevitable grave even as Belcher and Hawkins attempt to affirm their lives through their frantic—but abruptly silenced—speech. Fittingly, the closing passage of the story contains no conversation at all except Bonaparte's dialogue with himself. His lyrical thoughts contrast sharply with the friendly, colloquial conversations heard earlier, but the terrible beauty the reader sees through his eyes makes the reality of the murders an even greater horror. In the end, Bonaparte's cold, snowy isolation is complete, even from the reader.—**Claire Skowronski**

NEW HISTORICISM: Because new historicist critics assume that our experience of "*reality*" is inevitably social, and because they emphasize the way systems of power and domination both provoke and seek to control social conflicts, they tend to see a culture not as a single coherent entity but as a site of struggle, negotiation, or the constant exchange of energy. New historicists contend that no text, audience, or critic can stand apart from contemporary (i.e., both past and present) dynamics of power.

"The Bridal Night": A new historicist critic might approach this work by emphasizing how the lives of the characters are shaped by the fundamental (and all too often irreconcilable) ideological assumptions that compose the social forces of a community. Because new historicists are especially concerned with uses and abuses of power, they might particularly note how quickly (and lengthily) Denis is confined for mental illness once he refuses to conform to prescribed codes of social behavior. Alternatively, a new historicist might note how Miss Regan's selfless act of compassion for Denis also reveals a brave willingness to defy the rigid social conventions which, in her day, defined the "proper" relations between men and women. Indeed, almost the last comment of the story emphasizes how unusual it was to violate those conventions without suffering any punishment or criticism. The power of the community is paradoxically confirmed by its decision not to exercise that power in this one instance.—**Katie Magaw**

"Guests of the Nation": A new historicist might emphasize the myriad power relations—and the inevitability of experiencing such power-struggles in any society—evident in this story. First of all, the Irish hold British soldiers as prisoners of war, but the British forces have the Irish soldiers on the run, forcing the Irish to stay on the move (in their own homeland) in order to avoid capture themselves. Secondly, Donovan is a superior officer, but his men don't take him very seriously. Bonaparte, for example, "didn't like the tone" (7) Donovan took with him over the issue of guarding the prisoners, as if such a reason justifies a subordinate questioning a superior officer. On another level, a new historicist might choose to address the power-struggle going on in Bonaparte's mind as he wrestles with the question of friendship versus duty. A new historicist might suggest that Bonaparte is weak in both respects: he neither tries actively to save his friends in the end nor takes a definitive role in their murders. A new historicist might suggest that his indecision and lack of any strong convictions reflect the spirit of the Irish nation, tearing itself apart, caught between two religious faiths, both condemning and condoning killing, etc.—**Claire Skowronski**

MULTICULTURAL CRITICISM: Because multicultural critics emphasize the numerous differences that both shape and divide social *"real-*

ity," they tend to see all people (including writers, readers, and critics) as members of sometimes divergent, sometimes over-lapping groups. These groups, whether relatively fluid or relatively stable, can include such categories as races, sexes, genders, ages, and classes, and the critic should explore how such differences affect the ways in which literature is both written and read.

"The Bridal Night": A multiculturalist critic might argue that Winnie could conceivably be a lesbian or at least asexual. Numerous clues suggest this possibility. Mrs. Sullivan says, for instance, that Winnie's "'hand would never rock the cradle,'" and she jokes that Denis should tell Winnie that he is "'her intended'" (*CS* 21), as if the very notion is absurd. Also, although Winnie lacks any sexual interest in Denis, this is apparently not because she is involved with another man. She is almost always alone, perhaps because (if she has sexual relations at all) her partner must remain secret in such a small rural community. Nevertheless, others in the village may suspect her possible secret; certainly such suspicions would explain why, even after she spends the night in bed with Denis, "'no one would speak a bad word about what she did'" (*CS* 25). Perhaps they recognized, in the words of Mrs. Sullivan, that while "'another [woman might] . . . take pity on [Denis], knowing he would make her a fine steady husband,'" Winnie "'was not the sort, and well I knew it from the first days I laid eyes on her, that her hand would never rock the cradle'" (*CS* 21).—**Scott Johnson**

"Guests of the Nation": A multiculturalist critic might suggest that the friendships among Bonaparte, Noble, Belcher, and Hawkins represent a utopian ideal of enemy cultures coming together in harmony. However, a multiculturalist might also point out that although the reader gets a sense of genuine camaraderie among the soldiers, especially through their casual conversations and common language, the fact remains that Bonaparte first describes Belcher and Hawkins in terms of "their accents," which were so thick "you could cut [them] with a knife" (4). By emphasizing this difference in their speech, Bonaparte separates the soldiers, perhaps unconsciously, into groups of "us" and "them," an unfortunate division that inevitably paves the way for one group to oppress the other. A multiculturalist might note that the Irish have a history of rejecting the English language and speaking Gaelic in an effort to reject British rule, so Bonaparte's emphasis on the soldiers' accents may not be as innocuous as it first appears.—**Claire Skowronski**

POSTMODERNISM: Postmodernists are highly skeptical of large-scale claims to objective "truths" and doubt the validity of grand explanations. They see such claims as attempts to impose order on a "*reality*" that is, almost by definition, too shifting or fluid to be pinned down. Postmodernists assume that if writers, readers, and audiences abandoned their yearning for such order, they would more easily accept and enjoy the inevitable paradoxes and contradictions of life and art. The postmodern critic will look for (and value) any indications of a text's unstable heterogeneity.

"The Bridal Night": A postmodernist might respond to this story by celebrating the freedom implicit in Miss Regan's defiant gesture of genuine kindness. By acting as she does, she rejects the blindly repeated and all-embracing system of broad, often abstract social values that unambiguously dictate a prescribed form of behavior. Such a critic might argue that simplistic, unequivocal systems of values fail to do justice to the indeterminate complexities of human experience. For this reason, a postmodern critic might also admire the community's willingness to accept, and even embrace, the "strange and wonderful" ambiguity of Miss Regan's selfless act of compassion for Denis (*CS* 25). By passively and openly accepting Miss Regan's actions, they illustrate their recognition that it is futile to adhere to rigid codes of conduct when dealing with the complexities (and inevitable moral contradictions) created by life's dilemmas.—**Katie Magaw**

"Guests of the Nation": A postmodern critic might suggest that the struggle Bonaparte and Noble feel between duty and morality reflects the other struggles we all face when confronted with conflicting systems of value. Especially today, the traditional standards of value provided by religion, ideologies, or cultural mores may no longer seem to provide clear or unequivocal guides to conduct. Thus Hawkins' (admittedly superficial) commitments to communism and atheism are of little use or comfort to him in his moment of crisis. Significantly, however, neither are the much stronger, more traditional beliefs of Noble. Although in the end Noble is left praying, the reader is left with the impression that neither his sense of military duty nor his religion can completely reconcile him to his role in the killing. No single grand explanation can help him accept what has happened.—**Kathleen B. Durrer**

Frank O'Connor's "Lady Brenda": General Comments from Diverse Critical Perspectives

CONTRIBUTORS: PATRICIA ANGLEY, KATHLEEN B. DURRER, TIMOTHY FRANCISCO, ASHLEY GORDON, CLAIRE SKOWRONSKI, ONDRA THOMAS-KROUSE, MICHAEL PROBST, KAREN WORLEY PIRNIE, CLAUDIA WILSCH, JONATHAN WRIGHT

Frank O'Connor's short story "Lady Brenda," originally published in December 1958, has not received much attention and has not been reprinted in major collections of its author's fiction. However, "The Adventuress," an earlier and strikingly different version of the story (first published in 1948) *was* reprinted in a 1981 collection of O'Connor's works. "Lady Brenda," though, has not been easily accessible and thus has not attracted the attention it seems to merit.

The contrasts between the two versions are immediately apparent. "The Adventuress," for instance, begins as follows:

> My brothers and sisters didn't really like Brenda at all but I did. She was a couple of years older than I was and I was devoted to her. She had a long, grave, bony face and a power of concealing her real feelings about everything, even about me. I knew she liked me but she wasn't exactly what you'd call demonstrative about it. In fact there were times you might even say she was vindictive.
>
> That was part of her toughness. She was tough to the point of fool-hardiness. She would do anything a boy would do and a lot of things that few boys would do. It was never safe to dare her to anything . . .

The difference between this and the opening of "Lady Brenda" could hardly be more striking:

Joe Regan's sister Brenda was several years older than himself, and by long chalks she was the toughest of the family, though none of them was exactly what you would call a sissy. A sissy would have had very little chance with Joe's father. He was tall and gaunt and angular, a monk who had strayed into workaday clothes and grown a big mustache. In Mr. Regan's considered view of the universe, the whole town was in a conspiracy against him, and that included every one of his own family from the baby up—always excepting his wife whom he regarded as a friendly neutral. As long as Joe had known it, life at home was one long battle, with his father, in an imperialist frame of mind, trying to get at them, and his mother, acting as protecting power, trying to keep him off.

***

They had to be tough, there was no other way; but Brenda, whose principal task was looking after Joe, was tough by disposition. She was tall and gaunt and handsome like their father, and she would do anything a boy would do and a lot of things that most boys in their senses would not do. It was never safe to dare Brenda to anything. She scared Joe a great deal more than his father did.

In the revision, O'Connor shifts from first-person to third-person narration; from an immediate emphasis on Brenda to a diversionary (but thematically significant) emphasis on the colorful father; from straightforward and explicit statement to language full of metaphor and vivid phrasing; and from a sober tone to humorous diction that also immediately implies the potential for intriguing comic conflict. These, however, are just a few of the many differences the two versions reveal. The experience of teaching the two stories suggests that "Lady Brenda" works far better in class and appeals far more immediately to most readers than does "The Adventuress."

As it happens, "Lady Brenda" was much discussed during a special seminar in pluralistic critical theory sponsored at AUM by the Andrew W. Mellon Foundation in the summer of 1997, when the present book was in its final stages. Participants in the seminar included graduate students working on theses or dissertations, teachers with years of classroom experience, and even a few advanced undergraduates. "Lady Brenda" was used, to some extent, as a test case, and the fact that the story had hitherto received almost no critical attention made it, in some respects, a perfect litmus test for a variety of ways of reading. Nearly all the seminar's participants expressed real enthusiasm for O'Connor's story as well as a definite preference for the revised version.

It seems worthwhile, in fact, to append a few of these readers' reactions to a reprint of the story itself (see appendix 6). Their responses raise issues that may prove interesting to other readers, especially since many of the seminarians' comments suggest the usefulness of various current literary theories as ways of approaching O'Connor's works in general. (In this respect their comments are relevant to, and build on, the survey of critical theories offered in the preceding chapter of this book.) The students' comments are offered, then, to help stimulate thought (and perhaps even to help generate disagreement), not only about this particular story but about a variety of current approaches to literary interpretation.

***

In responding to O'Connor's "Lady Brenda," participants in the 1997 Mellon Seminar on Critical Pluralism were particularly interested in testing the usefulness of current literary theories as ways of reading and interpreting creative writing. **Patricia Angley**, for instance, adopted a *feminist* perspective when she suggested that

> Brenda is described as having masculine traits. . . . Attributing such traits or behavior to female characters is a method male writers often use to create "strong" female characters. . . . By constructing Brenda as he does, O'Connor creates a character who refuses to fit neatly into the boundaries imposed by her culture and who thus poses a critique of those boundaries. Must a girl always be timid, placating, and/or manipulative (like Brenda's mother, for instance)? . . . Joe sees his mother as a miracle

worker because she protects her children; he idealizes her. What he is idealizing, however, is a woman who cannot express herself freely for fear of what her husband, the ultimate family "authority," might do. Joe idealizes the woman in his life who stays clearly within cultural boundaries. Yet Joe also loves Brenda, even though her predictably unpredictable behavior frightens him.

Similar opinions were also expressed by **Claire Skowronski**, who contended that

> a feminist critic might applaud O'Connor's characterizations of Brenda, since she represents a strong female role model, in spite of her less savory actions (such as stealing). She is strong-willed and manipulative, demonstrating her ability to take command of a situation and use it to her advantage. She is resourceful, cunning, alert, and in tune with the personalities (particularly the flaws and weaknesses) of the people around her, giving her command of many situations. A feminist critic might note that, both historically and in contemporary society, these characteristics are generally considered desirable and encouraged in males in order to give them an "edge" in the business world. In creating a female character with these attributes, O'Connor demonstrates that women, too, reap the rewards—and experience the drawbacks—of possessing such a personality.

Karen Worley Pirnie also used a feminist approach to argue that

> many readers would be troubled by Brenda's intractable position, beginning with O'Connor's sarcastic title. Like all women in patriarchal societies, Brenda is in a "no win" situation: she is damned as "swanking" or frighteningly "tough" for her aspirations and assertive efforts to escape the "wisha" weakness of her mother (which seems manipulative and likely to drive Jim Regan "to his grave"). If we see the main plot conflict as involving Joe's view of his sister, his growth comes from seeing her less as "tough" and more as vulnerable, "going to cry," and "upset." Thus

Joe matures by perceiving his sister's traditionally female weakness. The male character advances at the cost of the female.

Timothy Francisco, on the other hand, used a *Marxist* perspective to present a reading of the story that both resembles and significantly departs from feminist interpretations. According to Francisco,

> At the heart of "Lady Brenda" lie deeply entrenched class and ideological stratifications, which the action of the story (indeed, the very title) interrogate and finally lament. Thus the title apparently encourages a response evocative of tales of chivalry, adventure, and romance—all powerfully classist genres which reestablish the status quo and conventional hierarchies under the guises of liberation and exploration. . . . [In O'Connor's story, both] Brenda and her father adhere to classic bourgeois notions of class and power. The latter asserts a blatant paranoia, which actually seems somewhat justified given the story's setting (in an Ireland still affected by imperialist colonialism) as well as the family's awkward dynamics. Brenda, meanwhile, by "swanking" and apparently seeking to subvert dominant class paradigms, actually reinforces them, as her successful charade in retaliation against the corner boy forces her to assume a stereotypical mantle of poverty and submissiveness to gain momentary access to the rich woman's domain. Class and market issues also surface through Brenda's virulent consumerism. She is a heroine to her brother, partly because she is generous with gifts and money, and, more important, she is shrewdly aware that money buys her a temporary reprieve from her lower-class status, as Coakley addresses her as "Miss Regan."
>
> . . . Brenda's pen-swank at the end of the story recapitulates the narrative's opening concerns with class and status as she tries, again through deception, to purchase a marker of status to which she feels she is entitled. But again, her attempt at subversion serves only to re-entrench the status quo, as she and Joe learn that no amount of "swanking" can change the nib of a cheap fountain pen.

Another participant who experimented with Marxist analysis to help explain the story was **Claudia Wilsch,** who likened the conflicts within the Regan family to the larger struggle between economic classes.

> From this perspective, Mr. Regan's children, an economically weak group symbolizing the proletariat, not only lack the solidarity necessary to confront representatives of the strong capitalist class but also succumb to the very values a Marxist might wish to see them oppose. Complaining that her sister does not "stick by [her]," Brenda points out the disloyalty of her siblings. A Marxist critic might see the reason for this split in the "proletariat" in the children's adherence to capitalist values. Colum's and Maeve's questions—Why should we give him a Christmas box?" and "What does he do for us?"—show that they appraise the worth of a human being by gauging the quality of the services the person renders, which in turn determines the "salary" he or she merits. . . . Brenda, on the other hand, appears to appreciate her father more. However, her attempt at procuring an expensive present ("the very best")—or at least one that *seems* expensive—reveals the capitalist in her. . . . [Similarly], by making money his primary concern and by expressing his dissatisfaction at the "dishonest" shopkeeper, Brenda's father not only manifests his own capitalist thinking but also shows that he thoroughly understands the capitalist class system in place. O'Connor's description of Mr. Regan as living "in a state of suspicion about life in general and shopkeepers in particular" and the father's question "Isn't that Rooney all out?" demonstrate that it comes as no surprise to him that his children have apparently been fooled by a businessman. In this manner, Mr. Regan implicitly communicates his acceptance of the notion that it is natural for capitalists to exploit others economically.
>
> Furthermore, a Marxist critic might suggest that, by complaining about the poor quality of his children's present, Mr. Regan alienates these "workers" from the product of their collective efforts. Not only does he fail to compensate the children emotionally for their "labor," thus exploiting them, but he also takes advantage of his superiority as the recipient and judge of the product of their work to weaken the

children's unity as a group opposing him.

This Marxist or materialist approach was also adopted by **Pirnie**, who argued that

> each of the three incidents [in the story] includes currency, from the sixpence given to Joe to the thirty shillings Brenda will finally pay for the pen. Reading the story as one of class conflict and economic determinism would therefore unify it. The title could be seen as ambiguous, perhaps expressing sympathy with Brenda's futile efforts to cross economic class lines. Focusing on the economic conflicts within the story makes the family's internal conflicts seem less personal and more tragic. This materialist analysis thus helps explain the flashes of sympathy we get for the bellicose Mr. Regan, as when we learn that "suspicion . . . nearly drove Jim Regan to his grave." He, like Brenda, seems to seek upward mobility, as is suggested by his change of name from the original O'Regan (still used by his sisters at home in Kanturk). Brenda's efforts to rally her siblings, although by trickery, might seem to express this same craving for economic advancement (symbolized by the ironically named "Standard" pen, available only to the "non-standard" bourgeoisie) . . . . Regardless of Frank O'Connor's personal politics, his story "Lady Brenda" supports a materialist reading better than any other.

Jonathan Wright, however, also seeking to explain Brenda's trickery or deceit, suggested that a *psychoanalytic* critic might argue that

> Brenda does not tell the truth because she is unable to cope with reality. Since reality is uncomfortable, she essentially escapes into a fantasy world that is far removed from the truth. She seems to be completely in control of herself (and of others such as Joe) when she dictates her own reality. Nevertheless, at the end of the story Brenda comes close to breaking down emotionally because she is forced to face the reality of rejection by her father and her siblings.

Wright himself, meanwhile, found significance in the fact that the story's central event occurs on Christmas day—a fact that ironically highlights the story's emphasis on materialism, pride, and combativeness and its absence of emphasis on genuine love and generosity. In this connection, Wright noted that "in an odd role reversal, Mr. Regan stares gleefully at the gift on his plate 'like a kid' while his children watch him closely for signs of approval."

Michael Probst, conversely, expressed a *formalist*'s admiration for O'Connor's subtle and complex characterization of the Regan family:

> The father, Jim, is stern and difficult to please. His paranoid attitude toward the world, his family, and shopkeepers in particular evoke images of the typical father who is harried by the never-ending pressures of providing for his family. Constantly aware of the demands imposed by his responsibilities, he is unable to find relief from his free-floating anxiety. Jim's wife, like her son Joe, is also something of a diplomat (though "double agent" might be a more accurate term). She too is in a conflicted role, torn between her husband's expectation of loyalty to him and her desire to protect her children from their father's subtle aggression. Finally, there are the relationships between the children and each other, and between them and their parents. We see the children struggling with the frequently discordant demands for conformity and acceptance—the desire to placate other siblings, curry the favor of parents, and avoid trouble with the outside world.

Ashley Gordon also praised the story from a *formalist* perspective. According to Gordon,

> one strength of the work is the narrator's voice, which engages the reader from the beginning. By using highly specific language, O'Connor helps establish a camaraderie between narrator and reader, creating a likable and human personality for the narrator, as if to imply that we are being *told* the story orally rather than reading it. Slang words and phrases such as "long chalks," "sissy," and "swanking" make us feel as

if we are the characters' neighbors. Such diction implies a tacit under-standing that the reader and narrator share the same background and a common vocabulary.

The narrator's conversational tone, colloquial phrasing, and occasional use of asides help make the story dramatic rather than didactic. O'Connor consistently *shows* his readers the characters' motives rather than merely *telling* them. Even when the narrator does resort to telling rather than showing, the use of qualifiers keeps the tone conversational and provides clues to unspoken feelings (particularly Joe's), as the following examples demonstrate:

> . . . none of them was *exactly* what you would call a sissy. . . .

***

> When there *really* came to be things to worry about, the suspicion of all that was concealed from him *nearly* drove Jim Regan to his grave.

***

> He knew that with Brenda you had always to pretend generosity even when you didn't feel it, and he was shrewd enough to realize that, since he was her favorite, he never *really* lost by it.

> Such phrasing not only makes the reader feel more closely involved with the story by continuing the casual diction but also implies that the narrator is himself (or herself?) a complicated observer of fundamentally complex characters and events.

Kathleen B. Durrer also used a *formalist* approach, this time to help explain the effectiveness of O'Connor's use of military language in the first paragraph:

> Although this terminology already suggests the father's battle with the family and particularly with Brenda, as the story unfolds we see that

far more serious battles are being fought, and that few, if any, are being won. Brenda is introduced in the opening sentence as the "toughest of the family," phrasing that immediately suggests the competition among the family members. However, Brenda's battles are not limited to the long-standing conflict with her father; they extend to her siblings, friends, and the surrounding community. Ironically, her battles closely resemble the ones her father constantly fights. She is described as looking like her father, and, like him, she also seems to view the world as a force to be dominated. Joe's insightful observations about his sister reveal that Brenda is not struggling to achieve acceptance from others but to be recognized as somehow better. Her perception of the shopkeepers as "robbers," her dismissal of any threat from the "bobbies," and her refusal to acknowledge any concept of right and wrong suggest that her battle extends beyond the boundaries of her own family and out into society in general. Her attitudes seem to parallel closely her father's own animosity to shopkeepers, monks (perhaps symbols of a moral authority), and "life in general." Ultimately, Brenda's efforts are also just as ineffectual as her father's. Although she extorts the money from her siblings to buy the more expensive pen, the gesture has lost any meaning. She wins neither the love of her father nor the support or respect of her siblings and is left with only Joe as a "friendly neutral" to accompany her in future campaigns. As Colum would say, Brenda and her father are sadly "lick alike."

Furthermore, **Claire Skowronski** contended that

a formalist critic might note that O'Connor's choice of title effectively conveys the complex unity of his short story. "Lady," of course, is ironic; the reader quickly learns that Brenda is a member of the lower working class, so the title "lady" speaks both to her disdain for her station in life and to her desire to taste something more. Her name itself supports the assertion that Brenda is both willing and able to take a bigger bite out of life: "Brenda" means "flame." Her personality is heated, passionate, and dangerous to those who get in her way; yet she draws people in, like moths to a candle flame. Joe, for instance, is both drawn to and repelled by his older sister's compelling personality.

Yet **Skowronski** also observed that

> a new historicist critic, deeply interested in questions of literary and social power, would perhaps suggest that O'Connor, widely published in commercial periodicals considered "women's magazines," deliberately set out to create a powerful female character to appeal to an influential audience, since he needed to attract such an audience to make his fiction marketable.

Finally, **Skowronski**—this time adopting the perspective of a *traditional historical* critic— proposed that such a critic might note

> that Joe's relationship with Brenda is consistent with O'Connor's own experiences growing up with a mother rather than a father as the strongest role model in his own life.

The varied responses to "Lady Brenda" by Angley, Durrer, Francisco, Gordon, Pirnie, Probst, Skowronski, Wilsch, and Wright seem useful not only as readings of this particular story but also as examples of how O'Connor's fiction might generally lend itself to a variety of interpretive approaches. The choice by several of these readers to pursue feminist approaches is perhaps not surprising in a story so obviously featuring a prominent female character. Nor is the decision of others to adopt a formalist perspective a matter of surprise, since the close analysis of artistic craftsmanship favored by formalist critics works well with the writings of most serious authors. Both feminist and formalist approaches might be fruitfully applied to many of O'Connor's other stories. Meanwhile, Wright's psychoanalytic speculations about Brenda's motives certainly seem worth pursuing, and indeed psychological approaches to O'Connor's whole *œuvre* seem promising, especially in view of O'Connor's own demonstrably strong interest in Freudian thought.

The fact that Francisco, Pirnie, and Wilsch all found Marxist or materialist perspectives useful in responding to "Lady Brenda" might at first seem surprising, especially given O'Connor's own publicly expressed lack of sympathy with Marxist politics. Much of his fiction, however, does seem to lend itself to materialist readings, since so many of his writings deal either explicitly or implicitly with economic tensions and relations between economic classes. Similarly, one can easily imagine how *new historicist* perspectives, such as Skowronski's, could easily be applied to O'Connor's stories in general and to "Lady Brenda" in particular. This story, after all, explores the complicated power relations within a single family, thereby suggesting that politics are not confined to the public sphere. In addition, a *traditional historical* approach (of the sort touched upon by Skowronski) would also work well with this story and with O'Connor's writings at large. As the Ireland of the first half of the twentieth century recedes in time, O'Connor's fiction is likely to need (and benefit from) the kind of contextual interpretation that historical research can best provide.

To say this is hardly to suggest, however, that either "Lady Brenda" or O'Connor's writings fail to resonate beyond their specific time or place. Probst's comments in particular (and the other formalist responses in general) suggest that one need not be a denizen of twentieth-century Ireland to appreciate the force of O'Connor's fiction, and the same argument might be made by *archetypal* (or "myth") critics. Any story (such as "Lady Brenda") that so prominently features protective mothers, aggressive fathers, adventurous quests, and imagery of battle is likely to have archetypal resonance, just as the story's emphasis on the complex relations of siblings is likely to seem relevant to persons in all cultures. Similarly, a *thematic* approach is almost always likely to prove useful in dealing with O'Connor's works, since he so often explores the same basic themes. Thus his favorite topic, human loneliness, obviously seems relevant to "Lady Brenda," especially to its bittersweet conclusion. However, *dialogical* readings can also work well with O'Connor's writings, especially in view of his well-known efforts to capture the real sounds of distinct human voices. The encounter between Brenda and Coakley in the stationery shop wonderfully exemplifies these efforts, while the different modulations or tones of Coakley's voice alone suggest the potential usefulness of dialogical theory.

Multicultural theory might apparently have little to say about a story such as "Lady Brenda," which seems to focus so totally on one segment of one distinct culture. Yet it is precisely such a limited focus that multicultural criticism can help illuminate, partly by reminding us of the groups or identities that O'Connor here ignores. Even this story, however, suggests the specific relevance of a multicultural perspective, especially if one notices (as Pirnie does) the subtle detail of Brenda's father's decision to Anglicize his name by changing it from "O'Regan" to "Regan." Details like these imply conflicting cultures, and even the opening emphasis on the need to be tough (and to avoid seeming a "sissy") suggests much about the notions of gender embedded within the story. For similar reasons, *structuralism* would prove a useful approach to a tale so obviously structured in terms of such binary oppositions as masculine/feminine, rich/poor, war/peace, strength/weakness, etc. And wherever structuralism seems applicable, *deconstruction* cannot be far behind, showing how apparently neutral descriptive categories that seem natural and inevitable are actually imposed, unstable hierarchies. Thus Brenda can be seen as a walking, talking contradiction of the oppositions just mentioned: she is a masculinized female who commands wealth (but not enough) and whose peace offering ignites another family conflict, to which she then reacts with both "weakness" and "strength." Clear and simple opposites, therefore, seem continually deconstructed or destabilized by O'Connor's story, and at the end Brenda seems, once again, both victorious and defeated. These and the story's other complexities, along with the diversity of interpretive perspectives to which it lends itself, thus help suggest the fruitfulness of a *reader-response* approach to O'Connor's fiction. How one interprets this work (and his others) is likely to depend greatly on the expectations one tacitly assumes when reading.

Even a story as apparently straightforward as "Lady Brenda," then, can be illuminated by viewing it from diverse theoretical perspectives. However, another way to approach this and other insufficiently examined works by O'Connor is to draw on the insights already offered by previous O'Connor critics who have discussed his other works. This approach was adopted by another Mellon seminarian, **Ondra Thomas- Krouse**, who used summarized critical comments reported elsewhere as points of departure for analyzing "Lady Brenda."[1]

According to Thomas-Krouse, for instance, James Matthews' claim that O'Connor sometimes depicts love as "a matter of wary diplomacy" (277) obviously applies to "Lady Brenda," especially to its descriptions of the uneasy relations between the father, mother, and siblings, whose interactions also illustrate Matthews' argument that O'Connor sometimes focuses on confrontations within families (275). Loneliness and alienation, two other common themes of O'Connor's writings (Tomory 120; Averill 297), also can be found in "Lady Brenda," according to Thomas-Krouse, who argued that these themes are not only implied in the presentation of the isolated mother but also become explicit in the final glimpse of a tearful Brenda. The conclusion, indeed, illustrates the claim that O'Connor often ends his works by focusing on a character's sudden realization of being alienated (Kilroy 110). In this connection, Thomas-Krouse additionally claimed that the story illustrates the assertion that O'Connor frequently depicts characters who search for meaning and love (Bordewyk 42). In her opinion, Brenda continually seeks her father's affection, while Joe seeks not only love from Brenda but also some sense of the larger meaning of her experiences. In fact, Thomas-Krouse also noted that O'Connor's frequent concern with surrogate parenthood (Matthews 234) is relevant here, since Brenda acts almost as a parent to Joe, who looks to her (more than to his mother) for guidance and affirmation. Furthermore, Thomas-Krouse observed that another common theme of O'Connor's fiction—the contrast between innocence and experience (Tomory 109)—seems relevant to the presentation of Joe, who at first appears naive but whose eyes are opened (during the

---

[1] See the section entitled "Selected Stories of Frank O'Connor: Synopses and Quick Critiques." Full bibliographical details concerning the authors cited here are given there.

course of the tale) to a more mature, if perhaps more jaundiced, vision
of life. Here as in other stories (Thomas-Krouse claimed), O'Connor
suggests that maturity is acquired through loss of innocence (Bordewyk
44): Brenda has "matured" by becoming increasingly like her father, and
with Brenda as a role model, Joe is also likely to mature by losing his
youthful innocence.

Thomas-Krouse also noted that the story exemplifies O'Connor's
occasional tendency to focus on eccentrics (Thompson 77), such as both
Brenda and her father; his habit of presenting self-centered fathers (Wohl
91-92) who perhaps reflect O'Connor's ambivalent feelings toward his
own father (Matthews 230-31); and his frequent efforts to treat the
depressing aspects of his own childhood in a light-hearted way (Matthews 109; 259). In the view of Thomas-Krouse, Brenda's father is so
used to trying to function as the head of his family that he has become
unaccustomed to receiving love, so that his instinctive reaction, when
presented with the Christmas gift, is to ask pointed questions and try to
take charge. His behavior thus illustrates the claim that in O'Connor's
fiction, foolish pride often prevents a desired communion (Tomory 95).
As always (according to Thomas-Krouse), Brenda tries to make the best
of a bad situation, and Joe obviously admires his strong-willed sibling.
Indeed, Brenda exemplifies O'Connor's frequent interest in (and respect
for) "mercurial, quick-witted, impulsive" girls (Matthews 298). His focus
on such a character here helps absolve this story from charges occasionally levelled at some of O'Connor's other tales, such as the claim that
his writing can be excessively maudlin (Matthews 266) or damagingly
sentimental (Tomory 96). In this story, meanings are *not* too openly
stated (Averill 303), nor is the tone here too preachy (Matthews 312).
Instead (according to Thomas-Krouse), O'Connor creates an ending that
leaves plenty of room for interpretation while still concluding with his
characteristic emphasis on a final revelation (Kilroy 110).

Thomas-Krouse's ability to mine the comments other O'Connor critics have made about other O'Connor stories in her own effort to interpret
"Lady Brenda" thus illustrates a method that might be fruitfully applied
to many works by O'Connor—works that have not yet been examined

in the detail they deserve. Here again the basic intellectual procedure of comparison and contrasts yields useful results. Whether measuring a particular story against the insights previous critics have offered about other works, or whether measuring such a story against the claims or suggestions of current literary theories, potential critics of O'Connor's fiction have a wealth of material (both primary and secondary) with which to work.—R.C.E.

Brian Friel's "Ebb Tide":
Specific Comments
from Diverse Critical Perspectives

CONTRIBUTORS: Jennifer Adger (JA); Amanda Allen (AA); Melissa Baker (MB); Kim Barron (KB); Ben Beard (BB); Janis Blaesing (JB); Krissy Blankenship (KB2); Kathleen Bohen (KB3); Shon Boling (SB2); Nataliya Bowden (NB); Spencer Brothers (SB); Tanya Brummett (TB); Melanie Clark (MC); Andrea Cook (AC); Todd Davis (TD); Paul Duke (PD); Heather Edwards (HE); Jeremy Fore (JF); Alan Griffith (AG); William Greene (WG); Kyla Gunter (KG); Drayton Hamilton (DH); Barbara Hartin (BH); Deborah Hill (DH2); Michael Hitch (MH); Kerrie Hopper (KH); Connie James (CJ); Jamey Johnson (JJ); Willie Mae Johnson (WMJ); Barrett Lee (BL); Monica Lee (ML); Anje Lister (AL); Marty Mace (MM); Mia Manning (MM2); John McGaughey (JM); Regina Moates (RM); Ann O'Clair (AMO); Mike Odom (MO); Margo Paraska (MP); Edward Pate (EP); Eleanor Planer (EP2); Lane Powell (LP); Neil Probst (NP); Will Quincy (WQ); Terri Richburg (TR); Peggy Russell (PR); Jay Sanson (JS); Lorelei Sanders (LS); Debbie Seale (DS); Tawanda Shaw (TS2); Brian Shefrin (BS); Charles Solomon (CS); Pat Steele (PS); Mark Stewart (MS); Teresa Stone (TS); Eric Thomason (ET); Barbrietta Turner (BT); Peter Walden (PW).

"Ebb Tide"

by Brian Friel

[1] **Tom Bonner was so old that there were times, especially during the summer days when the sea was a flat green, when he wondered whether he had ceased to exist. Then a light breeze would breathe round the side of the harbor wall and touch his face and neck and he would be reassured.**

A THEMATIC critic might note that even the two words of the story's title reflect the idea of aging and loss of vitality, which soon become important themes of the tale (PS; DS). Meanwhile, a FORMALIST critic, interested in a work's complex unity, would appreciate how the title already provides an image appropriate to the story's setting. Also, a FORMALIST might note that when the title is included in a comprehensive reading of the narrative, the story both begins and ends with the word "ebb." This repetition could reinforce the sense of a natural cycle—a cycle similar to that of an ocean moving through tides, and thus an image central to the meaning of this story (PS). In any case, the name **"Tom"** already sets a familiar, informal tone (NB; JJ), while the immediate description of him as **"old"** instantly introduces age as a main THEME of the story (DH; MO; PS; DS; JS; TB). This theme would also be of interest to MULTICULTURAL critics, who focus on sub-groups within the larger human population (BL; TS2). At the same time, the story's emphasis on aging would also interest an ARCHETYPAL critic, since the fear of aging and death is probably one of the most basic of all human emotions (PS; TS2). The contrast between Tom's old age and the vitality that is deserting him is already suggested by the reference to **"summer,"** a season traditionally associated with vigor and life, particularly by ARCHETYPAL critics (RCE). (At the same time, summer is also linked with fruition, maturity, and harvest in a way that spring, for instance, is not [TB].) In contrast to Tom's **"flat green" "summer days,"** it is conventionally during the summer months that people generally come out of their winter shells and interact more with other people (CJ). Friel's tendency to speak of large seasonal increments (**"summer"** here; "winter" in [8]) suggests the slowness with which Tom experiences time (MH), even as such phrasing also associates his life with the larger rhythms of nature (RCE). Perhaps the story's emphasis on life is also implied by the **"green"** color of the sea (PS; DS), although the fact that the sea (which is often associated with life and vitality [EP; TS2]) is also described as **"flat"** perhaps implies a kind of stagnancy resembling Tom's present existence (CJ; JJ; PS). The phrase **"flat green"** is almost oxymoronic, in the same way that "dull life" would be (MM2), and the words also imply a kind of sickliness (CJ). The word **"flat"** implies a lack of complexity or dimensions (TS). (Later, of course, the sea will seem anything but **"flat"** [AA]—a fact which will help reinforce the story's theme of man-vs.-nature [PS].) An ARCHETYPAL critic, concerned with humanity's relations with nature, might argue that the immensity and strength of the sea only emphasize, by contrast, Tom's small frailty (PS). A FORMALIST critic would admire how the first sentence, in which Tom **"wonder[s] whether he had ceased to exist,"** foreshadows phrasing in the middle of the story [5] (EP) as well as the story's very final sentence (EP; BT). An ARISTOTELIAN critic would admire the craftsmanship displayed by such careful placement of these important thematic statements (EP). The description of how a light **"breeze"** would **"breathe"** on Tom would appeal to a FORMALIST critic because of its effective, carefully crafted alliteration (BH; AMO; MM2), but the word **"breathe"** is especially noteworthy because it is just the first of many instances in which nature is personified in the tale (KB3; MM; MM2; MS). Indeed, perhaps this reference to breath also suggests the life-giving properties of nature (MM) and/or an easy, almost youthful vitality now missing from Tom (JS). Poignantly, it takes only a slight element of the weather (a **"breeze"**) for Tom to feel **"reassured"** that he is actually alive. For Tom, the **"breeze"** symbolizes warmth, love and affection. Nature embraces him metaphorically, yet we later learn that real human beings do not (CJ). This emphasis on a person's relations with nature would clearly be of great interest to ARCHETYPAL critics, who assume that this is perhaps the most important relationship in any human's life (AMO; MO; BT). In any case, the **"light breeze"** here contrasts strongly with the storm that will later transform Tom's existence (if only briefly). Similarly, the reference to the **"harbor wall"** creates a sense of being sheltered and protected—a sense that will later greatly diminish when Tom faces the storm [14]. Ironically, the **"harbor wall"** not only shelters Tom but also contributes to our sense that he is presently sheltered to the point of being almost numb from inactivity (TB; PS). However, just as Tom now feels slightly invigorated by the **"touch"** of the breeze (which is so gentle as to seem almost affectionate [RM] or even maternally **"reassur[ing]"** [PS]), so he will feel tremendously invigorated later when he is literally carried aloft by excited townspeople [14]. In both cases, physical contact with something outside himself helps **"reassure"** him of his own existence (MB). This theme of reassurance is one that will recur elsewhere in the tale. However, the mere fact that such reassurance is provoked here by a **"light breeze"** suggests how transitory, impermanent, and fickle it will be (TS). Here as later, Tom seems to have an especially close connection to nature (PS). At the same time, however, the gentle activity of the breeze emphasizes by contrast Tom's utter passivity and inaction (MO). Here, however, the weather is literally reassuring, whereas by the end of the tale it will seem far more dangerous and threatening—at least to the people of the town (JJ). Note how the rhythm of the final sentence here, with its "and . . . and . . . and" structure, imitates the very vitality it describes (MM2). Although nature seems **"reassur[ing]"** at this point in the story, later it will seem either threatening [8] and/or indifferent (MM2). The prominent emphasis given to the **"sea"** and **"breeze"** in this very first paragraph helps suggest the importance they will later have to the story as a whole (MH).

[2] **Life was now a routine of moving out to the front of his house and in again, according to the weather, like a barometer figure.**

The explicit statement that **"Life was now a routine"** would be of great interest to a THEMATIC critic, not only because this statement announces one of the main ideas of the story but also because it comes so early in the tale (WG). It thus helps direct our interpretation of details that come later. Just as the story itself has a kind of cyclical structure, so it opens by emphasizing an image suggesting a cycle that has now become meaningless and mindless (CJ). Tom's movement, likewise, has become regular but purposeless (TB). As we will discover later [6], however, Tom's life when he was a young man was anything but "routine" (MH). A FORMALIST critic would appreciate the complex unity created by the parallels between Tom's movement and the movement of the tides (CJ). At the same time, the reference to his **"routine"** helps prepare (by contrast) for the middle of the tale, when Tom's life will suddenly seem anything but boringly predictable (AG). Ironically, perhaps Tom himself is largely to blame for the monotonous routine of his existence; his tedious isolation may result at least as much from his own pessimism as from his age or physical disabilities (DS). In any case, the description of Tom as a kind of **"barometer figure"** not only makes him seem (paradoxically) an inanimate figure of motion (MM2) but also foreshadows his later, far more explicit usefulness to the townspeople as a predictor of weather (MO; NP). Here the "barometer" reference is merely a figure of speech; later Tom will function almost literally as a barometer (JJ). The use of the **"barometer"** image here makes Tom seem mechanical (PD) and inanimate—almost dead (MM). At the same time, the image once more suggests his intimate connection with nature (SB; KB2). Additionally, by the end of the story we will see how Tom comes to function not only as a source of information about the weather but also as a kind of barometer of significant changes in Irish society. Such changes would be of particular interest to a TRADITIONAL HISTORICAL CRITIC (TR).

[3] **The getting out was easy; without moving from his chair he could drag himself across the flagged floor of the kitchen, out through the door and down the steps to his favorite position in front of the**

kitchen window, from where he could look out across the bay, on a clear day, as far as Innisholme Island.

And there he could sit for a whole afternoon in the sun, like a dried-up stick that the tide had forgotten, just looking before him.

The use of the word **"easy"** to characterize how Tom manages to leave his house seems ironic, especially in light of the ensuing lengthy description. The **"flagged"** (or rough [JJ]) floor of his house symbolizes the present rough condition of his life (RCE). MULTICULTURAL critics would be interested in the fact that Tom is both elderly and disabled: he is therefore a member of a minority within a minority (TS2). A TRADITIONAL HISTORICAL CRITIC would be most likely to know the exact meaning of the word **"flagged."** Meanwhile, the reference to Tom's view of the **"bay"** and of **"Innisholme Island"** helps prepare for the exciting events with which the tale will conclude (RCE), since those events will center on crossing the bay to reach the island. A TRADITIONAL HISTORICAL CRITIC would want to know as much as possible about **"Innisholme Island."** Such a critic would want to know whether such a place "really" exists, and, if so, where it is located and what its existence might tell us about other "real" aspects of the story's setting (CJ; EP2; MM2; DS; BT). At the same time, the reference to the **"Island"** helps emphasize Tom's own physical and emotional isolation (DS; MM2). As we will soon see, Tom himself is a kind of island within a sea of people who are really not aware that he exists in the same area as they do. Perhaps there is even an implied pun on the word **"Innisholme,"** which sounds very much like the phrase "in his home" and thus re-emphasizes Tom's isolation (CJ; MM2): he does stay in (or near) his home almost constantly (CJ). (Even hearing the word as "Inn his home" would suggest a sense of transiency [MM2].) One could argue, however, that Tom isolates himself on a self-created island of discontent. His own distant attitude may have more to do with his isolated feelings than perhaps his age does (DS).

It is as if, in looking out across the bay, Tom is looking back on his former life—a life (we later discover) that once centered around that very same body of water (AMO). A FORMALIST would appreciate Friel's effective use of assonance in the phrase "**whole afternoon in the sun,**" in which the long, drawn-out vowel sounds mimic the long stretch of time they describe (RCE), while the comparison of Tom to a "**dried-up stick**" is especially effective since any such stick was once part of a living tree (PD; JM), just as Tom himself was once full of vitality and part of a larger community (PS). Ironically, although normally the "**sun**" is considered a life-giving force, particularly by ARCHETYPAL critics, here it threatens to sap Tom of his vitality (RCE). It is as if even the sea has "**forgotten**" Tom (HE), just as he is also largely forgotten by his neighbors, who in fact will later literally forget him [17] (RCE). The "**stick**" that has been "**forgotten**" by the tide will presumably be set in motion again when the tide comes back in, but we cannot be sure (at least at this point) that Tom will ever again feel any vitality or movement (JJ). The very word "tide" inevitably suggests death (TB). Once more Tom's present passivity is emphasized: he merely "**sit[s],**" "**just looking before him**" (RCE). The closest Tom now comes to being alive is watching others live (MM2). Indeed, a THEMATIC critic might note that this passage introduces the theme of watching the world go by from a stationary position. However, although Tom is no longer an active participant in that world, he is still interested in it and people in general. Sitting in front of his window, he sees only what passes by. One could nonetheless argue that he also sees things more acutely precisely because his perspective is so limited (DS).

[4] **Tom's house was at the end of a path that led to the pier. Occasionally visitors would drive down there and pour out of their cars and run out to the end of the pier and look down into the water and point out things to one another. Or they would shade their eyes and look out at Innisholme and plan a day trip sometime. Then, on their way back to their cars, they would notice Tom, just as they had noticed the other things, and they would talk to him, treating him with a curious respect as though he had secrets to reveal.**

But once they discovered that he was too old to be interesting they went off, laughing and chattering, to their cars.

The fact that Tom's house is at **"the end of a path"** seems symbolic, since Tom is clearly near the end of his own life (SB; BT). Perhaps his nearness to the sea suggests his nearness to death (AMO). The **"pier"** is a place for comings and goings, movements into and out of a wider world—precisely the kinds of movements of which Tom is no longer capable (TR). By opening the second sentence with the words **"Occasionally visitors,"** Friel doubly emphasizes the temporary, ephemeral quality of their haphazard presence (RCE). The fact that the visitors **"pour out"** contrasts their crowded companionship with Tom's loneliness (TS2). In addition, their varied, vigorous movements (**"drive . . . pour out . . . run"**) contrast pointedly with Tom's relative lack of movement, and thus make his life seem even more confined (JF). Note how the very length of the second sentence here mimics the excited activities it describes (RCE). In organizing this sentence, Friel effectively uses anaphora, the repetition of a key word or phrase (**"and . . . and . . . and . . . and"** [MP]). A MULTICULTURAL critic would be interested in the contact between Tom and the visitors, seeing that contact not just as an interaction between individuals but as a meeting of two differing cultures. This interaction would also interest a TRADITIONAL HISTORICAL critic for the same reasons (WMJ). The fact that the visitors are unnamed, combined with the fact that they **"pour out,"** makes them seem to lack individuality; they almost seem a mob (CS), and the words **"pour out"** even suggest that the visitors (presumably city folk) are naively over-eager, as if they are starved for any contact with nature (AL). (Later in the story Tom will experience a different kind of excited crowd of people rushing about [10], but at that point they will be locals, not visitors [RCE]). The fact that the visitors point to ambiguous, unnamed **"things"** suggests their ignorance of the local environment and culture (JM) and how unimportant both seem to them: local life is merely a quaint, temporary diversion from their normal existences (TR). Their experience of the sea is brief and superficial, unlike Tom's (MM2). By mentioning **"Innisholme"** island once more, Friel doesn't allow us to forget about a place that will later seem very important in this story (AMO). A TRADITIONAL HISTORICAL critic would know the particular significance of **"Innisholme,"** including its history

and contemporary associations (MO). When the visitors are said to plan
a **"day trip"** to Innisholme, both the adjective and the noun reemphasize
the tourists' merely temporary connections to the local landscape. Their
status as perpetual **"visitors"** and their interest in constantly making
"trip[s]" perhaps implies both an essential rootlessness and an empty
curiosity. In any case, their ability to move is once more implied, so that
again we see a contrast with Tom's relative immobility (RCE). The visitors
can **"plan"** a trip **"sometime,"** whereas Tom's ability to control his future
is as doubtful as the length of that future itself (AMO). The fact that the
visitors return to their **"cars"** not only associates them once more with the
mobility Tom lacks (PW) but also implies again, perhaps, their isolation
and distance from nature (NB). A TRADITIONAL HISTORICAL critic
would be interested to know how many people in Ireland owned cars
during the time in which the story is set and whether ownership of a car
implied an urban and relatively wealthy background. It seems unlikely,
for instance, that Tom himself now owns or has ever owned a car (RCE).
The visitors regard Tom as just another local curiosity; he is just one more
"thing" among the various **"other things"** they have seen that day (PD,
ML). It is almost as if they regard him as another natural object (MO),
as just another part of the local scenery (MM2). Tom observes nature,
while they observe Tom (NB). Note that they talk **"to"** him rather than
"with" him. The fact that they at first treat him **"with a curious respect
as though he had secrets to reveal"** not only foreshadows the story's
climactic events (JJ; DH) but also seems fitting in ways they cannot
understand, since we will later see that Tom does indeed possess a kind
of wisdom of which they know nothing (JJ; DH). For that reason, this
open reference to **"secrets"** would greatly interest a THEMATIC critic,
since secret wisdom later becomes one of the story's most prominent ideas
(MO). Tom's possession of such "secrets" contrasts with the visitors' own
superficiality (ET). This shallowness, in fact, makes Friel's description of
how they ultimately **"discovered"** that Tom is insufficiently **"interesting"**
seem more than a little ironic: it is they, not Tom, who are lacking in
interest (in several senses of that term [AG]). Paradoxically, they fail to
appreciate Tom's inevitable relevance to their own lives: they, too, will

someday grow old (MM2). The attitude of the visitors—who consider Tom **"too old to be interesting"**—obviously contrasts with the attitude of the narrator, who devotes an entire story to Tom and his thoughts (RCE). Their attitude also contrasts with the attitude later displayed by the townspeople, who will be very interested—if only briefly—in the wisdom Tom has acquired because of his age (PS). The reaction of the tourists would probably interest a READER-RESPONSE critic, since it would be easy to imagine many kinds of readers who might be offended by the tourists' attitude (TS2). The reference to Tom being **"old"** would obviously interest THEMATIC critics, since such phrasing reinforces a central idea of the tale: human aging (MO). At the same time, this theme would interest ARCHETYPAL critics, who might argue that the story derives part of its power from the basic human fear of growing old (DS). The visitors' view of Tom, like their view of the local surroundings, is cursory, superficial, and brief (TR). Once more their mobility is doubly emphasized by the description of how **"they went off . . . to their cars,"** while the reference to their **"laughing and chattering"** again suggests how flighty and superficial they are (HE). The word **"chattering,"** in particular, suggests nonsensical, useless talk (WG). In contrast, Tom speaks very little in this story, but when he does speak—especially near the end of the tale—his few words are full of significance and are eagerly listened to (RCE). His relationship with the visitors, like his relationship with the other townspeople, would interest a STRUCTURALIST critic, since in both cases the relationship is between persons representing the categorical opposites of youth and age—one of the most important "binary oppositions" by which human society is often structured (KB2; DS; JS). A STRUCTURALIST might also argue that just as the visitors cannot really comprehend Tom or his culture, so Tom may be equally incapable of comprehending them and theirs: Tom and the visitors are two halves of a larger binary opposition (EP). A DECONSTRUCTOR might argue that in the middle of this story we will see a blurring of the usually clear distinctions between these two categories: the old man will briefly become the figure of strength, while the young men will briefly seem needy and dependent (MB; DS).

[5] It was a different matter getting back into the kitchen again. Tom could not slide his chair up the three stone steps.

So he had to wait until some of the neighbors came along, or until some of the fishermen came in with a catch.

Very often it was dusk before they discovered him and they would say crossly: "What are you doing out here at this time of evening, Tom? Do you want to get your death?" As if death were something that struck you suddenly when the sun went down and not the gradual drifting away of all sensation.

Perhaps Tom, in order to prove both to himself and to others that he still exists, deliberately positions himself outside, where he cannot get back in the house without the assistance of the younger men. This routine may represent his attempt to get attention and receive the community's recognition that he is still alive (DS). A FEMINIST critic, interested in the operations of sexual stereotypes, might notice that Tom is associated here (and later) with the **"kitchen"**—traditionally considered a woman's domain. This linkage becomes even more significant later, when the elderly Tom is contrasted with the relative vigor of the other men of the village (DH). Friel magnifies Tom's helplessness by making an action that would be simple for most people—climbing three **"stone steps"**—seem impossible for Tom, and the very fact that the steps are made of such a hard material emphasizes the difficulty of the task (AMO). The fact that Tom **"had to wait"** symbolizes the general condition of his present existence (AMO), including his essential dependence on others (HE). A DECONSTRUCTOR might find it interesting that although Tom is presently dependent on his neighbors, later in the story this hierarchy will be destabilized, when Tom becomes the figure of authority. The fact that this new situation is itself soon reversed, however, would reinforce a deconstructor's sense that all hierarchical systems are potentially unstable (EP2). An ARCHETYPAL critic, concerned with basic human desires and fears, might argue that Tom's behavior shows how deeply rooted the human desire for attention is. Tom may be less interested in being out of doors than in being noticed and attended to. He is willing to take real physical risks in order to be the momentary object of his neighbors' brief attention (AC). The fact that he waits for the fishermen to come to him foreshadows the climax of the story, when they come to him for a different reason and in a different mood [9]. Here they come upon him in the growing darkness of **"dusk"**—a detail that contributes to the story's gloomy atmosphere and its sense of impending death (RCE). The reference to the **"fishermen [coming] in with a catch"** would interest a MARXIST critic since it reminds us that Tom is part of a community of people who must work hard for a living (WMJ), although Tom himself is now cut off from the ability to work and thus feels somewhat alienated from his society and therefore lacking in self-worth (RCE). Friel describes how the fishermen **"discovered"** Tom, much as the tourists **"discovered"** him three paragraphs earlier [4]; in both cases the verb emphasizes how easy it is for Tom to be forgotten or go unnoticed (TR). The fact that the fishermen now speak to Tom **"crossly"** makes it all the more ironic that they later adopt an entirely different tone when they need his help (TB; JJ). Their present tone is patronizing (NH), and their question—**"Do you want to get your death?"**—seems insensitive at best (JJ), although Tom does not seem to resent their attitude (AC). They address Tom almost as one might address a foolish child (TB). A MARXIST critic might suggest that if Tom were wealthy his neighbors would be unlikely to speak to him **"crossly"**; indeed, a rich Tom could afford to pay for the kind of care he must now merely hope for (RCE).

Tom's physical immobility makes him even more vulnerable to the weather than are the rest of the story's characters (PS). The image of the **"sun"** going **"down"** provides another symbol of death, of the literal decline of a source and symbol of life. Earlier Tom had been compared to a stick dried by the sun, but at least then he was in the light; now he is being literally overshadowed (LP). Meanwhile, the imagery of the **"gradual drifting away"** of sensation seems appropriate in a story concerned with the movement of the tides (PD), especially given the comparison of Tom earlier to a **"dried-up stick that the tide had forgotten"** (NP) [3]. Tom is threatened by a loss of **"all sensation"** both physically and emotionally

(RCE). Ironically, Tom probably wishes that death *were* sudden rather than being so painfully "**gradual**" (AMO). The last sentence of this passage seems simultaneously to express the narrator's opinion while also articulating Tom's own thoughts (AMO). A DIALOGICAL critic might find this sentence especially interesting, since it seems to be an instance of the author's—or at least the narrator's—voice directly intervening in the story to emphasize explicitly one of its major themes. The tone of this final sentence is less "objective" than the tone of most of the rest of the story (MM2). In any case, the phrase "gradual drifting away" would interest both THEMATIC and FORMALIST critics, since phrases such as this help reinforce a central meaning implied by the story's title (EP2).

> [6] **They would feel his hands, too, and say they were like stones. Then he would look at his hands as if they did not belong to him; big, gnarled, splayed things that once pulled oars and hauled lobster pots and shot nets and hoisted sails. Queer how they felt nothing now. Absolutely nothing. Even the rheumatism that bit into his legs ignored those hands. That puzzled him.**

It seems ironic that the neighbors would "**feel [Tom's] hands**," since Tom himself is increasingly incapable of such basic feeling (LP). Even such an apparently simple word as "**too**" suggests that their attentions to Tom have become part of a mere automatic routine (WG). The way they "**feel**" his hands seems less gentle and certainly less reassuring than the way Tom was "touch[ed]" by the breeze in the opening paragraph of the story (RCE). Once more "**stone**" imagery [5] is associated with Tom, as if to emphasize again his nearness to death, his lack of feeling, and the prospect that he will soon become a part of inanimate nature (PD; MO; PS; DS). The comparison of Tom's hands to "**stones**" suggests how heavy and cumbersome they have become and how much he himself has similarly become a burden to his neighbors (MS). Tom himself is now largely immobile, like a stone (MB). At the same time, the reference to the "**stones**" suggests another, darker sense in which Tom is constantly being linked to elements of nature (PS). At the same time, MARXIST critics would be interested in the ways this passage implies Tom's working-class background (TS2). Certainly the phrasing implies that Tom has had a long, hard life, and the references to his hands imply the story of his youth and past struggles. When he looks at his hands, he sees what they have become, but he also remembers what they once were and did. We get a nice double image in this passage, because we see both the old and the young Tom. Indeed, Tom's memory or memories are as important to the story as his thoughts about the present. These memories help us see Tom as someone other than just an old man (DS). The fact that Tom sees his hands as **"big, gnarled, splayed things"** suggests his image of himself and of his body: his **"hands"** are not just old hands; they are something ugly to him (DS). Meanwhile, the sense that Tom is turning into an inanimate object is intensified by the reference to his hands as **"things,"** and this impression is only emphasized further by the phrasing used to describe his vigorous youth: here the focus is on strong, active verbs (**"pulled . . . hauled . . . shot . . . hoisted"**) linked to concrete nouns (**"oars . . . pots . . . nets . . . sails"**) crisply tied together by the repeated conjunction **"and"** (NP). The movement of this sentence is almost wave-like (PS). Ironically, Friel had earlier used a similarly constructed sentence, full of active verbs, to describe the pointless, frenetic activities of the tourists [4], although the activities here associated with Tom are purposeful and serious. Sentence structure also reinforces meaning in the phrase **"Absolutely nothing,"** since the fragmentary syntax helps emphasize Tom's sense of personal fragmentation. Similarly, the movement from the sentence emphasizing forceful, active verbs to the description of the present condition of Tom's hands (**"Queer how they felt nothing now"**) not only introduces another fragment but is also effectively abrupt: the sudden shift juxtaposes the vigor of Tom's youth with the decrepitude of his old age (RCE). Meanwhile, a FORMALIST critic would appreciate the effectiveness of the repetition-with-change of the juxtaposition of **"nothing"** and **"Absolutely nothing"** (MB). Tom now feels as if he is merely a piece of his former self (MS); the numbness of his body resembles the numbness of his mind and spirit (SB2). Friel uses personification effectively (KB3; MP) when describing how rheumatism "**bit into**" Tom's legs even as it "**ignored**" his hands, so that the disease paradoxically displays both viciousness and indifference at the same time (NP). Paradoxically, pain would now be an almost welcome sensation to Tom (MO) since it would remind him that his body is still alive (NB). Ironically, Tom is partly ignored even by his disease, just as he is mostly ignored by the other people around him. He is "**puzzled**" by his rheumatism in much the same way that he himself is a puzzle to the inquisitive tourists (PD). Tom must struggle with the natural process of aging in the same way that the townspeople will later struggle with the natural process of the storm (PS).

[7] But the neighbors were kind, in a worldly way. They saw to it that he did not starve and they took turns to clear up his place. Once they had done these things for him, they could afford to forget about him, he was so old . . .

Immediately after emphasizing the relative indifference of Tom's rheumatism, Friel implies that the old man's neighbors are more "**kind,**" but then this adjective is immediately qualified by the phrase "**in a worldly way.**" This second phrase implies that their concern for Tom is dictated by conventional social rules rather than by deep personal feeling (MB; NB) and that their kindness involves material provisions rather than deep emotional attachment (KB2; SB; TB) or spiritual support (TB). Perhaps they are motivated primarily by a sense of guilt rather than by any deep compassion (AC). They ensure that Tom does "**not starve,**" but this very phrasing suggests how minimal their attentions are (HE). Tom, after all, is starved for attention as much as for food (AMO), but, as the word "**afford**" suggests, the neighbors regard time as a commodity (PD), and they feel that once they have taken "**turns**" doing certain materialistic "**things**" for Tom (thereby easing their own consciences [MM]), they can "**forget**" about him—much as the briefly inquisitive tourists soon neglected him earlier [4] (RM). His neighbors largely "**forget**" about him, just as his rheumatism earlier "**ignored**" [6] his hands (PD). Ironically, this emphasis on the way Tom's neighbors "**forget**" about him not only closes the first part of the story (a closure signalled by the ellipsis points ["..."]) but also precedes the second part of the tale, when Tom will once more suddenly seem—if only briefly—very important to the people around him (RCE).

Tom may be physically very weak, but, as we will soon discover, his mind is still strong (RM). A NEW HISTORICIST critic, interested in how differences of power affect human relations, might notice the implied contrast between Tom the "**old**" man and his younger neighbors: in this story age is largely (but not entirely) equated with weakness, while youth is equated with strength (KB; DH). A STRUCTURALIST critic, interested in categorical oppositions, would also take an interest in this division between age and youth, and so would MULTICULTURALIST critics, who are interested in the different experiences of diverse human groups (RCE). A THEMATIC critic would likewise note this emphasis on Tom being "**old**," since the contrast between youth and age is one of the central themes of the story (BH). Tom's age affects not only his self-perception but also the ways others perceive him (TS). Indeed, READER-RESPONSE critics might argue that different readers would respond in different ways to the present passage. Thus some readers might feel sorry for Tom because he is alone and cannot care for himself. On the other hand, other readers could note that he does have some people who care about him enough to help him get by, while some elderly people do not. These readers might feel that Tom is quite lucky not to be living in a nursing home or poor house, where the people who take care of him are merely hired to do so (AC). A TRADITIONAL HISTORICAL critic would want to know the degree to which nursing homes and other such facilities were available and used by members of Tom's class during the period in which Friel sets the story (EP2). An ARCHETYPAL critic might argue that Tom is bothered less by physical aging than by a worry that he has become unimportant and will leave nothing of value behind (CJ; MM2). Such a critic might also argue that this story taps into a basic human fear of being forgotten and ignored (EP2). Both archetypal and THEMATIC critics might suggest that much of the story's power is rooted in such common human experiences as age, death, depression, and the need to feel useful and able (EP2).

[8] **When the first of the winter gales struck one day early in October, the only people caught unawares were the few late visitors. They scurried back to their hotels with their beach wraps and their portable radios.**

A STRUCTURALIST critic might note how the contrast between the calm and stormy seas parallels the contrasts between Tom's passivity and his later rejuvenation. Such parallels function as part of the "semiotic system" by which the story is organized (PS). A STRUCTURALIST might also note that the contrasting reactions of the visitors and the residents to the **"winter gales"** is part of a larger structure of contrasts between the culture of the land-lubbers and the culture of these sea-faring folk: the opposition between land and sea is part of a larger series of oppositions that helps structure Friel's story (EP). The fact that the **"first"** winter storm strikes **"early in October"** suggests the fiercely inhospitable nature of the local climate: winter comes before fall is even finished. Such imagery not only contrasts with the gentle, placid summer imagery with which the story opened but also seems highly appropriate to a tale that is so much concerned with physical, social, and emotional death. Ironically, it is during this season most associated with dying that Tom will come to feel—if only briefly—most vigorously alive. Because a MULTICULTURAL critic is interested in exploring the ways in which race, sex, gender, age, class, or other differences affect the author or audience of a text, such a critic might focus on the fact that **"the only people caught unawares"** in the first winter gale were **"the few late visitors."** Since the group of people relaxing on the beach that day was more prosperous and modern than the local fishermen, they had never been compelled to read the ocean and sky for weather warnings (DH2). Their frightened reaction might draw the scorn of a MARXIST critic, who might see them as representing a leisured, bourgeois class and therefore as distinct from the more hardy working-class characters who otherwise populate the story (JA; JB; EP). An ARCHETYPAL critic might note how the fact that the tourists are "**caught unawares**" by the weather helps reinforce our earlier sense of them as fundamentally ignorant of (and divorced from) the basic rhythms of nature (RCE). A farmer or fisherman reading Friel's story might find it humorous that the visitors were surprised by the coming gale, while a more modernized or citified person might only sympathize with the visitors for being caught in a storm. Such differing responses would, of course, interest not only a MULTICULTURAL critic but also a READER-RESPONSE analyst (DH2). A THEMATIC critic, meanwhile, might find this passage interesting as an instance of the possibly historically new theme that humans, by virtue of their naive faith in technology, are often overwhelmed, humiliated, and confounded by natural forces (DH). Appropriately enough, the "**visitors**" or tourists are almost always described as being in motion (PN): earlier they had headed back to their cars, and now Friel describes sarcastically how they "**scurried**" back to the temporary shelter of "**hotels**," bringing with them their flimsy "**beach wraps**" and their modern "**portable radios**." Nearly all the details associated with the tourists suggest their distance from real nature—the degree to which they have cut themselves off from genuine contact with the physical environment in which Tom once immersed himself and which he still knows so well. Even the word "**scurried**" suggests their lack of individuality (CS) and strength: they move as a frightened group (TD), almost like tiny terrified animals (BH). At the same time, the word "**scurried**" emphasizes (by contrast) Tom's relative immobility (JA). The "**portable radios**" suggest the tourists' interest in mere entertainment and in merely superficial or distant communication. They are mere "**visitors**" to a place in which Tom, as we will soon see, still feels very much at home (RCE).

Because a MARXIST critic is interested in conflicts between economic classes and the ways that literature reflects, reinforces, or undermines conventional class relations, such a critic might particularly focus on the references to the "**visitors**" and their "**beach wraps**," "**hotels**," and "**portable radios**" (EP; DH2). Since these visitors are rich enough to be vacationing at a hotel and spending leisurely days sunning themselves on the beach with portable radios for entertainment, a Marxist critic might suggest that Friel is showing how the wealthy can spend their time pursuing pleasure and entertainment while poorer people must do hard physical labor to survive. A MARXIST critic might also note that the rich can run to comfort and safety as these vacationers run back to their hotel, while poor people such as the fishermen are forced to endure the harsh elements (DH2). A STRUCTURALIST might see the reference to the **"beach wraps"** and **"portable radios"** as parts of a larger code of oppositions between the wealth of the visitors and the relative poverty of the local villagers (EP).

[9] **Tom had not slithered out that day; he had smelled the storm coming the night before. He lay in bed and listened to the wind pounding on the roof and the breakers smashing on the rocks round at the Tor.**

He lay there for twenty-four hours, listening. Then, about noon on the second day, he heard people running past his door down to the pier. Above the roar of the Atlantic wind he could hear the urgency of their voices, shouting to one another.

The word **"slithered"** implies that Tom, like a snake, comes outside mainly to seek warmth (PD; JJ; TD). Such phrasing also suggests that his slow, sluggish, dragging movement (JA; AG) no longer seems fully human, and certainly the word contrasts with the immediately preced- ing description of the superficial tourists who quickly **"scurried"** back to their hotels (RCE). Since PSYCHOANALYTIC critics often see snakes as symbols of a potency that is frustrated or inert, they might find the word **"slithered"** particularly appropriate to Tom's current condition (EP). Alternatively, the snake imagery could be seen as implying (as it does in some cultures) a sense of potential renewal (EP). Because an ARCHE- TYPAL critic is interested in how certain basic fears, desires, images, and stories affect the ways humans perceive reality, such a critic might focus on Friel's use of the words **"slithered"** and **"smelled"** to evoke the image of an animal in the mind of the reader (JB DH2; EP). Just as an animal can smell fear or danger, so Tom can smell the approach of a storm. An ARCHETYPAL critic might compare Tom's instinctive reaction with the instincts of an animal (DH2; JB). The fact that Tom had **"smelled"** the storm coming not only reinforces his similarity to a snake (BS) but also implies his instinctive, almost animalistic connection to nature (NB; WQ). It is as if his sense of smell has become stronger as the rest of his senses (along with other aspects of his body) have weakened (SB).

The first half of the story had opened by emphasizing sunshine and gentle breezes, while this second half opens, in contrast, by emphasizing imagery of **"night"** and an approaching **"storm."** The **"storm"** will provide both the physical and the emotional climax of the tale. Whereas the tourists listen to their portable radios, Tom has **"listened"** to the **"pounding"** and **"smashing"** sounds of natural violence (RCE). Tom himself, like the rocks of **"Tor,"** will soon be **"pound[ed]"** by the storm (TS). Although water is conventionally associated with life, too much water (as here) is often a symbol of death. Therefore the destructive powers of the sea have always been greatly feared (EP). Because a FORMALIST critic is interested in the artistic form of a text and in how each subtle nuance contributes to a unified whole, such a critic might focus on the word **"breakers,"** since no other noun can describe as accurately the crashing, destructive waves of an Atlantic storm. For example, the damaging aspect of the storm would be weakened if the word **"breakers"** were replaced by "waves," or "billows," or even "whitecaps" (DH2). Nature, which had once **"reassured"** Tom [1], now seems almost personally threatening (AMO). A STRUCTURALIST CRITIC, interested in how we tend to understand our experiences in terms of opposites, might notice the heavy emphasis here and throughout the story on the contrast between activity and passivity. This contrast is exemplified by the description of how Tom **"lay"** in bed for twenty-four hours while the other men were **"running"** around outside (DH). Nevertheless, although Tom is physically passive (**"he lay there"**), he is highly active mentally (since he is constantly **"listening"**). The imagery here is almost cyclical (**"He lay there for twenty-four hours"**) and the diction becomes almost Biblical (**"Then, about noon on the second day"** [PD])—as if Friel intends to heighten the archetypal significance of the events he is describing (and is about to describe). Although many readers might argue that Tom is most alive during the storm, a DECONSTRUCTOR might challenge this standard reading by pointing out that Tom can at least leave the house when the sea is calm but that he is trapped inside during bad weather. Ironically, the fierce activity of nature renders Tom even more passive than he usually is (PS).

[10] **For a time he did not stir. A boat had broken her moorings, he thought. Or the buoy was adrift. But he knew a crowd must have gathered by now because at least twelve people had run past his door.**

He was about to ease himself on to his chair when somebody knocked. "Tom Bonner! Tom Bonner! Come quick! Down to the pier! The men want you," a child's voice piped through the keyhole.

"Eh? What is it?"

"Flares from Innisholme. One every ten minutes. The men are thinking of going out."

The fact that Tom does **"not stir"** contrasts effectively with all the activity (natural and human) going on outside; once more he is shown to be physically inactive but mentally alert. Note the cleverness with which Friel constructs the sentence stating that **"A boat had broken her moorings, he thought."** Until we reach the comma, we can mistakenly assume that the narrator is merely reporting a fact. After we reach the comma, however, we discover that Friel is only reporting Tom's speculation. The syntax therefore plays a subtle trick on us and thereby helps reinforce our sense of Tom's isolation. The use of two fragments (**"Or the buoy was adrift. But . . ."**) mimics the fragmentary nature of Tom's thinking here (RCE), but the fact that he **"knew"** that **"at least twelve people had run past his door"** shows how alert he is, how closely he pays attention to his environment despite his physical limitations (JJ). The fact that he **"was about to ease himself on to his chair when somebody knocked"** implies that he intended to involve himself in the action—and thus satisfy his need to be noticed—even before the child appeared at his door (MB). The energetic, excited **"child's voice"** only reinforces (by contrast) our sense of Tom's great age (RCE), while the child's command that Tom should **"Come quick"** seems unintentionally (but nonetheless heavily) ironic (BS). The command suggests how little the child knows about Tom's condition and thus perhaps symbolizes how little he is the object of the general community's attention (AC). Notice, by the way, how the child's ungrammatical call of "**Come quick**" seems far more appropriate to his character than "Come quickly" would have been (RCE). The fact that Tom is now being summoned by "**a child's voice**" may symbolize the sense of renewal and rejuvenation he is about to experience (PS). The fact that the community must make contact with Tom through a "**keyhole**" may perhaps symbolize the secret, almost precious knowledge he possesses (PS). Although Friel distinguishes between the "**child**" and the "**men**," in a sense even the men are now children when contrasted with the ancient and knowledgeable Tom (JJ). At the same time, such phrasing may suggest that Tom is no longer regarded as one of the "**men**"; he is set apart by his age and infirmity. The phrasing implies that "**the men**" are part of a group to which Tom no longer belongs (PS). Despite the fact that the story is set during a period of modern conveniences (such as cars and portable radios), when natural turmoil strikes, the islanders must still rely on the rather primitive but still effective tactic of firing "**[f]lares**" (MM), just as they must depend on Tom's ancient wisdom. The flares contribute to the story's larger pattern of light-and-dark imagery (the tale opens in daylight and closes in the midst of a symbolic nighttime), while the juxtaposition of the fire of the flares with the water of the storm and sea helps emphasize the elemental conflict Friel is here describing (RCE). The fact that the men are at this point merely "**thinking of going out**" implies their natural re-luctance and fear (AMO). A DIALOGICAL critic would be interested in the fact that up until this point, Tom has been literally silent; he has always been spoken to [5], but until now we have not heard him speak. Instead, everything we have learned about him has been reported by the narrator. Now, however, at the moment when Tom suddenly becomes important to his community, he also acquires a voice. Later, though, when he has fulfilled his function, he will once again become a subject of narration rather than a source of direct speech (KB2).

[11] **Tom knew that the men wanted his opinion. But they had**

forgotten that he could not walk the length of the kitchen to the front door.

"Tell them . . ." he began.

But the men had come to him. Feet shuffled outside and anxious faces peered in through the dirty square of window and searched the dark room for him.

"Flares from the island, Tom," shouted Mason. "It's probably the doctor they want for the lighthouse-keeper's wife. She's due this week, it seems."

Tom didn't answer.

The first two sentences here juxtapose Tom's physical weakness with the strength of his accumulated wisdom (KB). Here as earlier, Friel effectively uses sentence fragments (**"But they had forgotten . . . But the men had come"**) to suggest the quick, agitated nature of the thoughts and actions he describes. The fact that the men's feet **"shuffled"** reinforces our sense of their hasty, erratic movements (RCE), or perhaps the word implies the degree to which Tom and his neighbors have now traded places: they, not he, are the ones who now must shuffle (AMO). His relative calm emphasizes his close connection with the sea and nature: he is not as disturbed by the storm as his neighbors are, since he has faced many such storms in the past (PS). Meanwhile, the fact that they must peer through a **"dirty square of window"** implies that although his neighbors routinely "clear up his place" [7], they apparently have not done a very thorough or painstaking job. Perhaps their past failure to clean the window very thoroughly symbolizes their general neglect of Tom (AMO; KG). They lack a clear vision of him both literally and metaphorically (PW; JJ). The word **"forgotten"** might particularly interest a THEMATIC critic, because such critics are interested in the *ideas* that writers express and in the effect those ideas have on readers. Such a critic might therefore focus on the recurring theme of indifference or neglect towards Tom and might suggest that the idea of old people being forgotten and neglected could contribute to a reader's own fear of growing old. Such a response would obviously also interest READER-RESPONSE critics (DH2; DS). STRUCTURALIST critics, interested in the ways experience is understood in terms of opposite categories, might notice the implied opposition here (and throughout the story) between the prospect of new life and the imminence of Tom's death (DH; PS). The townspeople consider the baby's impending birth an emergency, but they generally pay little attention to Tom's impending death (TR), and it is part of the larger irony of the story that although Tom's ancient wisdom cannot prevent his own demise, it *can* help bring a new life successfully into the world (LP). The new infant will unknowingly benefit from the wisdom of the old man (AG), and this juxtaposition even perhaps introduces a hint of resurrection into the story (EP). The men show the same regard for the "**doctor**" that they presently (if only temporarily) show towards Tom: both are experts on whom the community must occasionally rely (RCE). Because of his crucial role in assisting with the baby's birth, Tom himself is in a sense reborn, if only momentarily: he gains a new sense of self-respect by regaining the respect of the community (PD). In any case, the juxtaposition of Tom's impending death with the birth of the new baby contributes to the pattern of cyclical ebb and flow that is crucial to the structure and meaning of this story. An ARCHETYPAL critic would be particularly interested in the ways the story deals with both birth and death—two of the most crucial rites of passage faced by all human beings (TS2).

[12] "We're thinking of trying the crossing," Mason said.

Tom worked himself to the edge of the bed and then on to the chair. He pulled a blanket over his shoulders. Then, muttering to himself, he dragged himself across the floor and pulled back the bolt on the door.

They poured into the kitchen with the wind, six of them in their yellow oilskins and thigh boots. Two scrawny boys hung about the threshold, watching.

"I was asleep," Tom said. It was a lie, but they were too full of the importance of their mission to detect it.

In this section Friel creates a small cross-section of masculine society: the young boys, the grown men, and the old man (MH). The fact that the men are said to be **"thinking of trying the crossing"** suggests again their natural nervousness and reluctance (AMO). Meanwhile, Tom's act of "muttering to himself" perhaps suggests that he is as dissatisfied with his neighbors as they are indifferent to him (TS2). Now that Tom feels needed, however, his body as well as his mind becomes active: note all the verbs of action linked to him here (**"worked," "pulled," "dragged," "pulled"**). This cluster of verbs recalls the similar cluster earlier used to describe Tom's actions as a young sailor [6]: it is as if he is regaining some of the vigor of his youth (SB). Like the crowd of tourists earlier who had "scurried" back to their hotels [8], the neighbors are now described as having **"poured"** into Tom's house; their ease and quickness of movement contrast with Tom's labored struggles. Indeed it was the tourists who were earlier described as having **"pour[ed] out of their cars"** [4]: the echo of that verb here, however, only helps emphasize the contrast between the visitors and the villagers. The villagers, dressed in their **"yellow oilskins and thigh boots,"** contrast starkly with the tourists with their **"beach wraps"** and **"portable radios"** [8]. For a STRUCTURALIST critic, this one specific contrast would be symptomatic of a whole series of differences between the lives of the villagers and the visitors (EP). Unlike Tom, they move as quickly and effortlessly as **"the wind."** Once more Friel emphasizes the whole spectrum of human ages, from the impending baby to the **"scrawny boys"** (who are standing at both a literal and metaphorical **"threshold"**) to the grown men and then to old Tom (RCE). The fact that the boys are **"scrawny"** could alternatively imply that they are simply skinny, or that they are malnourished, or that they are weak, or such phrasing could carry all three connotations at once (EP).

When Tom claims to have been **"asleep,"** perhaps he is motivated not only by a desire to protect his pride (MC) or reputation (AMO), but also because he does not want it to seem that his entire existence has involved paying attention to their activities (MC). He needn't worry, of course, since once again his neighbors pay him only the most superficial attention, even when they seem to need him most (KH). Because PSYCHOANALYTIC critics are interested in the complexity of the human mind's shaping and perceiving of reality and in how such complexity affects the ways texts are written and read, such critics might focus on the possible reasons that would induce Tom to lie when he claims to have been **"asleep."** For example, perhaps Tom is embarrassed by his own weakness and slowness as he stands before the strong, young, impatient fishermen, or perhaps he even wants them to recognize his lie and pity him for being so weak and old (DH2). In a deeper and symbolic sense Tom *has* been "asleep," but the need his community now shows for him helps awaken him to a new sense of usefulness and vitality (KB; LS). Another possible response is that Tom's behavior throughout this scene—his initial silence, his claim to have been asleep, his subsequent insistence that he be carried to the end of the pier before answering—makes him resemble an attention-hungry child. Ironically, he appears this way at precisely the moment when he is being sought out as a wise old man (MB).

[13] "The flares are coming regular," said Sweeney. "They need help bad, whatever it is."

They were all looking at him, waiting for him to speak. They wanted advice, and at the same time they wanted to shed their responsibility on to him, because be was old, and afterwards, if anything went wrong, they could say, "We only did what Bonner suggested." But they wanted advice first.

"Would a boat live in that northeast wind, Tom?" Mason asked.

Tom felt none of their anxiety; only importance that rose in him like hot blood and hurt his chest slightly and even made his dead hands tingle.

The fact that the flares **"are coming regular"** makes them resemble the contractions of imminent birth and thus heightens the suspense and anticipation (KH). The regularity of the flares is one of a number of details in the story (such as the waves and Tom's movements in and out of the house) that suggest a rhythmic, cyclical view of life (KB). Earlier the men had been described as being dressed in "yellow oilskins and

thigh boots" [12], but now the self-protection they seek is of an entirely
different kind (TR). Their willingness to **"shed their responsibility"**
onto Tom makes them seem even more callous (but perhaps also more
human) than their earlier indifference to him had made them seem, and
perhaps their callousness is another sign that they belong to a different
generation from his and thus represent (like the tourists) a fundamental
change in traditional Irish society (BB; NP). Such a possibility would
certainly interest a TRADITIONAL HISTORICAL critic. Meanwhile,
a PSYCHOANALYTIC critic might notice how the men of the village,
like Tom himself earlier [12], feel a need to protect their egos (JB)—in
their case by making Tom responsible for any potential failure. Whereas
animals **"shed"** automatically, humans must make a conscious choice to
do so, especially in this instance (NP). Paradoxically, their desire to escape
"responsibility" thus makes them seem all the more ethically responsible
for their desire to use Tom in this way (RCE). Whereas at first the men's
decision to turn to Tom for advice seemed a sign of their respect for
him, now their unspoken motive makes them actually seem somewhat
disrespectful (TB). An ARCHETYPAL critic might note how the men's
motives here combine both desire and fear—a desire to act and a fear of
being blamed if they act wrongly (AC). Earlier, when the men needed
his help, they had addressed him as "Tom" [11], but when they imagine
treating him in the future as a scapegoat (RM) he becomes merely **"Bonner"** (AMO). Now he is the center of their full attention (**"They were all
looking at him"**) whereas earlier they had largely ignored him, and later
they will largely do the same. Note the increasing moral complexity and
growing paradoxicality implied as this paragraph unfolds: first they are
said to want Tom's **"advice,"** a desire which makes them seem commend-
ably deferential and respectful; then they are said to want to **"shed their
responsibility onto him,"** an impulse that makes them seem somewhat
cold (but also flawed in a recognizably human way); then they are said
to be willing to scapegoat him in this fashion merely **"because he was
old,"** a motive that makes them seem almost heartless and cruel. In one
complexly unfolding sentence, Friel takes us fairly deeply into the heart
of darkness. Although these men are relatively young and vigorous when

contrasted with Tom, morally they now seem far weaker (RCE).

By making Mason ask whether a boat would "live" in such fierce weather, Friel not only uses personification effectively but perhaps also subtly implies Mason's understandable concern for his own life (RCE). At the same time, this usage may suggest that other lives may also be at stake—particularly the life of the baby and perhaps even the mother (PR). A THEMATIC critic might also note how the word "live" reinforces the story's larger concerns with life and death, while an ARCHETYPAL critic might argue that the word reflects the human habit of attributing life to non-living things (EP). Meanwhile, a FORMALIST might argue that the word "live" is more powerful in this context than "survive" would have been (TS2). When the men ponder the possibility of scapegoating the old man they think of him as "**Bonner,**" but when Mason needs the old man's help he addresses him familiarly as "**Tom**" (AMO). Earlier Tom had almost wished for physical pain, if only to confirm that he was still alive [6]; now he literally feels such confirming (if painful) vitality as his sense of being needed and useful returns (TB; MO). Ironically, the symptoms he experiences as he is rejuvenated resemble those of a heart attack (MH; AMO). The fact that his hands now "**tingle**" might suggest, to a NEW HISTORICIST, the revivifying influence of a feeling of renewed power (AC). As the baby on the island is waiting to be born, so is Tom now in a sense being reborn, and in both cases the sensation of birth is accompanied by pain (PW; MC).

[14] "Carry me to the end of the pier," he commanded.

"But Tom . . ." They wanted only advice: Go or Stay.

"Carry me to the end of the pier. Then I'll tell you what to do."

Four men carried him in his chair, shoulder high, across the gravel path and onto the pier. Somebody had thrown a waterproof cape around his head and shoulders so that only his thin white face peeped out occasionally when a gust of wind caught them. Waves broke on the back of the harbor wall and sent canopies of white spray cascading over them.

They stopped a few feet from the edge and lowered Tom to the ground. But they still held on to him in case the wind blew him into the water.

Tom's double command ("**Carry me to the end of the pier**") shows that he is now in charge (if only temporarily [RM; AMO]). His moment of power—however brief—would almost inevitably interest NEW HISTORICIST critics (AC). Tom's visit to the end of the pier, accompanied by the crowd of townspeople, is an ironic echo of the far more superficial visit earlier paid to the end of the pier by the crowd of tourists [4]. This echo would appeal to a FORMALIST critic since it contributes to the story's complex unity (CJ). On the one hand Tom's desire to view the condition of the sea for himself is eminently practical and logical, but clearly Tom is also taking advantage of this moment and is savoring his renewed importance to the community (MB). An ARCHETYPAL critic might argue that Tom's behavior here illustrates a basic human need and desire for attention and respect (MB; AC). The men seek "**only advice**": they want no more to do with Tom than is absolutely necessary (NP), but just as they seek to use him for their own purposes, he now uses them (RCE). The fact that he is carried "**in his chair, shoulder high**" makes him almost resemble a saint (TR) or a king (SB; AG; PS) and thus emphasizes the literally elevated status he now enjoys. He is treated almost as if he is sacred (EP; DS). The reference to the "**cape around [Tom's] head and shoulders**" perhaps reinforces the idea of royalty (while at the same time making him still seem like a protected child [MB]), and a FORMALIST might argue that even the word "**canopies**" has a regal connotation (PS). The fact that the cape is "waterproof" helps emphasize the theme of man vs. nature (DS), while the reference to Tom's "**thin white face**" emphasizes once more his frailty (PS). The juxtaposition of these images of strength and weakness would interest a DECONSTRUCTOR, since it would imply the instability not only of Tom's existence but of the story's meaning (PS). Tom's new sense of elevation—which is at once physical, psychological, and social—might be of particular interest to a LONGINIAN critic, who sees the desire for elevation as central to human nature (JA; MB; TS2). At the same time, however, the imagery also paradoxically seems funereal: it is as if the men are pall-bearers (NB) bearing a casket (JJ). This connotation is reinforced when the men are later described as having **"lowered Tom to the ground"** (JJ). In a sense, then, Tom's triumphant trip to the **"pier"** here ironically foreshadows the final journey that all persons must make (MH; EP). A DECONSTRUCTOR could argue that, even through the act of being raised up, Tom is still in a solitary position. As a kind of "sage" for the townspeople, Tom even now has no more true connections with them than when he was ignored (PS). Thus Friel variously manages to suggest, even at the moment of Tom's triumph, the final fate that inevitably (and probably soon) awaits him (LS).

The description of how **"[w]aves broke on the back of the harbor wall"** implies an intriguing and ironic parallel between Tom's present power and the power of the storm: in both cases that power is at its height but will soon diminish (LS). The image of Tom being borne aloft manages to capture quite nicely his present paradoxical status as someone who is simultaneously active and passive. In some respects he is as vital and strong now as he has been at any recent time in his life, but his frailty is also emphasized by the reference to his **"thin white face"** that **"peeped out occasionally"** from beneath the **"waterproof cape"** that an unnamed **"[s]omebody . . . had thrown . . . around his head and shoulders"** (RCE). A FORMALIST critic might note how Friel effectively contrasts Tom's **"thin white face"** with the **"canopies of white spray"** unleashed by the active, almost vital storm (AG). Meanwhile, an ARCHETYPAL critic, interested in humans' relations with nature, might notice that because the fishermen make their living from the sea, they show a very healthy respect for its power (JB).

[15] "Well, Tom? Would she make it?"

But Tom did not answer, although he had known what he was going to say from the moment they carried him outside the door and he saw the sky. Now he wanted to have them looking at him and waiting for him. He might never have the chance again. He needed to savor it.

"I say we try it," said Mason. "It's the least we can do is try it."

> **But the others awaited Tom's word, if only to postpone the attempt.**

The identity of the questioner here isn't specified: what is important is the question, not the person who speaks it. Once more the boat is personified (**"Would she make it?"**), as if to help emphasize that it is not only the boat but also the lives within it whose survival is at stake (RCE). At the same time, this phrase also reminds us that the lives of the expectant mother and her baby may also be at stake (PR). Early in the story Tom had been both an observer (of the harbor) and the superficially observed (an object of temporary curiosity to the tourists); now, however, he seeks to **"savor"** his status as the object of total attention (AMO). The word **"savor"** makes his response seem almost a physical sensation and his need seem almost a physical hunger (RCE). Tom seeks to enjoy this brief moment of role-reversal (KH), this brief moment of power (AC). It is not merely that he **"want[s]"** such attention: he positively **"need[s]"** it, partly because he knows it will be brief and impermanent: even at the moment when Tom is the center of attention, he realizes that this attention will not last. He now uses the men partly because he recognizes that they are merely using him and that he will cease to be important to them once his usefulness has been exploited. He is now using them as they are now using him [RM]. He is simultaneously the possessor of power and the subject of an almost pathetic need (DH2; EP2), and the word **"savor"** implies that his need is almost physical, not merely psychological. An ARCHETYPAL critic, who stresses the way literature responds to widely shared human impulses, might contend that nearly every reader has experienced in some way or another the kind of desire for recognition or regard that Tom displays here (DH2). Mason's impulse to **"try it"** can be read as brave and selfless but also, perhaps, as ill-considered or foolhardy. Similarly, Friel at first seems to imply that **"the others"** show deference and respect for **"Tom's word,"** but then he complicates our understanding of their intentions by suggesting that they merely (if understandably) wish **"to postpone the attempt"**: their apparent concern for Tom is thus shown to be rooted in a deeper self-concern. As so often is the case in this brief story, Friel will not settle for simplistic or uncomplicated explanations (RCE).

[16] **At last he spoke, looking across the waves that hid Innisholme from them.**

"Nobody goes nowhere yet," he said. "Not for two hours. You'll have nothing but a puff of wind then."

They were relieved. Their faces relaxed and they laughed and said: "Good old Tom," and "Takes the old ones," as if he had given them something. Then their dutiful solicitude for him returned and somebody said: "Better get him back in out of the wind," and they hoisted him up again and carried him back to his house.

Once they had him safely inside again they agreed that, since there were a couple of hours before they could set out, they might as well pass the time in O'Byrne's bar. So they thanked Tom again and told him he was a good one and there was not a man like him for telling the weather. Then they went off.

Friel puts his readers into the same position as the eager men; we, like they, must wait on Tom's word (RCE). The delay gives Tom's pronounce-ment almost the force of a proclamation (AC). The description of Tom **"looking across the waves that hid Innisholme"** recalls his similar (but also quite different) view at the very beginning of the story [3] and thus helps bring the work full circle. In the phrase **"Nobody goes nowhere yet,"** Friel conveys both Tom's idiomatic speech patterns and also his sense of authority and power (LS; AC). Ironically, Tom's prediction that the storm will soon be reduced to a mere **"puff of wind"** parallels the similar loss of power he himself will now experience (LS). The men are **"relieved"** not only because Tom has presumably given wise, experienced advice but also because he has justified their earlier desire "to postpone the attempt" [15]. In any case, they can also now blame him if the advice proves mistaken; in this sense Tom, although treated like a king, also becomes a kind of sacrificial scapegoat (DS). An ARCHETYPAL critic might argue that the reference to Tom as one of the **"old ones"** evokes the archetype of the Wise Old Man (JA). However, a DECONSTRUCTOR, interested in the ambiguities and contradictions embedded in language, might emphasize the tension implicit in the mens' comment, since "'**old ones**'" can be interpreted as showing both respect and condescension (BH). Indeed, a DECONSTRUCTOR might note how unstable the connotations of the word are during the course of the story: at first the term suggests weakness, then it is associated with wisdom, then it suggests weakness once more (EP). Imagine how different the effect would be if the man had said "'Takes the experienced ones.'" Instead, by emphasizing Tom's age, the man's intended compliment has the paradoxical effect of reminding Tom of his limitations (MB). Thus, even the compliments the men pay to Tom are somewhat ambiguous: by calling him "**Good old Tom**," they may imply that they affectionately regard him as "one of the boys"—one of themselves (MB). At the same time, their comments repeatedly remind us how "**old**" he actually is (TS2), while their renewed solicitude for him is "**dutiful**" rather than deeply heartfelt (MB). A FOR-MALIST critic, alert to the subtle links between different phrases in the story, might see a parallel between the "**dutiful solicitude**" Tom receives from the townspeople and the "**curious respect**" [4] he had earlier been shown by the tourists (DH).

Tom is now "**hoisted**" up almost as if he were a sack (AMO) and is quickly deposited back at his house and is then just as quickly left alone again: the men once more ignore him (AMO) as they head off to the "**bar**," a place of fellowship and community from which Tom is excluded (JJ). The men don't offer to take him with them or to bring back drinks for him (AMO), and even their act of "**thank[ing]**" him seems a bit routine, clichéd, and formulaic. The final sentence ("**Then they went off**") here is effectively abrupt and brief. Once more Tom is as isolated as he was at the beginning of the tale. He is valued for his usefulness ("**telling the weather**"—a phrase which reminds us of the very early comparison of Tom to a barometer figure [2]), and once he has been used he is abandoned (RCE). An ARCHETYPAL critic might argue that the "**wind**" in this story symbolizes the kind of power and energy (sometimes beneficent, sometimes threatening) that Tom himself no longer possesses. Ironically, he is personally most powerful when he is in the midst of the raging wind, but later he is carried back to his house of desiccation and death, from which the wind has been shut out (DH; RCE).

READER-RESPONSE critics might note that different readers might respond differently to the present passage. Thus some readers might be proud of Tom for utilizing his power over the men instead of just giving them his advice quickly and returning to his lonesome state. Other readers, however, might feel that Tom should have told the men what they wanted to hear and not have wasted any more of their time than necessary. Meanwhile, some readers also might see the men who seek Tom's advice about the storm as selfish. These readers might feel that the men should have been more attentive to Tom because he is an important part of their community and deserves better treatment. On the other hand, different readers might understand the men's need for quick help and believe that they treated Tom fairly in such a situation. The way persons feel about elderly people in general will probably greatly affect their response to Tom and his actions here (AC).

[17] **The kitchen was suddenly empty without them. Tom slid himself to one place and then another to escape the draft under the door, but it got at his feet and numbed them.**

With all the fuss, he thought, Mason's woman would probably forget to bring down his can of milk tonight. But there was no resentment in him; only an ebbing away of all feeling again until he was not quite sure whether he was awake or asleep.

Although a "**kitchen**" is the modern equivalent of a hearth and is thus in some ways the center of a home, Tom's kitchen is both literally and symbolically cold and "**empty**" (EP). Since he has no fire (or life-force) in his hearth, it is non-functional, and Tom's neighbors must ensure that he does not starve as a result of his neglected hearth. His minimal connection with the life-sustaining symbol of the hearth is reinforced by the fact that he begins his days by simply passing through his kitchen [3], and he cannot return to it at the end of the day without the assistance of his neighbors [5] (EP). Meanwhile, the present sudden departure of the townsfolk recalls the equally sudden departure of the tourists earlier [4]. It is as if the townspeople treat Tom only a little better than the visitors had done [TR]. Abandoned and isolated, he now seeks to "**escape the draft under the door**"—phrasing that effectively contrasts with the description of the caressing, reassuring breeze with which the story had opened [2]. Such phrasing also recalls his own recent prediction that the storm would soon be reduced to a "puff" [16] (RCE).

Whereas just moments earlier Tom had felt an "importance that rose in him like hot blood" [13], now the cold once more "**numb[s]**" his feet (NB) as he slips back into a kind of dormancy (JJ) that is not only physical but also emotional and psychological (MB). Just as the once-fierce wind has now been diminished to a minor "**draft**," so Tom himself has now lost his brief earlier power and importance. Ironically, this "**draft**" recalls the "**light breeze**" with which the story opened [1], but the echo only emphasizes the irony: the "**breeze**" had once revived Tom, whereas the "**draft**" is now a symbol and cause of his confinement (TS) as well as (perhaps) a symbol of his imminent demise (EP). Indeed, DECONSTRUCTORS might note the fluctuating instability of Tom's relations with nature: at times he is revived by those relations, but at other times they imply his impending death (PS). Tom now is consigned once more to a position of dependency (PD), and he is dependent not only on a female but on a female who by definition belongs to someone else ("**Mason's woman**"). A FEMINIST critic would of course be bothered by this phrase, which seems to make the anonymous "**woman**" a mere extension of her husband, almost a piece of his property (BH; CJ; WMJ; EP2). She is not even given the dignity of having her own name (CJ). A feminist might be annoyed by the suggestion that a small bit of excitement could cause this "**woman**" to forget her menial task (CJ; EP2). In this sense a feminist might note that women and old men are both treated as relatively powerless beings in this tale (BH). Tom, who was once himself a vigorous young man, now knows what it is like to be treated as if he were a woman—valued only to the extent that he is useful (RCE). At the same time, the woman is described in ways that make her seem almost motherly while making Tom seem almost a baby (MB; LP; PS), especially since she may (or may not) bring him merely a **"can of milk"** while the other men are off drinking beer or whiskey (JJ). A FEMINIST might note that even though Tom himself is weak and old, he can still condescend to a woman by assuming that she will **"probably forget"** her duty to serve him properly (BH). A STRUCTURALIST critic, interested in how binary opposites organize our experience, might also note this implied contrast between Tom's **"milk"** and the other men's liquor (DH).

Once more Tom is neglected (JJ). He experiences no positive feeling now, only the absence of a negative: he feels **"no resentment"** (RCE). His lack of **"resentment"** suggests the degree to which he has come to take such neglect for granted (AC). Or perhaps this lack of **"resentment"** implies that just as he is now physically motionless, so he is also spiritually at peace (MH). The description of his feeling **"ebbing away"** seems especially appropriate to the seaside setting of the tale: it is as if Tom feels like a piece of driftwood consigned to the beach (HE), and the very final words of the story closely echo those with which the tale began (PD). Everyone has used Tom and gotten what they needed out of him for the time being, and now he is of no more use. He is forgotten not only by the townspeople but also by himself (MB). The fact that Tom cannot be sure whether he is **"awake or asleep"** reminds us that at the very beginning of the tale [1] he wasn't even sure whether he was alive or dead (JJ; WQ). A THEMATIC critic would appreciate the way Friel carries this idea through from the start of the work to its end, while both a FORMALIST and an ARISTOTELIAN critic would appreciate how this echo brings the story full circle and contributes to its complex unity (JA; KB; BH; MO; EP2; LS). Meanwhile, a STRUCTURALIST critic might note the prominence Friel gives to these opposite possibilities (JB), whereas a DECONSTRUCTOR might notice how the story blurs and breaks down this apparent opposition (RCE).

An ARCHETYPAL critic, interested in humans' interactions with nature, would find the very title of the story significant, especially since it is echoed here at the end of the tale through the word **"ebbing."** An ebb tide is the tide going out, and, being a tide, it is something natural and regular and ineluctable. The image is thus highly appropriate to Tom's decline and impending death: his tide is ebbing, and perhaps the story implies that this same movement is an inevitable pattern of all human lives (DH). Ironically, because of the contrast with the excitement he has just experienced, Tom may now feel even more isolated than he did before the townspeople took their brief interest in him (PS). At the end of the story Tom has come back, full circle, to the monotonous life with which the tale began. Although he could have let both the literal and metaphorical "storms" reawaken him to an appreciation of life, it is possible to argue that he lacks both the imagination and the optimism to embrace this experience and appreciate it fully. Instead, he simply allows himself to sink right back into his original feelings of stagnation, uselessness, and helplessness (DS). A HORATIAN critic, partly interested in literature as a mode of instruction and as a means of appealing to diverse audiences, might argue that one lesson this story teaches is a lesson directed at the young—a lesson about how it feels to become old (DS).

Appendix 1:

"The Story of an Hour"

by Kate Chopin

Knowing that Mrs. Mallard was afflicted with a heart trouble, great care was taken to break to her as gently as possible the news of her husband's death.

It was her sister Josephine who told her, in broken sentences; veiled hints that revealed in half concealing. Her husband's friend Richards was there, too, near her. It was he who had been in the newspaper office when intelligence of the railroad disaster was received, with Brently Mallard's name leading the list of "killed." He had only taken the time to assure himself of its truth by a second telegram, and had hastened to forestall any less careful, less tender friend in bearing the sad message.

She did not hear the story as many women have heard the same, with a paralyzed inability to accept its significance. She wept at once, with sudden, wild abandonment, in her sister's arms. When the storm of grief had spent itself she went away to her room alone. She would have no one follow her.

There stood, facing the open window, a comfortable, roomy armchair. Into this she sank, pressed down by a physical exhaustion that haunted her body and seemed to reach into her soul.

She could see in the open square before her house the tops of trees that were all aquiver with the new spring life. The delicious breath of rain was in the air. In the street below a peddler was crying his wares. The notes of a distant song which some one was singing reached her faintly, and countless sparrows were twittering in the eaves.

There were patches of blue sky showing here and there through the clouds that had met and piled one above the other in the west facing her window.

She sat with her head thrown back upon the cushion of the chair, quite motionless, except when a sob came up into her throat and shook her, as a child who has cried itself to sleep continues to sob in its dreams.

She was young, with a fair, calm face, whose lines bespoke repression and even a certain strength. But now there was a dull stare in her eyes, whose gaze was fixed away off yonder on one of those patches of blue sky. It was not a glance of reflection, but rather indicated a suspension of intelligent thought.

There was something coming to her and she was waiting for it, fearfully. What was it? She did not know; it was too subtle and elusive to name. But she felt it, creeping out of the sky, reaching toward her through the sounds, the scents, the color that filled the air.

Now her bosom rose and fell tumultuously. She was beginning to recognize this thing that was approaching to possess her, and she was striving to beat it back with her will—as powerless as her two white slender hands would have been.

When she abandoned herself a little whispered word escaped her slightly parted lips. She said it over and over under her breath: "free, free, free!" The vacant stare and the look of terror that had followed it went from her eyes. They stayed keen and bright. Her pulses beat fast, and the coursing blood warmed and relaxed every inch of her body.

She did not stop to ask if it were or were not a monstrous joy that held her. A clear and exalted perception enabled her to dismiss the suggestion as trivial.

She knew that she would weep again when she saw the kind, tender hands folded in death; the face that had never looked save with love upon her, fixed and gray and dead. But she saw beyond that bitter moment a long procession of years to come that would belong to her absolutely. And she opened and spread her arms out to them in welcome.

There would be no one to live for her during those coming years; she would live for herself. There would be no powerful will bending hers in that blind persistence with which men and women believe they have a right to impose a private will upon a fellow creature. A kind intention or a cruel intention made the act seem no less a crime as she looked upon it in that brief moment of illumination.

And yet she had loved him—sometimes. Often she had not. What did it matter! What could love, the unsolved mystery, count for in face of this possession of self-assertion which she suddenly recognized as the strongest impulse of her being!

"Free! Body and soul free!" she kept whispering.

Josephine was kneeling before the closed door with her lips to the keyhole, imploring for admission. "Louise, open the door! I beg; open the door—you will make yourself ill. What are you doing, Louise? For heaven's sake open the door."

"Go away. I am not making myself ill." No; she was drinking in a very elixir of life through that open window.

Her fancy was running riot along those days ahead of her. Spring days, and summer days, and all sorts of days that would be her own. She breathed a quick prayer that life might be long. It was only yesterday she had thought with a shudder that life might be long.

She arose at length and opened the door to her sister's importunities. There was a feverish triumph in her eyes, and she carried herself unwittingly like a goddess of Victory. She clasped her sister's waist, and together they descended the stairs. Richards stood waiting for them at the bottom.

Some one was opening the front door with a latchkey. It was Brently Mallard who entered, a little travel-stained, composedly carrying his gripsack and umbrella. He had been far from the scene of accident, and did not even know there had been one. He stood amazed at Josephine's piercing cry; at Richards' quick motion to screen him from the view of his wife.

But Richards was too late.

When the doctors came they said she had died of heart disease—of joy that kills.

Appendix 2:

"Caline"

by Kate Chopin

The sun was just far enough in the west to send inviting shadows. In the center of a small field, and in the shade of a haystack which was there, a girl lay sleeping. She had slept long and soundly, when something awoke her as suddenly as if it had been a blow. She opened her eyes and stared a moment up in the cloudless sky. She yawned and stretched her long brown legs and arms, lazily. Then she arose, never minding the bits of straw that clung to her black hair, to her red bodice, and the blue cotonade skirt that did not reach her naked ankles.

The log cabin in which she dwelt with her parents was just outside the enclosure in which she had been sleeping. Beyond was a small clearing that did duty as a cotton field. All else was dense wood, except the long stretch that curved round the brow of the hill, and in which glittered the steel rails of the Texas and Pacific road.

When Caline emerged from the shadow she saw a long train of passenger coaches standing in view, where they must have stopped abruptly. It was that sudden stopping which had awakened her; for such a thing had not happened before within her recollection, and she looked stupid, at first, with astonishment. There seemed to be something wrong with the engine; and some of the passengers who dismounted went forward to investigate the trouble. Others came strolling along in the direction of the cabin, where Caline stood under an old gnarled mulberry tree, staring. Her father had halted his mule at the end of the cotton row, and stood staring also, leaning upon his plow.

There were ladies in the party. They walked awkwardly in their high-heeled boots over the rough, uneven ground, and held up their skirts mincingly. They twirled parasols over their shoulders, and laughed immoderately at the funny things which their masculine companions were saying.

They tried to talk to Caline, but could not understand the French patois with which she answered them.

One of the men—a pleasant-faced youngster—drew a sketch book from his pocket and began to make a picture of the girl. She stayed motionless, her hands behind her, and her wide eyes fixed earnestly upon him.

Before he had finished there was a summons from the train; and all went scampering hurriedly away. The engine screeched, it sent a few lazy puffs into the still air, and in another moment or two had vanished, bearing its human cargo with it.

Caline could not feel the same after that. She looked with new and strange interest upon the trains of cars that passed so swiftly back and forth across her vision, each day; and wondered whence these people came, and whither they were going.

Her mother and father could not tell her, except to say that they came from "loin là bas," and were going "Djieu sait é où."

One day she walked miles down the track to talk with the old flagman, who stayed down there by the big water tank. Yes, he knew. Those people came from the great cities in the north, and were going to the city in the south. He knew all about the city; it was a grand place. He had lived there once. His sister lived there now; and she would be glad enough to have so fine a girl as Caline to help her cook and scrub, and tend the babies. And he thought Caline might earn as much as five dollars a month, in the city.

So she went; in a new cotonade, and her Sunday shoes; with a sacredly guarded scrawl that the flagman sent to his sister.

The woman lived in a tiny, stuccoed house, with green blinds, and three wooden steps leading down to the banquette. There seemed to be hundreds like it along the street. Over the house tops loomed the tall masts of ships, and the hum of the French market could be heard on a still morning.

Caline was at first bewildered. She had to readjust all her preconceptions to fit the reality of it. The flagman's sister was a kind and gentle task-mistress. At the end of a week or two she wanted to know how the girl liked it all. Caline liked it very well, for it was pleasant, on Sunday afternoons, to stroll with the children under the great, solemn sugar sheds; or to sit upon the compressed cotton bales, watching the stately steamers, the graceful boats, and noisy little tugs that plied the waters of the Mississippi. And it filled her with agreeable excitement to go to the French market, where the handsome Gascon butchers were eager to present their compliments and little Sunday bouquets to the pretty Acadian girl; and to throw fistfuls of lagniappe into her basket.

When the woman asked her again after another week if she were still pleased, she was not so sure. And again when she questioned Caline the girl turned away, and went to sit behind the big, yellow cistern, to cry unobserved. For she knew now that it was not the great city and its crowds of people she had so eagerly sought; but the pleasant-faced boy, who had made her picture that day under the mulberry tree.

Appendix 3:

"La Belle Zoraïde"

by Kate Chopin

The summer night was hot and still; not a ripple of air swept over the *marais* [marsh]. Yonder, across Bayou St. John, lights twinkled here and there in the darkness, and in the dark sky above a few stars were blinking. A lugger that had come out of the lake was moving with slow, lazy motion down the bayou. A man in the boat was singing a song.

The notes of the song came faintly to the ears of old Manna-Loulou, herself as black as the night, who had gone out upon the gallery to open the shutters wide.

Something in the refrain reminded the woman of an old, half-forgotten Creole romance, and she began to sing it low to herself while she threw the shutters open:

> "Lisett' to kité la plaine.
> Ma perdi bunhair á moué;
> Ziés à moué semblé fontaine,
> Dépi no pa miré toué."

> [Lizette, {since} you have left the plain
> I have lost my happiness;
> My eyes are like a fountain,
> Since I cannot look at you.]

And then this old song, a lover's lament for the loss of his mistress, floating into her memory, brought with it the story she would tell to Madame, who lay in her sumptuous mahogany bed, waiting to be fanned and put to sleep to the sound of one of Manna-Loulou's stories. The old negress had already bathed her mistress's pretty white feet and kissed them lovingly, one, then the other. She had brushed her mistress's beautiful hair, that was as soft and shining as satin, and was the color of Madame's wedding-ring. Now, when she reëntered the room, she moved softly toward the bed, and seating herself there began gently to fan Madame Delisle.

Manna-Loulou was not always ready with her story, for Madame would hear none but those that were true. But tonight the story was all there in Manna-Loulou's head—the story of la belle Zoraïde—and she told it to her mistress in the soft Creole patois whose music and charm no English words can convey.

"La belle Zoraïde had eyes that were so dusky, so beautiful, that any man who gazed too long into their depths was sure to lose his head, and even his heart sometimes. Her soft, smooth skin was the color of *café-au-lait*. As for her elegant manners, her svelte and graceful figure, they were the envy of half the ladies who visited her mistress, Madame Delariviére.

"No wonder Zoraïde was as charming and as dainty as the finest lady of la rue Royale: from a toddling thing she had been brought up at her mistress's side; her fingers had never done rougher work than sewing a fine muslin seam; and she even had her own little black servant to wait upon her. Madame, who was her godmother as well as her mistress, would often say to her: —

"'Remember, Zoraïde, when you are ready to marry, it must be in a way to do honor to your bringing up. It will be at the Cathedral. Your wedding gown, your *corbeille* [hope chest], all will be of the best; I shall see to that myself. You know, M'sieur Ambroise is ready whenever you say the word, and his master is willing to do as much for him as I shall do for you. It is a union that will please me in every way.'

"Monsieur Ambroise was then the body servant of Doctor Langlé. La belle Zoraïde detested the little mulatto, with his shining whiskers like a white man's, and his small eyes, that were cruel and false as a snake's. She would cast down her own mischievous eyes, and say:

"'Ah, nénaine [Godmother], I am so happy, so contented here at your side just as I am. I don't want to marry now; next year, perhaps, or the next.' And Madame would smile indulgently and remind Zoraïde that a woman's charms are not everlasting.

"But the truth of the matter was, Zoraïde had seen la beau Mézor dance the Bamboula in Congo Square. That was a sight to hold one rooted to the ground. Mézor was as straight as a cypress tree and as proud looking as a king. His body, bare to the waist, was like a column of ebony and it glistened like oil.

"Poor Zoraïde's heart grew sick in her bosom with love for le beau Mézor from the moment that she saw the fierce gleam of his eye, lighted by the inspiring strains of the Bamboula, and beheld the stately movements of his splendid body swaying and quivering through the figures of the dance.

"But when she knew him later, and he came near to her to speak with her, all the fierceness was gone out of his eyes, and she saw only kindness in them and heard only gentleness in his voice, for love had taken possession of him also, and Zoraïde was more distracted than ever. When Mézor was not dancing Bamboula in Congo Square, he was hoeing sugar cane, barefooted and half-naked, in his master's field outside of the city. Doctor Langle was his master as well as M'sieur Ambroise's.

"One day, when Zoraïde kneeled before her mistress, drawing on Madame's silken stockings, that were of the finest, she said:

"'Nénaine, you have spoken to me often of marrying. Now, at last, I have chosen a husband, but it is not M'sieur Ambroise, it is le beau Mézor that I want and no other.' And Zoraïde hid her face in her hands when she said that, for she guessed, rightly enough, that her mistress would be very angry.

"And indeed, Madame Delarivíére was at first speechless with rage. When she finally spoke it was only to gasp out, exasperated:

"'That Negro! that Negro! Bon Dieu Seigneur [Good Lord God], but this is too much!'

"'Am I white, nénaine?' pleaded Zoraïde.

"'You white! *Malheureuse!* [Miserable one!] You deserve to have the lash laid upon you like any other slave; you have proven yourself no better than the worst.'

"'I am not white,' persisted Zoraïde, respectfully and gently. 'Doctor Langle gives me his slave to marry, but he would not give me his son. Then, since I am not white, let me have from out of my own race the one whom my heart has chosen.'

"However, you may well believe that Madame would not hear to that. Zoraïde was forbidden to speak to Mézor, and Mézor was cautioned against seeing Zoraïde again. But you know how the Negroes are, Ma'zélle Titite," added Manna-Loulou, smiling a little sadly. "There is no mistress, no master, no king nor priest who can hinder them from loving when they will. And these two found ways and means.

"When months had passed by, Zoraïde, who had grown unlike herself—sober and preoccupied—said again to her mistress: —

"'Nénaine, you would not let me have Mézor for my husband; but I have disobeyed you, I have sinned. Kill me if you wish, Nénaine; forgive me if you will; but when I heard le beau Mézor say to me, "Zoraïde, mo l'aime toi [I love you]," I could have died, but I could not have helped loving him.'

"This time Madame Delariviére was so actually pained, so wounded at hearing Zoraïde's confession, that there was no place left in her heart for anger. She could only utter confused reproaches. But she was a woman of action rather than of words, and she acted promptly. Her first step was to induce Doctor Langle to sell Mézor. Doctor Langle, who was a widower, had long wanted to marry Madame Delariviére, and he would willingly have walked on all fours at noon through the Place d'Armes if she wanted him to. Naturally he lost no time in disposing of le beau Mézor, who was sold away into Georgia, or the Carolinas, or one of those distant countries far away, where he could no longer hear his Creole tongue spoken, nor dance Calinda, nor hold la belle Zoraïde in his arms.

"The poor thing was heartbroken when Mézor was sent away from her, but she took comfort and hope in the thought of her baby that she would soon be able to clasp to her breast.

"La belle Zoraïde's sorrows had now begun in earnest. Not only sorrows but sufferings, and with the anguish of maternity came the shadow of death. But there is no agony that a mother will not forget when she holds her first-born to her heart, and presses her lips upon the baby flesh that is her own, yet far more precious than her own.

"So, instinctively, when Zoraïde came out of the awful shadow she gazed questioningly about her and felt with her trembling hands upon either side of her. 'Oú li, mo piti a moin? where is my little one?' she asked imploringly. Madame who was there and the nurse who was there both told her in turn, 'To piti á toi, li mouri' ('Your little one is dead'), which was a wicked falsehood that must have caused the angels in heaven to weep. For the baby was living and well and strong. It had at once been removed from its mother's side, to be sent away to Madame's plantation, far up the coast. Zoraïde could only moan in reply, 'Li mouri, li mouri,' and she turned her face to the wall.

"Madame had hoped, in thus depriving Zoraïde of her child, to have her young waiting-maid again at her side free, happy, and beautiful as of old. But there was a more powerful will than Madame's at work—the will of the good God, who had already designed that Zoraïde should grieve with a sorrow that was never more to be lifted in this world. La belle Zoraïde was no more. In her stead was a sad-eyed woman who mourned night and day for her baby. 'Li mouri, li mouri,' she would sigh over and over again to those about her, and to herself when others grew weary of her complaint.

"Yet, in spite of all, M'sieur Ambroise was still in the notion to marry her. A sad wife or a merry one was all the same to him so long as that wife was Zoraïde. And she seemed to consent, or rather to submit, to the approaching marriage as though nothing mattered any longer in this world.

"One day, a black servant entered a little noisily the room in which Zoraïde sat sewing. With a look of strange and vacuous happiness upon her face, Zoraïde arose hastily. 'Hush, hush,' she whispered, lifting a warning finger, 'my little one is asleep; you must not awaken her.'

"Upon the bed was a senseless bundle of rags shaped like an infant in swaddling clothes. Over this dummy the woman had drawn the mosquito bar, and she was sitting contentedly beside it. In short, from that day Zoraïde was demented. Night nor day did she lose sight of the doll that lay in her bed or in her arms.

"And now was Madame stung with sorrow and remorse at seeing this terrible affliction that had befallen her dear Zoraïde. Consulting with Doctor Langle, they decided to bring back to the mother the real baby of flesh and blood that was now toddling about, and kicking its heels in the dust yonder upon the plantation.

"It was Madame herself who led the pretty, tiny little 'griffe' girl to her mother. Zoraïde was sitting on a stone bench in the courtyard, listening to the soft splashing of the fountain, and watching the fitful shadows of the palm leaves upon the broad, white flagging.

"'Here,' said Madame, approaching, 'here, my poor dear Zoraïde, is your own little child. Keep her; she is yours. No one will ever take her from you again.'

"Zoraïde looked with sullen suspicion upon her mistress and the child before her. Reaching out a hand she thrust the little one mistrustfully away from her. With the other hand she clasped the rag bundle fiercely to her breast; for she suspected a plot to deprive her of it.

"Nor could she ever be induced to let her own child approach her; and finally the little one was sent back to the plantation, where she was never to know the love of mother or father.

"And now this is the end of Zoraïde's story. She was never known again as la belle Zoraïde, but ever after as Zoraïde la folle, whom no one ever wanted to marry—not even M'sieur Ambroise. She lived to be an old woman, whom some people pitied and others laughed at—always clasping at her bundle of rags—her 'piti.'

"Are you asleep, Ma'zélle Titite?"

"No, I am not asleep; I was thinking. Ah, the poor little one, Man Loulou, the poor little one! better had she died!"

But this is the way Madame Delisle and Manna-Loulou really talked to each other:

"Vou pré droumi, Ma'zélle Titite?"

"Non, pa pré droumi; mo yapré zongler. Ah, la pauv' piti, Man Loulou. La pauv' piti! Mieux li mouri!"

Appendix 4:

"Guests of the Nation"

by Frank O'Connor

1

At dusk the big Englishman, Belcher, would shift his long legs out of the ashes and say "Well, chums, what about it?" and Noble or me would say "All right, chum" (for we had picked up some of their curious expressions), and the little Englishman, Hawkins, would light the lamp and bring out the cards. Sometimes Jeremiah Donovan would come up and supervise the game and get excited over Hawkins's cards, which he always played badly, and shout at him as if he was one of our own, "Ah, you divil, you, why didn't you play the tray?"

But ordinarily Jeremiah was a sober and contented poor devil like the big Englishman, Belcher, and was looked up to only because he was a fair hand at documents, though he was slow enough even with them. He wore a small cloth hat and big gaiters over his long pants, and you seldom saw him with his hands out of his pockets. He reddened when you talked to him, tilting from toe to heel and back, and looking down all the time at his big farmer's feet. Noble and me used to make fun of his broad accent, because we were from the town.

I couldn't at the time see the point of me and Noble guarding Belcher and Hawkins at all, for it was my belief that you could have planted that pair down anywhere from this to Claregalway and they'd have taken root there like a native weed. I never in my short experience seen two men to take to the country as they did.

They were handed on to us by the Second Battalion when the search for them became too hot, and Noble and myself, being young, took over with a natural feeling of responsibility, but Hawkins made us look like fools when he showed that he knew the country better than we did.

"You're the bloke they calls Bonaparte," he says to me. "Mary Brigid O'Connell told me to ask you what you done with the pair of her brother's socks you borrowed."

For it seemed, as they explained it, that the Second used to have little evenings, and some of the girls of the neighborhood turned in, and, seeing they were such decent chaps, our fellows couldn't leave the two Englishmen out of them. Hawkins learned to dance "The Walls of Limerick," "The Siege of Ennis," and "The Waves of Tory" as well as any of them, though, naturally, we couldn't return the compliment, because our lads at that time did not dance foreign dances on principle.

So whatever privileges Belcher and Hawkins had with the Second they just naturally took with us, and after the first day or two we gave up all pretense of keeping a close eye on them. Not that they could have got far, for they had accents you could cut with a knife and wore khaki tunics and overcoats with civilian pants and boots. But it's my belief that they never had any idea of escaping and were quite content to be where they were.

It was a treat to see how Belcher got off with the old woman of the house where we were staying. She was a great warrant to scold, and cranky even with us, but before ever she had a chance of giving our guests, as I may call them, a lick of her tongue, Belcher had made her his friend for life. She was breaking sticks, and Belcher, who hadn't been more than ten minutes in the house, jumped up from his seat and went over to her.

"Allow me, madam," he says, smiling his queer little smile, "please allow me"; and he takes the bloody hatchet. She was struck too paralytic to speak, and after that, Belcher would be at her heels, carrying a bucket, a basket, or a load of turf, as the case might be. As Noble said, he got into looking before she leapt, and hot water, or any little thing she wanted, Belcher would have it ready for her. For such a huge man (and though I am five foot ten myself I had to look up at him) he had an uncommon shortness—or should I say lack?—of speech. It took us some time to get used to him, walking in and out, like a ghost, without a word. Especially because Hawkins talked enough for a platoon, it was strange to hear big Belcher with his toes in the ashes come out with a solitary "Excuse me, chum," or "That's right, chum." His one and only passion was cards, and I will say for him that he was a good cardplayer. He could have fleeced myself and Noble, but whatever we lost to him Hawkins lost to us, and Hawkins played with the money Belcher gave him.

Hawkins lost to us because he had too much old gab, and we probably lost to Belcher for the same reason. Hawkins and Noble would spit at one another about religion into the early hours of the morning, and Hawkins worried the soul out of Noble, whose brother was a priest, with a string of questions that would puzzle a cardinal. To make it worse, even in treating of holy subjects, Hawkins had a deplorable tongue. I never in all my career met a man who could mix such a variety of cursing and bad language into an argument. He was a terrible man, and a fright to argue. He never did a stroke of work, and when he had no one else to talk to, he got stuck in the old woman.

He met his match in her, for one day when he tried to get her to complain profanely of the drought, she gave him a great come-down by blaming it entirely on Jupiter Pluvius (a deity neither Hawkins nor I had ever heard of, though Noble said that among the pagans it was believed that he had something to do with the rain). Another day he was swearing at the capitalists for starting the German war when the old lady laid down her iron, puckered up her little crab's mouth, and said: "Mr. Hawkins, you can say what you like about the war, and think you'll deceive me because I'm only a simple poor countrywoman, but I know what started the war. It was the Italian Count that stole the heathen divinity out of the temple in Japan. Believe me, Mr. Hawkins, nothing but sorrow and want can follow the people that disturb the hidden powers."

A queer old girl, all right.

2

We had our tea one evening, and Hawkins lit the lamp and we all sat into cards. Jeremiah Donovan came in too, and sat down and watched us for a while, and it suddenly struck me that he had no great love for the two Englishmen. It came as a great surprise to me, because I hadn't noticed anything about him before.

Late in the evening a really terrible argument blew up between Hawkins and Noble, about capitalists and priests and love of your country.

"The capitalists," says Hawkins with an angry gulp, "pays the priests to tell you about the next world so as you won't notice what the bastards are up to in this."

"Nonsense, man!" says Noble, losing his temper. "Before ever a capitalist was thought of, people believed in the next world."

Hawkins stood up as though he was preaching a sermon.

"Oh, they did, did they?" he says with a sneer. "They believed all the things you believe, isn't that what you mean? And you believe that God created Adam, and Adam created Shem, and Shem created Jehoshaphat. You believe all that silly old fairytale about Eve and Eden and the apple. Well, listen to me, chum. If you're entitled to hold a silly belief like that, I'm entitled to hold my silly belief—which is that the first thing your God created was a bleeding capitalist, with morality and Rolls-Royce complete. Am I right, chum?" he says to Belcher.

"You're right, chum," says Belcher with his amused smile, and got up from the table to stretch his long legs into the fire and stroke his moustache. So, seeing that Jeremiah Donovan was going, and that there was no knowing when the argument about religion would be over, I went out with him. We strolled down to the village together, and then he stopped and started blushing and mumbling and saying I ought to be behind, keeping guard on the prisoners. I didn't like the tone he took with me, and anyway I was bored with life in the cottage, so I replied by asking him what the hell we wanted guarding them at all for. I told him I'd talked it over with Noble, and that we'd both rather be out with a fighting column.

"What use are those fellows to us?" says I.

He looked at me in surprise and said: "I thought you knew we were keeping them as hostages."

"Hostages?" I said.

"The enemy have prisoners belonging to us," he says, "and now they're talking of shooting them. If they shoot our prisoners, we'll shoot theirs."

"Shoot them?" I said.

"What else did you think we were keeping them for?" he says.

"Wasn't it very unforeseen of you not to warn Noble and myself of that in the beginning?" I said.

"How was it?" says he. "You might have known it."

"We couldn't know it, Jeremiah Donovan," says I. "How could we when they were on our hands so long?"

"The enemy have our prisoners as long and longer," says he.

"That's not the same thing at all," says I.

"What difference is there?" says he.

I couldn't tell him, because I knew he wouldn't understand. If it was only an old dog that was going to the vet's, you'd try and not get too fond of him, but Jeremiah Donovan wasn't a man that would ever be in danger of that.

"And when is this thing going to be decided?" says I.

"We might hear tonight," he says. "Or tomorrow or the next day at latest. So if it's only hanging round here that's a trouble to you, you'll be free soon enough."

It wasn't the hanging round that was a trouble to me at all by this time. I had worse things to worry about. When I got back to the cottage the argument was still on. Hawkins was holding forth in his best style, maintaining that there was no next world, and Noble was maintaining that there was; but I could see that Hawkins had had the best of it.

"Do you know what, chum?" he was saying with a saucy smile. "I think you're just as big a bleeding unbeliever as I am. You say you believe in the next world, and you know just as much about the next world as I do, which is sweet damn-all. What's heaven? You don't know. Where's heaven? You don't know. You know sweet damn-all! I ask you again, do they wear wings?"

"Very well, then," says Noble, "they do. Is that enough for you? They do wear wings."

"Where do they get them, then? Who makes them? Have they a factory for wings? Have they a sort of store where you hands in your chit and takes your bleeding wings?"

"You're an impossible man to argue with," says Noble. "Now, listen to me—" And they were off again.

It was long after midnight when we locked up and went to bed. As I blew out the candle I told Noble what Jeremiah Donovan was after telling me. Noble took it very quietly. When we'd been in bed about an hour he asked me did I think we ought to tell the Englishmen. I didn't think we should, because it was more than likely that the English wouldn't shoot our men, and even if they did, the brigade officers, who were always up and down with the Second Battalion and knew the Englishmen well, wouldn't be likely to want them plugged. "I think so too," says Noble. "It would be great cruelty to put the wind up them now."

"It was very unforeseen of Jeremiah Donovan anyhow," says I.

It was next morning that we found it so hard to face Belcher and Hawkins. We went about the house all day scarcely saying a word. Belcher didn't seem to notice; he was stretched into the ashes as usual, with his usual look of waiting in quietness for something unforeseen to happen, but Hawkins noticed and put it down to Noble's being beaten in the argument of the night before.

"Why can't you take a discussion in the proper spirit?" he says severely. "You and your Adam and Eve! I'm a Communist, that's what I am. Communist or anarchist, it all comes to much the same thing." And for hours he went round the house, muttering when the fit took him. "Adam and Eve! Adam and Eve! Nothing better to do with their time than picking bleeding apples!"

3

I don't know how we got through that day, but I was very glad when it was over, the tea things were cleared away, and Belcher said in his peaceful way: "Well, chums, what about it?" We sat round the table and Hawkins took out the cards, and just then I heard Jeremiah Donovan's footsteps on the path and a dark presentiment crossed my mind. I rose from the table and caught him before he reached the door.

"What do you want?" I asked.

"I want those two soldier friends of yours," he says, getting red.

"Is that the way, Jeremiah Donovan?" I asked.

"That's the way. There were four of our lads shot this morning, one of them a boy of sixteen."

"That's bad," I said.

At that moment Noble followed me out, and the three of us walked down the path together, talking in whispers. Feeney, the local intelligence officer, was standing by the gate.

"What are you going to do about it?" I asked Jeremiah Donovan.

"I want you and Noble to get them out; tell them they're being shifted again; that'll be the quietest way."

"Leave me out of that," says Noble under his breath.

Jeremiah Donovan looks at him hard.

"All right," he says. "You and Feeney get a few tools from the shed and dig a hole by the far end of the bog. Bonaparte and myself will be after you. Don't let anyone see you with the tools. I wouldn't like it to go beyond ourselves."

We saw Feeney and Noble go round to the shed and went in ourselves. I left Jeremiah Donovan to do the explanations. He told them that he had orders to send them back to the Second Battalion. Hawkins let out a mouthful of curses, and you could see that though Belcher didn't say anything, he was a bit upset too. The old woman was for having them stay in spite of us, and she didn't stop advising them until Jeremiah Donovan lost his temper and turned on her. He had a nasty temper, I noticed. It was pitch-dark in the cottage by this time, but no one thought of lighting the lamp, and in the darkness the two Englishmen fetched their topcoats and said good-bye to the old woman.

"Just as a man makes a home of a bleeding place, some bastard at headquarters thinks you're too cushy and shunts you off," says Hawkins, shaking her hand.

"A thousand thanks, madam," says Belcher. "A thousand thanks for everything"—as though he'd made it up.

We went round to the back of the house and down towards the bog. It was only then that Jeremiah Donovan told them. He was shaking with excitement.

"There were four of our fellows shot in Cork this morning and now you're to be shot as a reprisal."

"What are you talking about?" snaps Hawkins. "It's bad enough being mucked about as we are without having to put up with your funny jokes."

"It isn't a joke," says Donovan. "I'm sorry, Hawkins, but it's true," and begins on the usual rigmarole about duty and how unpleasant it is.

I never noticed that people who talk a lot about duty find it much of a trouble to them.

"Oh, cut it out!" says Hawkins.

"Ask Bonaparte," says Donovan, seeing that Hawkins isn't taking him seriously. "Isn't it true, Bonaparte?"

"It is," I say, and Hawkins stops.

"Ah, for Christ's sake, chum."

"I mean it, chum," I say.

"You don't sound as if you meant it."

"If he doesn't mean it, I do," says Donovan, working himself up.

"What have you against me, Jeremiah Donovan?"

"I never said I had anything against you. But why did your people take out four of our prisoners and shoot them in cold blood?"

He took Hawkins by the arm and dragged him on, but it was impossible to make him understand that we were in earnest. I had the Smith and Wesson in my pocket and I kept fingering it and wondering what I'd do if they put up a fight for it or ran, and wishing to God they'd do one or the other. I knew if they did run for it, that I'd never fire on them. Hawkins wanted to know was Noble in it, and when we said yes, he asked why Noble wanted to plug him. Why did any of us want to plug him? What had he done to us? Weren't we all chums? Didn't we understand him and didn't he understand us? Did we imagine for an instant that he'd shoot us for all the so-and-so officers in the so-and-so British Army?

By this time we'd reached the bog, and I was so sick I couldn't even answer him. We walked along the edge of it in the darkness, and every now and then Hawkins would call a halt and begin all over again, as if he was wound up, about our being chums, and I knew that nothing but the sight of the grave would convince him that we had to do it. And all the time I was hoping that something would happen; that they'd run for it or that Noble would take over the responsibility from me. I had the feeling that it was worse on Noble than on me.

4

At last we saw the lantern in the distance and made towards it. Noble was carrying it, and Feeney was standing somewhere in the darkness behind him, and the picture of them so still and silent in the bogland brought it home to me that we were in earnest, and banished the last bit of hope I had.

Belcher, on recognizing Noble, said: "Hallo, chum," in his quiet way, but Hawkins flew at him at once, and the argument began all over again, only this time Noble had nothing to say for himself and stood with his head down, holding the lantern between his legs.

It was Jeremiah Donovan who did the answering. For the twentieth time, as though it was haunting his mind, Hawkins asked if anybody thought he'd shoot Noble.

"Yes, you would," says Jeremiah Donovan.

"No, I wouldn't, damn you!"

"You would, because you'd know you'd be shot for not doing it."

"I wouldn't, not if I was to be shot twenty times over. I wouldn't shoot a pal. And Belcher wouldn't—isn't that right, Belcher?"

"That's right, chum," Belcher said, but more by way of answering the question than of joining in the argument. Belcher sounded as though whatever unforeseen thing he'd always been waiting for had come at last.

"Anyway, who says Noble would be shot if I wasn't? What do you think I'd do if I was in his place, out in the middle of a blasted bog?"

"What would you do?" asks Donovan.

"I'd go with him wherever he was going, of course. Share my last bob with him and stick by him through thick and thin. No one can ever say of me that I let down a pal."

"We had enough of this," says Jeremiah Donovan, cocking his revolver. "Is there any message you want to send?"

"No, there isn't."

"Do you want to say your prayers?"

Hawkins came out with a cold-blooded remark that even shocked me and turned on Noble again.

"Listen to me, Noble," he says. "You and me are chums. You can't come over to my side, so I'll come over to your side. That show you I mean what I say? Give me a rifle and I'll go along with you and the other lads."

Nobody answered him. We knew that was no way out.

"Hear what I'm saying?" he says. "I'm through with it. I'm a deserter or anything else you like. I don't believe in your stuff, but it's no worse than mine. That satisfy you?"

Noble raised his head, but Donovan began to speak and he lowered it again without replying.

"For the last time, have you any messages to send?" says Donovan in a cold, excited sort of voice.

"Shut up, Donovan! You don't understand me, but these lads do. They're not the sort to make a pal and kill a pal. They're not the tools of any capitalist."

I alone of the crowd saw Donovan raise his Webley to the back of Hawkins's neck, and as he did so I shut my eyes and tried to pray. Hawkins had begun to say something else when Donovan fired, and as I opened my eyes at the bang, I saw Hawkins stagger at the knees and lie out flat at Noble's feet, slowly and as quiet as a kid falling asleep, with the lantern-light on his lean legs and bright farmer's boots. We all stood very still, watching him settle out in the last agony.

Then Belcher took out a handkerchief and began to tie it about his own eyes (in our excitement we'd forgotten to do the same for Hawkins), and, seeing it wasn't big enough, turned and asked for the loan of mine. I gave it to him and he knotted the two together and pointed with his foot at Hawkins.

"He's not quite dead," he says. "Better give him another."

Sure enough, Hawkins's left knee is beginning to rise. I bend down and put my gun to his head; then, recollecting myself, I get up again. Belcher understands what's in my mind.

"Give him his first," he says. "I don't mind. Poor bastard, we don't know what's happening to him now."

I knelt and fired. By this time I didn't seem to know what I was doing. Belcher, who was fumbling a bit awkwardly with the handkerchiefs, came out with a laugh as he heard the shot. It was the first time I heard him laugh and it sent a shudder down my back; it sounded so unnatural.

"Poor bugger!" he said quietly. "And last night he was so curious about it all. It's very queer, chums, I always think. Now he knows as much about it as they'll ever let him know, and last night he was all in the dark."

Donovan helped him to tie the handkerchiefs about his eyes. "Thanks, chum," he said. Donovan asked if there were any messages he wanted sent.

"No, chum," he says. "Not for me. If any of you would like to write to Hawkins's mother, you'll find a letter from her in his pocket. He and his mother were great chums. But my missus left me eight years ago. Went away with another fellow and took the kid with her. I like the feeling of a home, as you may have noticed, but I couldn't start again after that."

It was an extraordinary thing, but in those few minutes Belcher said more than in all the weeks before. It was just as if the sound of the shot had started a flood of talk in him and he could go on the whole night like that, quite happily, talking about himself. We stood round like fools now that he couldn't see us any longer. Donovan looked at Noble, and Noble shook his head. Then Donovan raised his Webley, and at that moment Belcher gives his queer laugh again. He may have thought we were talking about him, or perhaps he noticed the same thing I'd noticed and couldn't understand it.

"Excuse me, chums," he says. "I feel I'm talking the hell of a lot, and so silly, about my being so handy about a house and things like that. But this thing came on me suddenly. You'll forgive me, I'm sure."

"You don't want to say a prayer?" asked Donovan.

"No, chum," he says. "I don't think it would help. I'm ready, and you boys want to get it over."

"You understand that we're only doing our duty?" says Donovan.

Belcher's head was raised like a blind man's, so that you could only see his chin and the tip of his nose in the lantern-light.

"I never could make out what duty was myself," he said. "I think you're all good lads, if that's what you mean. I'm not complaining."

Noble, just as if he couldn't bear any more of it, raised his fist at Donovan, and in a flash Donovan raised his gun and fired. The big man went over like a sack of meal, and this time there was no need of a second shot.

I don't remember much about the burying, but that it was worse than all the rest because we had to carry them to the grave. It was all mad lonely with nothing but a patch of lantern-light between ourselves and the dark, and birds hooting and screeching all round, disturbed by the guns. Noble went through Hawkins's belongings to find the letter from his mother, and then joined his hands together. He did the same with Belcher. Then, when we'd filled in the grave, we separated from Jeremiah Donovan and Feeney and took our tools back to the shed. All the way we didn't speak a word. The kitchen was dark and cold as we'd left it, and the old woman was sitting over the hearth, saying her beads. We walked past her into the room, and Noble struck a match to light the lamp. She rose quietly and came to the doorway with all her cantankerousness gone.

"What did ye do with them?" she asked in a whisper, and Noble started so that the match went out in his hand.

"What's that?" he asked without turning round.

"I heard ye," she said.

"What did you hear?" asked Noble.

"I heard ye. Do ye think I didn't hear ye, putting the spade back in the houseen?"

Noble struck another match and this time the lamp lit for him.

"Was that what ye did to them?" she asked.

Then, by God, in the very doorway, she fell on her knees and began praying, and after looking at her for a minute or two Noble did the same by the fireplace. I pushed my way out past her and left them at it. I stood at the door, watching the stars and listening to the shrieking of the birds dying out over the bogs. It is so strange what you feel at times like that you can't describe it. Noble says he saw everything ten times the size, as though there were nothing in the whole world but that little patch of bog with the two Englishmen stiffening into it, but with me it was as if the patch of bog where the Englishmen were was a million miles away, and even Noble and the old woman, mumbling behind me, and the birds and the bloody stars were all far away, and I was somehow very small and very lost and lonely like a child astray in the snow. And anything that happened to me afterwards, I never felt the same about again.

Appendix 5:

"The Bridal Night"

by Frank O'Connor

It was sunset, and the two great humps of rock made a twilight in the cove where the boats were lying high up the strand. There was one light only in a little whitewashed cottage. Around the headland came a boat and the heavy dipping of its oars was like a heron's flight. The old woman was sitting on the low stone wall outside her cottage.

"'Tis a lonesome place," said I.

"'Tis so," she agreed, "a lonesome place, but any place is lonesome without one you'd care for."

"Your own flock are gone from you, I suppose?" I asked.

"I never had but the one," she replied, "the one son only," and I knew because she did not add a prayer for his soul that he was still alive.

"Is it in America he is?" I asked. (It is to America all the boys of the locality go when they leave home.)

"No, then," she replied simply. "It is in the asylum in Cork he is on me these twelve years."

I had no fear of trespassing on her emotions. These lonesome people in the wild places, it is their nature to speak; they must cry out their sorrows like the wild birds.

"God help us!" I said. "Far enough!"

"Far enough," she sighed. "Too far for an old woman. There was a nice priest here one time brought me up in his car to see him. All the ways to this wild place he brought it, and he drove me into the city. It is a place I was never used to, but it eased my mind to see poor Denis well-cared-for and well-liked. It was a trouble to me before that, not knowing would they see what a good boy he was before his madness came on him. He knew me; he saluted me, but he said nothing until the superintendent came to tell me the tea was ready for me. Then poor Denis raised his head and says: 'Leave ye not forget the toast. She was ever a great one for her bit of toast.' It seemed to give him ease and he cried after. A good boy he was and is. It was like him after seven long years to think of his old mother and her little bit of toast."

"God help us," I said for her voice was like the birds', hurrying high, immensely high, in the colored light, out to sea to the last islands where their nests were.

"Blessed be His holy will," the old woman added, "there is no turning aside what is in store. It was a teacher that was here at the time. Miss Regan her name was. She was a fine big jolly girl from the town. Her father had a shop there. They said she had three hundred pounds to her own cheek the day she set foot in the school, and—'tis hard to believe but 'tis what they all said: I will not belie her—'twasn't banished she was at all, but she came here of her own choice, for the great liking she had for the sea and the mountains. Now, that is the story, and with my own eyes I saw her, day in day out, coming down the little pathway you came yourself from the road and sitting beyond there in a hollow you can hardly see, out of the wind. The neighbors could make nothing of it, and she being a stranger, and with only the book Irish, they left her alone. It never seemed to take a peg out of her, only sitting in that hole in the rocks, as happy as the day is long, reading her little book or writing her letters. Of an odd time she might bring one of the little scholars along with her to be picking posies.

"That was where my Denis saw her. He'd go up to her of an evening and sit on the grass beside her, and off and on he might take her out in the boat with him. And she'd say with that big laugh of hers: 'Denis is my beau.' Those now were her words and she meant no more harm by it than the child unborn, and I knew it and Denis knew it, and it was a little joke we had, the three of us. It was the same way she used to joke about her little hollow. 'Mrs. Sullivan,' she'd say, 'leave no one near it. It is my nest and my cell and my little prayer-house, and maybe I would be like the birds and catch the smell of the stranger and then fly away from ye all.' It did me good to hear her laugh, and whenever I saw Denis moping or idle I would say it to him myself: 'Denis, why wouldn't you go out and pay your attentions to Miss Regan and all saying you are her intended?' It was only a joke. I would say the same thing to her face, for Denis was such a quiet boy, no way rough or accustomed to the girls at all—and how would he in this lonesome place?

"I will not belie her; it was she saw first that poor Denis was after more than company, and it was not to this cove she came at all then but to the little cove beyond the headland, and 'tis hardly she would go there itself without a little scholar along with her. 'Ah,' I says, for I missed her company, 'isn't it the great stranger Miss Regan is becoming?' and Denis would put on his coat and go hunting in the dusk till he came to whatever spot she was. Little ease that was to him, poor boy, for he lost his tongue entirely, and lying on his belly before her, chewing an old bit of grass, is all he would do till she got up and left him. He could not help himself, poor boy. The madness was on him, even then, and it was only when I saw the plunder done that I knew there was no cure for him only to put her out of his mind entirely. For 'twas madness in him and he knew it, and that was what made him lose his tongue—he that was maybe without the price of an ounce of 'baccy—I will not deny it: often enough he had to do without it when the hens would not be laying, and often enough stirabout and praties was all we had for days. And there was she with money to her name in the bank! And that wasn't all, for he was a good boy; a quiet, good-natured boy, and another would take pity on him, knowing he would make her a fine steady husband, but she was not the sort, and well I knew it from the first day I laid eyes on her, that her hand would never rock the cradle. There was the madness out and out.

"So here was I, pulling and hauling, coaxing him to stop at home, and hiding whatever little thing was to be done till evening the way his hands would not be idle. But he had no heart in the work, only listening, always listening, or climbing the cnuceen to see would he catch a glimpse of her coming or going. And, oh, Mary, the heavy sigh he'd give when his bit of supper was over and I bolting the house for the night, and he with the long hours of darkness forninst him—my heart was broken thinking of it. It was the madness, you see. It was on him. He could hardly sleep or eat, and at night I would hear him, turning and groaning as loud as the sea on the rocks.

"It was then when the sleep was a fever to him that he took to walking in the night. I remember well the first night I heard him lift the latch. I put on my few things and went out after him. It was standing here I heard his feet on the stile. I went back and latched the door and hurried after him. What else could I do, and this place terrible after the fall of night with rocks and hills and water and streams, and he, poor soul, blinded with the dint of sleep. He travelled the road a piece, and then took to the hills, and I followed him with my legs all torn with briars and furze. It was over beyond by the new house that he gave up. He turned to me then the way a little child that is running away turns and clings to your knees; he turned to me and said: 'Mother, we'll go home now. It was the bad day for you ever you brought me into the world.' And as the day was breaking I got him back to bed and covered him up to sleep.

"I was hoping that in time he'd wear himself out, but it was worse he was getting. I was a strong woman then, a mayen-strong woman. I could cart a load of seaweed or dig a field with any man, but the nightwalking broke me. I knelt one night before the Blessed Virgin and prayed whatever was to happen, it would happen while the light of life was in me, the way I would not be leaving him lonesome like that in a wild place.

"And it happened the way I prayed. Blessed be God, he woke that night or the next night on me and he roaring. I went in to him but I couldn't hold him. He had the strength of five men. So I went out and locked the door behind me. It was down the hill I faced in the starlight to the little house above the cove. The Donoghues came with me: I will not belie them; they were fine powerful men and good neighbors. The father and the two sons came with me and brought the rope from the boats. It was a hard struggle they had of it and a long time before they got him on the floor, and a longer time before they got the ropes on him. And when they had him tied they put him back into bed for me, and I covered him up, nice and decent, and put a hot stone to his feet to take the chill of the cold floor off him.

"Sean Donoghue spent the night sitting beside the fire with me, and in the morning he sent one of the boys off for the doctor. Then Denis called me in his own voice and I went into him. 'Mother,' says Denis, 'will you leave me this way against the time they come for me?' I hadn't the heart. God knows I hadn't. 'Don't do it, Peg,' says Sean. 'If 'twas a hard job trussing him before, it will be harder the next time, and I won't answer for it.'

"'You're a kind neighbor, Sean,' says I, 'and I would never make little of you, but he is the only son I ever reared and I'd sooner he'd kill me now than shame him at the last.'

"So I loosened the ropes on him and he lay there very quiet all day without breaking his fast. Coming on to evening he asked me for the sup of tea and he drank it, and soon after the doctor and another man came in the car. They said a few words to Denis but he made them no answer and the doctor gave me the bit of writing. 'It will be tomorrow before they come for him,' says he, 'and 'tisn't right for you to be alone in the house with the man.' But I said I would stop with him and Sean Donoghue said the same.

"When darkness came on there was a little bit of a wind blew up from the sea and Denis began to rave to himself, and it was her name he was calling all the time. 'Winnie,' that was her name, and it was the first time I heard it spoken. 'Who is that he is calling?' says Sean. 'It is the schoolmistress,' says I, 'for though I do not recognize the name, I know 'tis no one else he'd be asking for.' 'That is a bad sign,' says Sean. 'He'll get worse as the night goes on and the wind rises. 'Twould be better for me go down and get the boys to put the ropes on him again while he's quiet.' And it was then something struck me, and I said: 'Maybe if she came to him herself for a minute he would be quiet after.' 'We can try it anyway,' says Sean, 'and if the girl has a kind heart she will come.'

"It was Sean that went up for her. I would not have the courage to ask her. Her little house is there on the edge of the hill; you can see it as you go back the road with the bit of garden before it the new teacher left grow wild. And it was a true word Sean said for 'twas worse Denis was getting, shouting out against the wind for us to get Winnie for him. Sean was a long time away or maybe I felt it long, and I thought it might be the way she was afeared to come. There are many like that, small blame to them. Then I heard her step that I knew so well on the boreen beside the house and I ran to the door, meaning to say I was sorry for the trouble we were giving her, but when I opened the door Denis called out her name in a loud voice, and the crying fit came on me, thinking how lighthearted we used to be together.

"I couldn't help it, and she pushed in apast me into the bedroom with her face as white as that wall. The candle was lighting on the dresser. He turned to her roaring with the mad look in his eyes, and then went quiet all of a sudden, seeing her like that overright him with her hair all tumbled in the wind. I was coming behind her. I heard it. He put up his two poor hands and the red mark of the ropes on his wrists and whispered to her: 'Winnie, asthore, isn't it the long time you were away from me?'

"'It is, Denis, it is indeed,' says she, 'but you know I couldn't help it.'

"'Don't leave me anymore now, Winnie,' says he, and then he said no more, only the two eyes lighting out on her as she sat by the bed. And Sean Donoghue brought in the little stooleen for me, and there we were, the three of us, talking, and Denis paying us no attention, only staring at her.

'Winnie,' says he, 'lie down here beside me.'

"Oye, says Sean, humoring him, 'don't you know the poor girl is played out after her day's work? She must go home to bed.'

"'No, no, no,' says Denis and the terrible mad light in his eye. 'There is a high wind blowing and 'tis no night for one like her to be out. Leave her sleep here beside me. Leave her creep in under the clothes to me the way I'll keep her warm.'

"'Oh, oh, oh, oh,' says I, 'indeed and indeed, Miss Regan, 'tis I'm sorry for bringing you here. 'Tisn't my son is talking at all but the madness in him. I'll go now,' says I, 'and bring Sean's boys to put the ropes on him again.'

"'No, Mrs. Sullivan,' says she in a quiet voice. 'Don't do that at all. I'll stop here with him and he'll go fast asleep. Won't you, Denis?'

"'I will, I will,' says he, 'but come under the clothes to me. There does a terrible draught blow under that door.'

"'I will indeed, Denis,' says she, 'if you'll promise me to go to sleep.'

"'Oye, whisht, girl,' says I. ''Tis you that's mad. While you're here you're in my charge, and how would I answer to your father if you stopped in here by yourself?'

"'Never mind about me, Mrs. Sullivan,' she said. 'I'm not a bit in dread of Denis: I promise you there will no harm come to me. You and Mr. Donoghue can sit outside in the kitchen, and I'll be all right here.'

"She had a worried look but there was something about her there was no mistaking. I wouldn't take it on myself to cross the girl. We went out to the kitchen, Sean and myself, and we heard every whisper that passed between them. She got into the bed beside him: I heard her. He was whispering into her ear the sort of foolish things boys do be saying at that age, and then we heard no more only the pair of them breathing. I went to the room door and looked in. He was lying with his arm about her and his head on her bosom, sleeping like a child, sleeping like he slept in his good days with no worry at all on his poor face. She did not look at me and I did not speak to her. My heart was too full. God help us, it was an old song of my father's that was going through my head: 'Lonely Rock is the one wife my children will know.'

"Later on, the candle went out and I did not light another. I wasn't a bit afraid for her then. The storm blew up and he slept through it all, breathing nice and even. When it was light I made a cup of tea for her and beckoned her from the room door. She loosened his hold and slipped out of bed. Then he stirred and opened his eyes.

"'Winnie,' says he, 'where are you going?'

"'I'm going to work, Denis,' says she. 'Don't you know I must be at school early?'

"'But you'll come back to me tonight, Winnie?' says he.

"'I will, Denis,' says she. 'I'll come back, never fear.'

"And he turned on his side and went fast asleep again.

"When she walked into the kitchen I went on my two knees before her and kissed her hands. I did so. There would no words come to me, and we sat there, the three of us, over our tea, and I declare for the time being I felt 'twas worth it all, all the troubles of his birth and rearing and all the lonesome years ahead.

"It was a great ease to us. Poor Denis never stirred, and when the police came he went along with them without commotion or handcuffs or anything that would shame him, and all the words he said to me was: 'Mother, tell Winnie I'll be expecting her.'

"And isn't it a strange and wonderful thing? From that day to the day she left us there did no one speak a bad word about what she did, and the people couldn't do enough for her. Isn't it a strange thing and the world as wicked as it is, that no one would say the bad word about her?"

Darkness had fallen over the Atlantic, blank gray to its farthest reaches.

Appendix 6:

"Lady Brenda"

by Frank O'Connor

Joe Regan's sister Brenda was several years older than himself, and by long chalks she was the toughest of the family, though none of them was exactly what you would call a sissy. A sissy would have had very little chance with Joe's father. He was tall and gaunt and angular, a monk who had strayed into workaday clothes and grown a big mustache. In Mr. Regan's considered view of the universe, the whole town was in a conspiracy against him, and that included every one of his own family from the baby up—always excepting his wife whom he regarded as a friendly neutral. As long as Joe had known it, life at home was one long battle, with his father, in an imperialist frame of mind, trying to get at them, and his mother, acting as protecting power, trying to keep him off.

That didn't mean that life wasn't sufficiently exciting. Protect her flanks as she might, Joe's mother never could keep one or another of the children from showing a light in some position covered by his father, or his father from discovering a new firing point from which for days on end he could decimate the children. But his mother's defenses were superb. No reconnaissance of his father's ever brought back prisoners or information; his intelligence system was blown to bits—and Joe's mother rationalized it all to herself as "not worrying poor Dad." When there really came to be things to worry about, the suspicion of all that was concealed from him nearly drove Jim Regan to his grave.

They had to be tough, there was no other way; but Brenda, whose principal task was looking after Joe, was tough by disposition. She was tall and gaunt and handsome like their father, and she would do anything a boy would do and a lot of things that most boys in their senses would not do. It was never safe to dare Brenda to anything. She scared Joe a great deal more than his father did.

For instance, the two of them would be sitting by the tram-stop in the evening when some corner-boy would start to jeer at her, and then anything might happen. One evening a fellow named Wright accused her of swanking—people were always accusing her of that—and Brenda began to boast more and more of her grand acquaintances. Everyone in the big houses by the tram-stop were friends of her family. Joe began trying to get her away, but you couldn't detach Brenda from a row.

"Go on!" bawled Wright. "Prove it! Go up to Lacy's house and prove it."

"Come on, Joe," Brenda said lightly.

"Don't, Brenda, don't!" sniveled Joe.

"Why wouldn't I?" snapped Brenda, angrier with him than with Wright. "Don't be a blooming baby!"

"They might send for the bobbies," said Joe. Everything about Brenda suggested policemen to Joe.

"Well, let them send for the bobbies," Brenda replied contemptuously.

Away she went up the steps to the house while Joe in terror watched from the gate. He knew if it was only the maid answered, she could get away by pretending she had come to the wrong house, but instead a lady came out. Brenda spoke to her a few minutes and then the two of them came down the steps together. Joe was astonished at the way Brenda spoke, just like a grownup.

"You turn down here by the church," said the lady. "Then take the turn to the right when you reach the old bridge, and you're almost opposite the station. Is this your little brother?"

"Yes," Brenda said with a sad smile at Joe. "I have to look after him. My mother died last year, and my father is thinking of putting him in an orphanage."

"You should really hurry and get home before dark," said the lady. "Here's something for you, sonny," she added, giving Joe sixpence.

They walked off in silence, Brenda looking mockingly at Wright who was sitting on the wall, a picture of mortification.

"Keep the tanner," she said good-naturedly to Joe. "It was only that I didn't want to give that fellow the satisfaction."

It was like Brenda to give sixpence away in that lordly way of hers, but all the same it wasn't wishing to Joe. For weeks he went round in dread the lady might see him with his mother and find out that he wasn't an orphan. He felt it was fated that one of those days Brenda would get him into the hands of the bobbies.

One year Brenda took it into her head that they should give their father a proper Christmas present, not the miserable pincushions and things the girls had made him previously.

"Why should we give him a Christmas box?" snapped Colum. Colum was the eldest of the family and very conscious of his superiority, particularly with the girls.

"What does he do for us?" asked Maeve who always supported Colum.

"Doesn't he keep us, woman?" asked Brenda. "Sure only for him we wouldn't be here at all."

"That's no good reason for giving him a Christmas box," growled Colum. "What could we give him?"

"He wants a fountain pen," said Brenda, who, as usual, had it all worked out.

"Pity about him!" said Colum.

"Ye needn't be so blooming mean," said Brenda, beginning to get into a wax. "Rooney's have very nice pens for ten and six. What is it only two bob a man? Ye'll get more than that out of the aunts."

The aunts were the O'Regan sisters from Kanturk who always stayed with their brother during the Christmas shopping, and, on the strength of their half crowns, it was decided to give Mr. Regan the fountain pen. Brenda collected the subscriptions and Joe paid up like a man. He knew that with Brenda you had always to pretend generosity even when you didn't feel it, and he was shrewd enough to realize that, since he was her favorite, he never really lost by it. It was the same about the pen. She not only allowed him to go to town with her to buy it, as well as that, she took him to a toyshop and out of her own money bought him an air gun. That was another peculiar thing about Brenda. Not even the other girls ever knew how much money she really had, and if anyone asked questions she always replied with lies. But Joe liked her just the same. It would be a long day before ever he got anything out of Colum or Maeve.

After that they went back up Patrick Street in the twilight, and into Rooney's, which was a combined stationery and bookshop. Brenda made straight for an assistant called Coakley who lived near them and who was friendly with her father; a tall chap with pince-nez, black curly hair and a pencil behind his ear. He leaned across the counter, laughing at Brenda, and Joe could see that he liked her.

"And what can I do for you, Miss Regan?" he asked, and Joe nearly died with pride to hear her so addressed.

"You can show us a few fountain pens," she said with a queenly air as if she had never been called anything else.

"Well," Coakley said eagerly, producing a tray from under the counter, "to make a long story short, you can't do better than the best." Then he produced another tray. "Of course, we have the cheaper ones as well, but they're not a patch on those."

"How much is this?" asked Brenda frowning, taking one from the first tray.

"Thirty bob," Coakley said, leaning his elbows on the counter.

"'Tis too dear," said Brenda, putting it back.

"That's a Standard," said Coakley. "'Tis a lot of money, of course, but 'tis worth it. That other stuff, I wouldn't waste your time recommending it to you."

"They all look much alike to me," said Brenda, taking up one of the cheaper pens.

"Ah, Miss Regan," Coakley said bitterly, "they're only got up like that to please the mugs. 'Tisn't the appearance that counts at all, but the nib." Then he took a fountain pen from his breast pocket and unscrewed the cap. It looked as if it would hold a half pint. "See that pen?" he asked, holding it out to Brenda. "Go on! Look at it! Guess how long I have that!"

"How long?" she asked curiously.

"Fifteen years," Coakley replied dramatically. "Fifteen blooming years. I bought that pen out of the first week's money I ever earned, and I give you my word there wasn't much of it left when I bought it. They were cheaper then, of course. That's so old that they're not even making them any more. They mend it for me as a personal favor, because I'm in the business. I had that through the war, in gaol and everything. I did every blessed thing with that pen only stop a bullet with it, and, I declare to God, I believe if I did that itself, I could have written home afterward with it to tell the story. I'm not telling you a word of a lie, Miss Regan. If you offered me the full price of that pen at this minute I wouldn't sell it to you. That's a Standard for you! There isn't another pen on the market you could say the same about."

He took it back from her, looked at it lovingly, screwed back the cap and returned it to his breast pocket. Joe could see he was really fond of the pen and that Brenda was impressed in spite of herself.

"Give it to us for a quid and I'll take it," she said coolly.

"A quid?" he replied, taken aback by her tone. "You might as well ask me to give it to you for nothing. Thirty bob is the price of those pens, and God knows I wouldn't tell you a lie."

"Don't be so blooming mean," said Brenda, a bit put out at her failure in her first attempt at bargaining. "What's ten bob one way or the other to ye?"

"What's ten bob to us?" he echoed blankly. Then he raised his hand to his mouth, reached a bit farther across the counter and indicated a small fat man serving at the far end of the shop. "Do you know Mr. Rooney?" he whispered.

"No," replied Brenda. "Why?"

"You ought to go up and ask him that question," Coakley said, and went into a stifled guffaw that shook every bit of him. "Just ask him what's ten bob to him, one way or the other. I'd love to see his face!"

"Anyway," said Brenda, seeing that this line was a complete wash-out, "you can split the difference. I'd give you the thirty bob, honest to God, but I'm after buying an air gun for the kid."

"Listen, Miss Regan," Coakley said with genuine earnestness, throwing himself over the counter again and speaking in a confidential whisper. "I'd do it like a shot, only 'twould be as much as my blooming job is worth. Your father will tell you. He knows the way I'm situated. I wouldn't tell you a lie."

Joe thought that Brenda would still take the good pen even if it meant throwing in his air gun to make up the price. By that time he would not have minded. He was fond of Brenda, and he could see that she was having a terrible time with her pride. It went through her to offer their father anything that was not the very best. It was as though she wasn't quite the thing herself. Then she gave a shrug.

"Ah, I'll take the ten and a tanner one so," she said. "It looks all right anyway."

"Oh, it is, it is," Coakley said, shaking his head and trying to put things in the best light. "I wouldn't give it to you at all if it wasn't. As a matter of fact, 'tis quite a decent little pen considering the price. We're selling them by the hundred."

Even Joe could see that this was a most unfortunate remark because in his sister's eyes nobody valued what everyone had. She was a natural aristocrat. It was dark when they came out and stood on the edge of the footpath with the lights reflected in the wet streets all round them. Brenda set her jaw and shook her head.

"I was an idiot to go to Coakley," she said with finality and turned to go.

"But why, Brenda?" asked Joe.

"He knows us too well," she said shortly. "If we might have gone to a stranger I could have fecked one of the good pens."

The panic Joe knew so well was beginning to rise in him again. They had still a good bit of Patrick Street to walk, and he knew his extraordinary sister so well that he realized there was every possibility of her staging a smash and grab raid on some other shop, with policemen chasing after them through town. The very thought of it made him sick.

"We'd get caught," he said sagaciously.

"Ah, you never think of anything only getting caught," Brenda said and gave him a savage dig. "Old baby!"

"Anyway," he said, trying to assert himself, "'twould be wrong."

"What'd be wrong about it?" she retorted. "As if they were going to miss one pen out of all they have! Robbers!"

He saw that was the wrong approach too. It was never much use talking to Brenda about right or wrong. He summed up all his cunning.

"I think the pen we got is better," he said.

"It is not better, you idiot!" said Brenda viciously. "Only for you and your blooming old air gun I'd have had enough for it, too. Not," she added in bitter meditation, "that *I'd* get any thanks for it. That crowd at home think I'm going to offer Daddy any old thing as if that was all we thought of him. Then they blame him if he gives one of us a clout. Is it any wonder the man would give us a clout and the little we make of him? God, it makes me sick!"

On Christmas morning Mr. Regan came downstairs in what for him was a very benevolent mood. Christmas was always a trying time for him. Between the universal claims for Christmas boxes, his sisters, and his children home from school, he could not help feeling put-upon. His wife had worked hard on him that morning, and he had almost been persuaded into promising not to do anything to upset the occasion for the children. He looked at the little parcel on his own plate and studied it for a moment.

"Hullo," he said with a pleasant grin. "What's this?"

"Something Santa brought for you," said Brenda. Then he sat down, undid the wrapping, opened the little box and saw the pen.

"Oh, now, that's very nice," he said with real glee, just like a kid. "That's the very thing I want. Which of ye thought of that?"

"Brenda did," Joe said quickly to make sure that no one robbed his sister of the credit.

"That was very thoughtful of her," said Mr. Regan, making a really gracious bow. "Very thoughtful of all of you," he added, giving each of them a grin in turn. "How much was it?" he asked briskly. That was more like him.

"Really, Jim," said Mrs. Regan with a laugh. "Such a thing to ask!"

"Why wouldn't I?" he asked, beginning to frown.

"The price is on the box," Brenda said quietly.

"Oh, begor, so it is," said Mr. Regan, glancing at it.

"Thirty bob!" he added, impressed in spite of himself. His patrols had never brought back information about the economic state of the enemy's troops, and most of the time he seemed to think they lived off the country. Joe looked at Colum, Maeve and Brigid, and he saw that they were impressed too, only in a different way. They were looking at Brenda to see what she was up to now. She didn't look as if she was ever up to anything. She just sat there with a radiant look that would have suggested sanctity except to someone that knew her.

"Where did you get it?" her father asked with a trace of suspicion.

"Rooney's," Brenda replied lightly.

"Rooney's?" her father echoed as he unscrewed the cap of the pen and looked at the nib. "Rooney's have Standard pens for that."

"I know," Brenda said composedly. "Joe and myself looked at them but we didn't like them. The assistant didn't like them much either. Isn't that right, Joe?"

"That's right," Joe said loyally. "Them were the best, Daddy."

"*They* were the best, dear," his mother said comfortably. "Wisha, Jim," she added. "I don't know is that school any good at all. The monks don't seem to teach them anything."

The children knew that their mother was sketching a diversion on her flank, but their father did not follow it up. Monks were another of his phobias. Any other time he'd have had quite a lot to say on the subject of monks, but not just then. He lived in a state of suspicion about life in general and shopkeepers in particular. He sucked in his cheeks, breathed through his nose and looked at that pen as though it could tell him what dirty trick the world was trying to play on him now. He rubbed his forehead briskly and turned on Brenda again.

"Which assistant was that?" he asked. "Coakley?"

"No," said Brenda. "A fellow we didn't know."

"Hah!" exclaimed her father, nodding as he began to see deeper into the plot. "I thought as much. I'd be surprised if Coakley had anything to do with that. Isn't that Rooney all out?" he said to his wife. "He saw the unfortunate children coming and knew he could impose on them."

"Wisha, nonsense!" she replied lightly. "He couldn't stand over a thing like that."

"But you don't mean to tell me that—that thing is worth thirty shillings?" he snarled, handing her the pen.

"Wisha, really, Jim," his wife said indignantly, "what way is that to talk about the children's present?"

"Now, I'm not complaining about the children at all," he said vindictively. "I know the intention was good. What I'm complaining of is Willie Rooney and his sanctimonious air, and I'm going to show him that he can't treat me like that."

"Sure, if you don't like it, they'll change it," said his wife.

"I'll do it after the holidays," Brenda said quickly.

"You'll only let yourself be fooled again," said her father.

"She's no fool at all," her mother said with a touch of asperity.

"Oh, all right, all right," said Mr. Regan, as cross as two cats at being deprived of such a neat excuse for a row. "Here, Brenda," he added, replacing the pen in the box, "put that away carefully till Thursday, and then take it back. Mind, now, and don't use it. Go to Coakley. You know Coakley? Pay attention to what I'm telling you. Have nothing to say to the other assistants. Go to Coakley and say I sent you, and that he's to give you a Standard pen instead of that one. He'll see you're not codded again."

Then Mr. Regan was perfectly happy, having ruined the whole day on the family.

"That's the last Christmas present that old show is going to get from me," said Maeve.

"Never mind him," snapped Colum. "What do you say to this one, changing the price on the box?"

"Ah," said Maeve contemptuously, "we might have known what she'd do with it. Always swanking."

Brenda was laughing at them. At least, she seemed to be laughing, but she frightened Joe.

"Anyway," she said. "I want another four bob now from each of ye."

"Try and get it." said Colum.

"Oh, I'm going to get it all right," said Brenda, tossing her head. "If ye don't give it to me I'll go and tell my father that ye put me up to it."

"I wouldn't put it past you," said Maeve with a sneer.

"I suppose you think I wouldn't?" asked Brenda.

They had gone too far, and they knew it. It was in the highest degree unsafe to challenge Brenda to do anything, because there was nothing you could positively say she would not do, and what was worse, nothing you could positively say her father would not believe. As Colum said once, they were lick alike. Joe knew it was wrong, and he was sorry that Brenda made the rest of them feel that way about her, but he could not help admiring her spirit.

They paid up and walked out on her. Joe emptied his pockets and offered her everything he had. It was his way of showing that he didn't really mind.

"Keep it," she said sharply. "I had it all the time, and I'd have paid it too if only they had the decency to stick by me." Then she smiled, a bitter sort of smile, and Joe thought with interest that she was probably going to cry. "The trouble with our family," she went on, "is that they have all small minds. You're the only one that hasn't, but you're only a baby, and I suppose you'll grow up like the rest."

Joe thought that unkind, but he could see she was upset.

Appendix 7:

"Ebb Tide"

by Brian Friel

Tom Bonner was so old that there were times, especially during the summer days when the sea was a flat green, when he wondered whether he had ceased to exist. Then a light breeze would breathe round the side of the harbor wall and touch his face and neck and he would be reassured.

Life was now a routine of moving out to the front of his house and in again, according to the weather, like a barometer figure.

The getting out was easy; without moving from his chair he could drag himself across the flagged floor of the kitchen, out through the door and down the steps to his favorite position in front of the kitchen window, from where he could look out across the bay, on a clear day, as far as Innisholme Island.

And there he could sit for a whole afternoon in the sun, like a dried-up stick that the tide had forgotten, just looking before him.

Tom's house was at the end of a path that led to the pier. Occasionally visitors would drive down there and pour out of their cars and run out to the end of the pier and look down into the water and point out things to one another. Or they would shade their eyes and look out at Innisholme and plan a day trip sometime. Then, on their way back to their cars, they would notice Tom, just as they had noticed the other things, and they would talk to him, treating him with a curious respect as though he had secrets to reveal.

But once they discovered that he was too old to be interesting they went off, laughing and chattering, to their cars.

It was a different matter getting back into the kitchen again. Tom could not slide his chair up the three stone steps.

So he had to wait until some of the neighbors came along, or until some of the fishermen came in with a catch.

Very often it was dusk before they discovered him and they would say crossly: "What are you doing out here at this time of evening, Tom? Do you want to get your death?" As if death were something that struck you suddenly when the sun went down and not the gradual drifting away of all sensation.

They would feel his hands, too, and say they were like stones. Then he would look at his hands as if they did not belong to him; big, gnarled, splayed things that once pulled oars and hauled lobster pots and shot nets and hoisted sails. Queer how they felt nothing now. Absolutely nothing. Even the rheumatism that bit into his legs ignored those hands. That puzzled him.

But the neighbors were kind, in a worldly way. They saw to it that he did not starve and they took turns to clear up his place. Once they had done these things for him, they could afford to forget about him, he was so old . . . .

When the first of the winter gales struck one day early in October, the only people caught unawares were the few late visitors. They scurried back to their hotels with their beach wraps and their portable radios.

Tom had not slithered out that day; he had smelled the storm coming the night before. He lay in bed and listened to the wind pounding on the roof and the breakers smashing on the rocks round at the Tor.

He lay there for twenty-four hours, listening. Then, about noon on the second day, he heard people running past his door down to the pier. Above the roar of the Atlantic wind he could hear the urgency of their voices, shouting to one another.

For a time he did not stir. A boat had broken her moorings, he thought. Or the buoy was adrift. But he knew a crowd must have gathered by now because at least twelve people had run past his door.

He was about to ease himself on to his chair when somebody knocked. "Tom Bonner! Tom Bonner! Come quick! Down to the pier! The men want you," a child's voice piped through the keyhole.

"Eh? What is it?"

"Flares from Innisholme. One every ten minutes. The men are thinking of going out."

Tom knew that the men wanted his opinion. But they had forgotten that he could not walk the length of the kitchen to the front door.

"Tell them . . ." he began.

But the men had come to him. Feet shuffled outside and anxious faces peered in through the dirty square of window and searched the dark room for him.

"Flares from the island, Tom," shouted Mason. "It's probably the doctor they want for the lighthouse-keeper's wife. She's due this week, it seems."

Tom didn't answer.

"We're thinking of trying the crossing," Mason said.

Tom worked himself to the edge of the bed and then on to the chair. He pulled a blanket over his shoulders. Then, muttering to himself, he dragged himself across the floor and pulled back the bolt on the door.

They poured into the kitchen with the wind, six of them in their yellow oilskins and thigh boots. Two scrawny boys hung about the threshold, watching.

"I was asleep," Tom said. It was a lie, but they were too full of the importance of their mission to detect it.

"The flares are coming regular," said Sweeney. "They need help bad, whatever it is."

They were all looking at him, waiting for him to speak. They wanted advice, and at the same time they wanted to shed their responsibility on to him, because he was old, and afterwards, if anything went wrong, they could say, "We only did what Bonner suggested." But they wanted advice first.

"Would a boat live in that northeast wind, Tom?" Mason asked.

Tom felt none of their anxiety; only importance that rose in him like hot blood and hurt his chest slightly and even made his dead hands tingle.

"Carry me to the end of the pier," he commanded.

"But Tom . . ." They wanted only advice: Go or Stay.

"Carry me to the end of the pier. Then I'll tell you what to do."

Four men carried him in his chair, shoulder high, across the gravel path and onto the pier. Somebody had thrown a waterproof cape around his head and shoulders so that only his thin white face peeped out occasionally when a gust of wind caught them. Waves broke on the back of the harbor wall and sent canopies of white spray cascading over them.

They stopped a few feet from the edge and lowered Tom to the ground. But they still held on to him in case the wind blew him into the water.

"Well, Tom? Would she make it?"

But Tom did not answer, although he had known what he was going to say from the moment they carried him outside the door and he saw the sky. Now he wanted to have them looking at him and waiting for him. He might never have the chance again. He needed to savor it.

"I say we try it," said Mason. "It's the least we can do is try it."

But the others awaited Tom's word, if only to postpone the attempt.

At last he spoke, looking across the waves that hid Innisholme from them.

"Nobody goes nowhere yet," he said. "Not for two hours. You'll have nothing but a puff of wind then."

They were relieved. Their faces relaxed and they laughed and said: "Good old Tom," and "Takes the old ones," as if he had given them something. Then their dutiful solicitude for him returned and somebody said: "Better get him back in out of the wind," and they hoisted him up again and carried him back to his house.

Once they had him safely inside again they agreed that, since there were a couple of hours before they could set out, they might as well pass the time in O'Byrne's bar. So they thanked Tom again and told him he was a good one and there was not a man like him for telling the weather. Then they went off.

The kitchen was suddenly empty without them. Tom slid himself to one place and then another to escape the draft under the door, but it got at his feet and numbed them.

With all the fuss, he thought, Mason's woman would probably forget to bring down his can of milk tonight. But there was no resentment in him; only an ebbing away of all feeling again until he was not quite sure whether he was awake or asleep.

Appendix 8:

Literary Theories: A Very Brief Overview

PLATONIC CRITICISM: Because Plato prizes an accurate, objective understanding of *reality*, he sees "creative" writers and "literary" texts as potential distractions since they may lead the already-emotional audience to neglect proper pursuit of philosophical truth, which the critic should seek, explain, and defend by using logic and reason.

ARISTOTELIAN CRITICISM: Because Aristotle values the *text* as a highly crafted complex unity, he tends to see the author as a craftsman, the audience as capable of appreciating such craftsmanship, the text as a potentially valuable means of understanding the complexity of "reality," and the critic as a specialist conversant with all aspects of the poetic craft.

HORATIAN CRITICISM: Because Horace emphasizes the need to satisfy a diverse *audience*, he tends to see the author as attempting to please and/or teach them, the text as embodying principles of custom and moderation (so as to please the widest possible audience), "reality" as understood in traditional or conventional terms, and the critic as a fatherly advisor who tries to prevent the author from making a fool of himself.

LONGINIAN CRITICISM: Because "Longinus" (whose real identity is unknown) stresses the ideally lofty nature of the sublime (i.e., elevated) *author*, he tends to view the text as an expression of the author's power, the audience as desiring the ecstasy a great author can induce, social "reality" as rooted in a basic human nature that everywhere and always has a yearning for elevation, and the critic as (among other things) a moral and spiritual advisor who encourages the highest aspirations of readers and writers alike.

TRADITIONAL HISTORICAL CRITICISM: Because traditional historical critics tend to emphasize the ways social *realities* influence the writer, the writer's creation of a text, and audience's reactions to it, they stress the critic's obligation to study the past as thoroughly and objectively as possible to determine how the text might have been understood by its original readers.

THEMATIC CRITICISM: Because thematic critics stress the importance of ideas in shaping social and psychological *reality*, they generally look for the ways those ideas are expressed by (and affect) the texts that writers create. They assume that audiences turn to texts for enlightenment as well as entertainment and that writers either express the same basic ideas repeatedly or that the evolution of their thinking can be traced in different works.

FORMALISM: Because formalists value the *text* as a complex unity in which all the parts contribute to a rich and resonant effect, they usually offer highly detailed ("close") readings intended to show how the work achieves a powerful, compelling artistic form. Formalist critics help audiences appreciate how a work's subtle nuances contribute to its total effect.

PSYCHOANALYTIC CRITICISM: Freudian or psychoanalytic critics emphasize the key role of the human mind in perceiving and shaping *reality* and believe that the minds of writers, audiences, and critics are highly complex and often highly conflicted (especially in sexual terms, and particularly in terms of the moralistic "super-ego," the rational ego, and the irrational "id"). They contend that such complexity inevitably affects the ways texts are written and read. The critic, therefore, should analyze how psychological patterns affect the ways in which texts are created and received.

ARCHETYPAL OR "MYTH" CRITICISM: Because archetypal critics believe that humans experience *reality* in terms of certain basic fears, desires, images (symbols), and stories (myths), they assume that writers will inevitably employ such patterns; that audiences will react to them forcefully and almost automatically; and that critics should therefore study the ways such patterns affect writers, texts, and readers.

MARXIST CRITICISM: Because Marxist critics assume that conflicts between economic classes inevitably shape social *reality*, they emphasize the ways these struggles affect writers, audiences, and texts. They assume that literature will either reflect, reinforce, or undermine (or some combination of these) the dominant ideologies (i.e., standard patterns of thought) that help structure social relations. Marxist critics study the complex relations between literature and society, ideally seeking to promote social progress.

STRUCTURALIST CRITICISM: Because structuralist critics assume that humans structure (or make sense of) *reality* by imposing patterns of meaning on it, and because they assume that these structures can only be interpreted in terms of the codes the structures embody, they believe that writers will inevitably rely on such codes to create meaning, that texts will inevitably embody such codes, and that audiences will inevitably use such codes to interpret texts. To understand a text, the critic must be familiar with the systematic codes that shape it; he must master the system(s) the text implies.

FEMINIST CRITICISM: Because feminist critics assume that our experience of *reality* is inevitably affected by categories of sex and gender (such as divisions between male and female, heterosexual and homosexual, etc.), and because they assume that (heterosexual) males have long enjoyed dominant social power, they believe that writers, texts, and audiences will all be affected (usually negatively) by "patriarchal" forces. The critic's job will be to study (and even attempt to counter-act) the impact of patriarchy.

DECONSTRUCTION: Because Deconstructive critics assume that "*reality*" cannot be experienced except through language, and because they believe that language is inevitably full of contradictions, gaps, and dead-ends, they believe that no writer, text, audience, or critic can ever escape from the unsolvable paradoxes language embodies. Deconstruction therefore undercuts the hierarchical assumptions of any other critical system (such as structuralism, formalism, Marxism, etc.) that claims to offer an "objective," "neutral," or "scientific" perspective on literature.

READER-RESPONSE CRITICISM: Because reader-response critics assume that literary texts are inevitably interpreted by individual members of the *audience* and that these individuals react to texts in ways that are sometimes shared, sometimes highly personal (and sometimes both at once), they believe that writers exert much less control over texts than we sometimes suppose, and that critics must never ignore the crucial role of audience response(s).

DIALOGICAL CRITICISM: Because dialogical critics assume that the (worthy) *text* almost inevitably embodies divergent points of view, they believe that elements within a text engage in a constant dialogue or give-and-take with other elements, both within and outside the text itself. The writer, too, is almost inevitably engaged in a complex dialogue, through the text, with his potential audience(s), and the sensitive critic must be alert to the multitude of voices a text expresses or implies.

NEW HISTORICISM: Because new historicist critics assume that our experience of *reality* is inevitably social, and because they emphasize the way systems of power and domination both provoke and control social conflicts, they tend to see a culture not as a single coherent entity but as a site of struggle, negotiation, or the constant exchange of energy. New historicists contend that no text, audience, or critic can stand apart from contemporary (i.e., both past and present) dynamics of power.

MULTICULTURAL CRITICISM: Because multicultural critics emphasize the numerous differences that both shape and divide social *reality*, they tend to see all people (including writers, readers, and critics) as members of sometimes divergent, sometimes over-lapping groups. These groups, whether relatively fluid or relatively stable, can include such categories as races, sexes, genders, ages, and classes, and the critic should explore how such differences affect the ways in which literature is both written and read.

POSTMODERNISM: Postmodernists are highly skeptical of large-scale claims to objective "truths" and thus doubt the validity of grand explanations. They see such claims as attempts to impose order on a *reality* that is, almost by definition, too shifting or fluid to be pinned down. Postmodernists assume that if writers, readers, and audiences abandoned their yearning for such order, they would more easily accept and enjoy the inevitable paradoxes and contradictions of life and art. The postmodern critic will look for (and value) any indications of a text's instabilities.